The Population of the South

The Population of the South
Structure and Change in Social Demographic Context

Edited by
Dudley L. Poston, Jr., and Robert H. Weller

Dudley L. Poston, who received his Ph.D. in sociology from the University of Oregon in 1968, is associate professor of sociology and associate director of the Population Research Center at the University of Texas at Austin. He is coauthor of *Sustenance Organization and Migration in Nonmetropolitan Areas*. Robert H. Weller is professor of sociology at Florida State University. He received his Ph.D. from Cornell in 1967 and is coauthor of *An Introduction to Demography*.

University of Texas Press, Austin

First Edition, 1981

Library of Congress Cataloging in Publication Data

Main entry under title:
The Population of the South.
  Bibliography: p.
  Includes index.
  1. Southern States—Population—Addresses, essays, lectures.
I. Poston, Dudley L., 1940–   II. Weller, Robert H.
HB3511.P66   304.6'0975   80-18454
ISBN 0-292-76467-7

For reasons of economy, the tables in this book were printed
from camera-ready copy provided by the editors.

Contents

Preface

DANIEL O. PRICE

Books on demography of the South are not a new idea. Vance's *Human Geography of the South* (1932) might be listed as the first such volume, although there were certainly earlier publications containing material on the subject.[1] Vance's volume *All these People: The Nation's Human Resources in the South* (1945) is probably the most important single volume on southern demography. During the Depression, President Roosevelt characterized the South as "the nation's number one economic problem" since the region contained a disproportionate number of the nation's one-third that was "ill-clothed, ill-housed, and ill-fed." Until about 1975 more than half the blacks in the United States resided in the South. The country as a whole had more than half its population living in urban areas in 1920, but the South did not reach this level of urbanization until 30 years later. It is no wonder that the demography of the South has been of major interest to so many people for so long a time.

This volume follows in a long tradition. Among the early research workers in this area (in addition to Vance) were Otis Durant Duncan in Oklahoma, Wilson Gee at the University of Virginia, Horace Hamilton at both Texas A.&M. and North Carolina State University, Carl Rosenquist at the University of Texas, T. Lynn Smith at both Vanderbilt and the University of Florida, and B. O. Williams at the University of Georgia. Moreover, between this early group and the authors of the current volume, there are too many southern demographers to enumerate. It is thus of interest to ask whether there is a need for another book on southern demography, or even the broader question, whether there is a need for another book on the South?

As a consequence of the South's unique place in American history (the only region that fought a war against the rest of the country), there have probably been more books written about the South than about any other region of the nation. The expression "the New South" was powerfully presented by Henry Grady, editor of the *Atlanta Constitution*, to a New York audience in 1886, although the expression had been used even before that. Every generation of writers since has used the term. The idea of the changing South has been the only common element among the users of the expression.

The present volume looks at the changing South, and, for the most part, it traces patterns of demographic change that show convergence with the rest of the United States. If the demographic characteristics of the South have converged with those of the rest of the country, is there a justification for this volume?

At one point on Interstate Highway 77 in southern Virginia, a driver will be startled to realize that he is on IH 77 going north and also on IH 81 going south. After a short period of merging, these two highways continue on their separate ways, one north and the other south. Do we have any evidence that the present convergence of demographic characteristics of the South with those of the rest of the country represents a temporary similarity and that there may be divergence of some characteristics in the future, or is there evidence of conformity, possibly due to increased communication? The present volume provides a basis for examining these alternatives.

Although the authors of this volume do not reach consensus about the merging of characteristics of the South with those of the rest of the nation, the majority do feel that the South will continue to be different in its demographic characteristics, and several even provide rationales for this expectation. Only time, of course, will provide the answer, but continued differentiation within the United States should not be surprising. Vance saw convergence as a desirable goal.

> The South wants to share the Nation's future. It is not the existence of regional inequalities that disturbs the South so much. It is their persistence over the generations (Vance, 1945:477).

Nevertheless, with this question of convergence or differentiation still unanswered, we not only have justification for the present volume but the requirement that somewhere in the future there must be at least one more book on southern demography to examine whether the characteristics of the South have merged with or become differentiated from those of the rest of the nation.

NOTE

1. For example, see Rupert B. Vance, *Human Factors in Cotton Culture* (University of North Carolina Press, 1929), and Holland Thompson, *The New South* (Yale University Press, 1919).

The Population of the South

I
Demographic Change in the South

DUDLEY L. POSTON, JR., WILLIAM J. SEROW, AND
ROBERT H. WELLER

Population growth in the South has elicited a great deal of attention recently. In the early 1970s the national press began to give increasingly more attention to the rise of the Sunbelt, particularly its cities. Journalists apparently had been caught by surprise in reviewing the results of the 1970 U.S. *Census of Population*, which notes for the first time that cities in the northeastern corridor were losing population and metropolitan areas in the South were gaining.

> Not only were the old central cities of the Northeast sick and decaying, but entire metropolitan areas were losing population and jobs to a younger and more vigorous section of the country. The "Cowboys" were vanquishing the "Yankees" in a "second war between the states" (Perry and Watkins, 1974 : 14).

For the most part, demographers and other social scientists were not surprised with these "new" developments, for they had known of these demographic and economic shifts for some time. At least since midcentury, the country had been tilting toward the South; so the growth of the Sunbelt and the decline of the Northeast were not unexpected developments to the more trenchant observers.

However, developments have also occurred recently that are not entirely a continuation of the trends since midcentury. The reversal in the 1970s which involved net population movements from metropolitan areas, a phenomenon experienced in all regions of the country, deserves particular attention. Since 1970 there has been relatively more population growth in the nonmetropolitan counties of the United States than in the metropolitan counties. The nonmetropolitan areas registered a net population gain of more than 1.8 million persons between 1970 and 1974 (Beale, 1975 : 1; Zuiches and Brown, 1975 : 9; and Frisbie and Poston, 1976 : 354).

These changes have been due to substantial increases in the out-migration rates from metropolitan areas, coupled with a significant decline in out-migration rates from nonmetropolitan areas. Moreover, the changes have not been caused exclusively by alterations in the sizes and age structures of the two types of areas, but by "real changes in outmigration rates at practically all ages in both areas" (Tucker, 1976:442).

In many ways the relatively longstanding interregional population shifts to the South are related to these more recent developments involving the growth of nonmetropolitan America. For instance, data show that the metropolitan areas most responsible for the migration reversals are the larger and older ones in the North, not those in the South. Thus, the growth of the nonmetropolitan South has not occurred at the expense of the metropolitan South. Both sections now share in the region's overall growth dynamics.

In an attempt to provide a perspective for these and other discussions of southern population change which will appear later in this volume, this chapter will begin with a basic overview of demographic change in the South since 1870. Changes in the relative size and growth rate of the South and the rest of the United States over the past century will be considered first, followed by individual discussions of fertility, mortality, and migration. We will next address the topic of population redistribution in the South and the balance of the nation since 1970, focusing particularly on the South, its divisions and states.

These discussions will provide a foundation for setting the book's chapters in perspective. The last part of this introductory chapter will address each in brief form in an attempt to place them within a social demographic context of structure and change.

DEMOGRAPHIC CHANGES SINCE 1870

The 1870 *Census of Population*, when corrected for underenumeration throughout the vanquished Confederacy, showed that slightly more than one-third of the nation's inhabitants (including all of the present-day territory except Alaska and Hawaii) lived in the South. As illustrated in table 1.1, this percentage declined steadily through most of the following century, with the exception of a slight upturn during the 1890s and a more significant upturn during the Depression decade of the 1930s. During the 1960s the prevailing pattern was reversed once again. But since then there have

TABLE 1.1 Total Population and Average Annual Rate of Increase, South and Non-South 1870–1975

	South			Non-South[a]	
Year	Population (thousands)	% Average Annual Intercensal Growth Rate	% of Nation	Population (thousands)	% Average Annual Intercensal Growth Rate
1870[b]	13,548	—	34.0	26,270	—
1880	16,517	2.0	32.9	33,639	2.5
1890	20,028	1.9	31.8	42,951	2.5
1900	24,554	2.0	32.2	51,689	1.9
1910	29,389	1.8	31.9	62,840	2.0
1920	33,126	1.2	31.2	72,896	1.5
1930	37,858	1.3	30.7	85,345	1.6
1940	41,666	1.0	31.5	90,499	0.6
1950	47,197	1.3	31.2	104,129	1.4
1960	54,973	1.5	30.7	124,350	1.8
1970	62,795	1.3	30.9	140,417	1.2
1975	68,041	1.6	31.9	144,991	0.6

Source: U.S. Bureau of the Census, Historical Statistics of the United States, Colonial Times to 1970, Washington, D.C.: Government Printing Office, 1975, ser. A2 and A172; U.S. Bureau of the Census, "Estimates of the Population of States, by Age: July 1, 1975 and 1976," Current Population Reports, ser. P-25, no. 646, February 1977, table 2.

[a] Includes Alaska from 1890 and Hawaii from 1900.

[b] Adjusted for underenumeration.

been marked increases in the proportion of the national population living in the South (U.S. Bureau of the Census, 1977b), with most of the region's increased share of the national population occurring toward the end of the decade. The South has long had a disproportionately large share of the nation's military population (nearly half in 1970), and the buildup in military strength during the Vietnam conflict had an appreciable effect on relative population growth in the South during the late 1960s (J. Long, 1976; Serow, 1976).

The cause for the decline in the relative size of the South over so many decades, as well as the recent growth in its numbers, must ultimately be identified with patterns of net migration. We will return later to a consideration of these patterns over the decades since 1870. First, however, we will examine the long-term patterns in fertility and mortality.

Fertility
From a historical perspective, the South has long led "the nation in large families and high birth rates" (Vance, 1945:64). In the absence of more precise data for much of the period under consideration, we have analyzed fertility change and differentials with the child-woman ratio (children aged 0–4 per 1,000 women aged 15–44). This measure differs somewhat from that employed in a later chapter by Rindfuss on southern fertility where he presents total fertility rates estimated from census data based on the "own children" method. However, the same overall conclusion emerges from both sets of data; namely, the convergence of southern and nonsouthern fertility.

The child-woman ratio in the South has been considerably higher than that of the non-South for all years prior to 1950 (see table 1.2), but the differences since midcentury between the South and non-South have been minimal, principally because of a more dramatic decline in the South. Moreover, this southern fertility decline in recent years has occurred along with a decrease in the South's share of national nonwhite population and an increase in the proportion of Southerners who live in urban areas. As recently as 1950, more than half of all Southerners lived in rural areas—a level consistent with that of the non-South in 1900. Similarly, in the early portion of the period under consideration, nearly all nonwhite Americans lived in the South. By 1970 only about one-half of all blacks lived there. The 1970 census, in fact, represented the first

TABLE 1.2 Child-Woman Ratios by Race and Urban-Rural Residence, South and Non-South, 1870–1970 (Children 0–4 per 1,000 women 15–44)

	South						Non-South					
	Total	White	Nonwhite	Urban	Rural	% Rural	Total	White	Nonwhite	Urban	Rural	% Rural
1870[a]	696.9	NA	NA	NA	NA	87.8	600.8	NA	NA	NA	NA	68.0
1880[a]	741.5	711.4	792.6	NA	NA	87.8	545.9	547.5	506.6	NA	NA	64.0
1890	645.5	620.7	648.5	NA	NA	83.7	479.0	486.8	400.3	NA	NA	56.1
1900	636.0	638.1	635.6[b]	NA	NA	82.0	467.7	460.6	391.4[b]	NA	NA	50.1
1910	606.6	622.7	569.3[b]	364.5	676.9	77.5	436.9	440.3	381.4[b]	374.2	518.0	43.6
1920	537.2	546.9	465.0	335.9	615.9	71.9	445.6	446.1	317.4	391.1	533.4	38.3
1930	461.5	470.5	493.3	314.0	550.1	65.9	364.8	357.5	396.5	315.5	460.1	34.1
1940	395.1	384.1	429.9	264.0	471.1	63.3	305.0	300.9	408.8	254.5	401.7	34.3
1950	517.3	497.2	589.0	439.4	591.0	51.4	461.0	458.1	513.9	420.3	560.6	29.0
1960	575.0	530.1	735.4	548.4	607.7	41.5	560.8	551.8	676.8	537.5	630.3	25.1
1970	406.9	382.3	506.7	390.2	440.1	35.4	403.0	396.0	471.3	391.7	441.9	22.5

Source: Decennial Census of Population, various years.

[a] Excludes Oklahoma.

[b] Black only.

TABLE 1.3   Child-Woman Ratios by Race and Urban-Rural
Residence, Southern, Nonsouthern, 1970

	South		Non-South	
	Child-Woman Ratio[a]	% of Total Population	Child-Woman Ratio[a]	% of Total Population
Total	406.9	100.0	403.0	100.0
Urban	390.2	64.6	391.7	77.5
Rural	440.1	35.6	441.9	22.5
White	382.0	80.4	396.0	90.9
Urban	366.8	51.4	383.0	68.9
Rural	409.4	29.0	436.7	22.0
Black	506.5	19.2	472.1	7.5
Urban	479.8	12.9	470.8	7.3
Rural	553.5	8.4	543.1	0.2

Source: 1970 Census of Population Characteristics of the
Population United States Summary, part 1, section 2, table
269.

[a]Data are derived from a sample and may differ slightly from
complete count data.

time in which a majority of nonwhite Americans did not live in
the South.

More detailed data illustrating the sources of the differences in
fertility which remain between the South and the non-South in
1970 are given in table 1.3. Among whites the southern child-
woman ratios were slightly lower in both rural and urban sectors
than they were in the respective sectors of the non-South. However, child-woman ratios for urban and rural southern blacks were
only modestly greater than the corresponding levels for nonsouthern urban and rural blacks. Because the southern blacks were
more rural in 1970 than the nonsouthern blacks, their overall fertility level was about 7 percent higher.

Mortality
Unlike fertility, analyses of geographic differences in mortality levels absolutely require the availability of vital statistics data on
such characteristics of the decedent as age, race, sex. However it

was not until 1933, when Texas joined, that all states were part of the death registration system. Indeed, only one of the seventeen states (including the District of Columbia) comprising the Census South was permanently in the registration system prior to 1900, and only six were members by 1920 (Linder and Grove, 1947:96).

Therefore, the mortality data available by region for 1919–1920 are very limited, although they do show that the mortality level in the South was comparable to levels in the rest of the nation. However, this comparability was produced by two offsetting differences in population composition. First, mortality was much higher among blacks than whites. Because blacks were disproportionately located in the South, southern mortality levels were pressured upward. Second, at that particular stage of demographic development, the level of mortality was positively related to the degree of urbanization and industrialization within the area, and this positive relationship obtained within each racial group (Thompson and Whelpton, 1933). Because the South was comparatively rural and nonindustrialized vis-à-vis the rest of the country, it had a relative advantage in mortality experience, thus partially offsetting the disadvantage created by the relative concentration of blacks in the South.

The data available for 1939–1941 are more reliable and more extensive; yet these show a pattern similar to that just discussed for 1919–1920. Differences between life table values for the South and the nation, by residence, race, and sex, were negligible (Vance, 1945:352–353), and data show the same patterns for 1950 (Bogue, 1959).

Although the South had a higher mortality level than the rest of the nation, the differences are largely attributable to differences in racial composition. For whites, mortality in the South was equal to or less than that of all whites (in terms of age-adjusted crude death rates). However, for nonwhites, adjusted death rates of Southerners were somewhat greater than those of non-Southerners, a trend which apparently has been continuing to recent years. A 1973 study by the Statistical Bureau of the Metropolitan Life Insurance Company found mortality among nonwhites aged 35 and over to be higher in the South than in the rest of the nation.

Moriyama (1964) found that southern states were more likely than other states to be characterized by dramatic increases in crude death rates (unadjusted for age) during the late 1950s and early 1960s. However, by 1970 crude death rates (unadjusted for differences in race or age) in the South were not appreciably different from those throughout the nation (NCHS, 1971). Allowing for the greater proportion of nonwhites still residing in the South and the tendency of some parts of the South (such as Florida) to attract disproportionately large numbers of older immigrants, it seems fairly safe to conclude that there are no appreciable differences in mortality between the South and the remainder of the nation. Rosenberg and Burnham arrive at a similar conclusion after a much more detailed analysis in a later chapter in this volume.

Migration
For the first fifty years after 1870, net immigration played a crucial role in explaining the growth of American population. Between 1870 and 1920, at least 138,000 (in 1878) were admitted to the United States each year, with a maximum of nearly 1.3 million (in 1907). The foreign-born population increased from 5.5 million in 1870 to 14.2 million in 1930. If the indirect (through reproduction) and direct influences of immigration in total population are entertained, about one-half of the current United States population is attributable to the estimated net immigration of 35 million persons to the United States between 1790 and 1970 (Gibson, 1975).

Relatively few of these immigrants located in the South. At any one time during the 1870–1970 interval, no more than 3 percent of the South's population was foreign born. The children of immigrants accounted for no more than 6 percent of the South's white population at any one time. By contrast, the foreign-born population accounted for 20 percent of the non-South in 1920, but since then the proportion has been diminishing. The share of the non-South white population that was second generation ethnic was 30 percent during the early years of the century, but it too has fallen.

The differences in racial composition between the South and the rest of the nation are not sufficient explanations for the failure of the South to attract immigrants. Both whites and nonwhites in the South have been much more likely to claim the U.S. as their birthplace than persons residing in the other areas of the nation. However, recent decades have seen relative and absolute increases in the number of foreign born (of both races) in the South, with corresponding relative and absolute declines in the non-South. Part of this recent upsurge in foreign-born Southerners is likely attributable to refugees from Cuba who have settled in Florida; another part may reflect the redistribution of population from North to South which has occurred recently.

Several years ago Everett S. Lee described three broad movements that characterized the internal redistribution of population within the United States:

> First and greatest was the migration from east to west which consolidated the country and dispelled threats to American sovereignty. Even as the West was being populated, the second movement, that to cities, set in, transforming us from a nation of farmers into an industrial power. The third great movement was the migration from the South to the North, a movement which of late has taken on special significance because it has become primarily a migration of Negroes. All three movements continue today (Lee, 1964:124).

In the years since Lee's remarks, the nation has witnessed a reversal of the second and third broad movements. But to some extent, these reversals are part and parcel of the same phenomenon.

As Lee notes, for decades following the Civil War, the South exhibited a pronounced and continuous pattern of out-migration. A foreshadowing of future events, however, was noted by Shryock in 1964, when he observed that the South (the South Atlantic and West South Central Divisions) received a slight net in-migration between 1949 and 1950. (Contrary to usual practice, the 1950 census asked place of residence for the preceding year rather than for five years earlier. The obvious reason for this temporary shift was World War II.)

In table 1.4 we have presented data reflecting two measures of population redistribution: net lifetime migration and net intercensal migration. Net lifetime migration applies only to persons born in this country and is measured as the difference between the native (U.S. born) population born in a state, division, or region, and the native population currently residing in that state, division, or region. When the latter exceeds the former, there is net in-migration. Table 1.4 illustrates that, as Lee suggested, out-migration from the South has been heavier and more extensive in the nonwhite population. The rapid increase in net lifetime out-migration among nonwhites during the 1940s strongly suggests that military service and war-related industry drew many native Southerners, particularly nonwhites, from the South.

These data report several reversals of net lifetime migration, but among the most interesting are the rapid declines in net out-migration for whites in the South since 1960. Although a large portion is the result of retirement and other migration to Florida (U.S. Bureau of the Census, 1973a:table 7), the lifetime migration loss of the southern white population is now close to zero. Long and Hansen

TABLE 1.4 Net Lifetime and Net Intercensal Migration, by Race: South, 1870–1970 (thousands of persons)

	White		Nonwhite or Black		
	Net Lifetime	Net Intercensal[b]	Net Lifetime(NW)	Net Intercensal(NW)	Net Intercensal(B)
1870[a]	-671	--	-134	--	
1880[a]	-543	99.4	-176	-60.4	
1890	-421[a]	-182.5	-219[a]	-69.7	
1900	-126	119.1	-315	-168.0	
1910	-47	-2.3	-397	-170.5	
1920	-196	-389.0	-733	-454.4	
1930	-801[c]	-546.1[c]	-1,395[c]	-749.0	
1940	-1,061	-294.9[c]	-1,485	-347.5	
1950	-1,512	-502.7[d] (-538)[e]	-2,485	-1,279.1[d]	(-1,602)[e]
1960	-1,732	-234.4[f] (57)[e]	-3,096	-1,202.3[f]	(-1,477)[e]
1970	-517	1,807[e]	-3,225	-1,380[e]	

Source: Historical Statistics, ser. C15–24 and C25–75.

[a] Excludes Oklahoma.
[b] Native white prior to 1950.
[c] Mexicans classified with other races.
[d] Lee et al. (1957), pp. 107–231.
[e] Current Population Reports, ser. P-25, nos. 72, 304, 406.
[f] Eldridge (n.d.), table A-1.

(1975 : 161) have attributed the recent reversal of white migration to three factors: "Increased return movement between 1955–1960 and 1965–70 were important in this changeover, but slightly more important numerically were 1) decreased out-migration of native southerners and 2) increased in-migration of persons not born in the South." As Cahill (1976) has observed, ". . . the holding power of the South and its ability to attract natives of other regions appear to be increasing." We focus in more detail on these post-1970 changes in the next section.

Table 1.4 also presents estimates of intercensal net migration for the South since 1870. On balance, the South was a net donor of population to the rest of the country between 1880 and 1960. With the exception of the final decade of the nineteenth century, the South lost more white and black migrants than it gained for all decades up to 1960. Except for the Depression of the 1930s, net out-migration for whites was in the vicinity of a half-million persons for the decades ending in 1930 and 1950. During the 1950s there was a modest net in-migration of whites; during the 1960s the net inflow was nearly 2 million persons. As noted earlier, the net out-migration of blacks was spurred by both World Wars, with some reduction during the 1930s. However, the absolute volume has been declining since 1940. Since 1970 the net migration of blacks from the South has been near zero (U.S. Bureau of the Census, 1975) and appears "to be changing in much the same general way as white migration did earlier, with change in net migration being the joint result of decreases in out-migration rates and increases in net in-migration rates" (Long and Hansen, 1975 : 611).

To this point the discussion of demographic change in the South has been restricted mainly to the period ending in 1970. However, we have noted briefly the demographic events which occurred since 1970, and it was pointed out that in many ways the post-1970 situation in the South and elsewhere is not at all a continuation of trends established earlier. We turn now to a more detailed consideration of the dynamics of southern demographic change between 1970 and 1975.

DEMOGRAPHIC CHANGES SINCE 1970

Between 1970 and 1975, the population of the South increased by over 5 million persons, more than half of the nearly 10 million increase for the total United States over the same period. Of the

TABLE 1.5 Population and Components of Population Change

Region	July 1, 1975	April 1, 1970
U.S.	213,121	203,304
Northeast	49,461	49,061
North Central	57,669	56,593
South	68,113	62,812
West	37,878	34,838

Source: U.S. Bureau of the Census, Current Population of the Population of States with Components of Change: Washington, D.C.: Government Printing Office.

more than 5 million increase in the South, about half was attributable to reproductive change, the other half to net migration. In no other region were both the volume of overall growth and the share due to net migration as high as in the South.

Table 1.5 presents components of population change data for the U.S. and its component regions for the 1970–1975 period. While slightly less than half the growth in the West resulted from net migration, its total population increase was much less than that of the South. The other two regions, the Northeast and the North Central, gained population between 1970 and 1975. However, their increases were wholly due to reproductive change, for both lost more persons through migration than they gained. The population increase of 400,000 in the Northeast occurred despite a net migration loss of nearly 700,000. The North Central region increased its population by more than 1 million, while experiencing a net migration loss of nearly 900,000. Were it not for a considerable excess of births over deaths in these two regions, both would have shown for the United States and Its Regions, 1970–1975 (thousands)

Change 1970–1975		Components of Population Change 1970–1975			
		Births	Deaths	Net Migration	
Number	%			Number	%
9,817	4.8	17,490	10,200	2,527	1.2
401	0.8	3,668	2,581	-686	-1.4
1,076	1.9	4,801	2,848	-878	-1.6
5,301	8.4	5,895	3,218	2,624	4.2
3,039	8.7	3,126	1,553	1,467	4.2

Reports, Population Estimates and Projections. Estimates 1960 to 1975. Ser. P-25, no. 640, November 1976.

net population losses between 1970 and 1975 (U.S. Bureau of the Census, 1976b).

Clearly, the South has been the region of maximum growth in the U.S. between 1970 and 1975, a point made especially apparent with the data in table 1.5. To gain a deeper appreciation of these dynamics of demographic change, we focus next on the geographic divisions and states comprising the region. Table 1.6 provides components of population change data for the three geographic divisions of the South and its sixteen states and the District of Columbia for 1970–1975. The South Atlantic Division grew by nearly 10 percent over the five years, and more than half of this increase (6.1 percent) was due to net migration. There were nearly 1.9 million net in-migrants to the South Atlantic between 1970 and 1975. These increases, however, were not shared equally by the eight states and the district comprising the division. Indeed, more than half the division's overall population increase and more than three-fourths of its increase due to net migration occurred in Florida.

TABLE 1.6   Population and Components of Population Change

Division and State	July 1, 1975	April 1, 1970
South	68,113	62,812
South Atlantic	33,715	30,679
Delaware	579	548
Maryland	4,098	3,924
District of Columbia	716	757
Virginia	4,967	4,651
West Virginia	1,803	1,744
North Carolina	5,451	5,084
South Carolina	2,818	2,591
Georgia	4,926	4,588
Florida	8,357	6,791
East South Central	13,544	12,808
Kentucky	3,396	3,221
Tennessee	4,188	3,926
Alabama	3,614	3,444
Mississippi	2,346	2,217
West South Central	20,855	19,325
Arkansas	2,116	1,923
Louisiana	3,791	3,642
Oklahoma	2,712	2,559
Texas	12,237	11,199

Source: U.S. Bureau of the Census, Current Population of the Population of States with Components of Change: Washington, D.C.:   Government Printing Office.

r the Southern United States; 1970-1975 (thousands)

| Change 1970-1975 | | Components of Population Change 1970-1975 | | | |
Number	Percent	Births	Deaths	Net Migration Number	Net Migration Percent
5,301	8.4	5,895	3,218	2,624	4.2
3,036	9.9	2,762	1,585	1,859	6.1
31	5.7	47	26	9	1.7
174	4.4	310	172	37	0.9
-40	-5.4	63	43	-61	-8.1
315	6.8	401	211	125	2.7
59	3.4	152	105	11	0.7
367	7.2	472	242	137	2.7
227	8.8	265	125	88	3.4
338	7.4	465	224	97	2.1
1,565	23.0	587	438	1,416	20.8
736	5.7	1,218	685	202	1.6
175	5.4	295	177	57	1.8
262	6.7	352	205	115	2.9
170	4.9	329	180	21	0.6
129	5.8	242	123	9	0.4
1,530	7.9	1,915	948	563	2.9
191	10.0	182	114	125	6.5
148	4.1	364	177	-38	-1.1
152	6.0	226	141	68	2.6
1,037	9.3	1,143	515	409	3.7

ports, Population Estimates and Projections.   Estimates
60 to 1975. Ser. P-25, no. 640, November 1976.

There were more than 1.4 million net in-migrants to the state of Florida between 1970 and 1975.

The West South Central Division grew by 1.5 million persons in the first half of the 1970s, and more than a third of this increase (563,000) was due to net migration. By far the largest actual share belonged to Texas, where there was an overall population increase of more than 1 million and a gain due to net migration of more than 400,000. The East South Central Division increased by 736,000 overall, with 202,000 due to net migration. In both actual and relative terms, Tennessee held the largest shares of these increases.

The major locations of population increase in the South between 1970 and 1975 were Florida and Texas. These two states together accounted for nearly half the South's overall population increase and nearly 70 percent of its migration increase. Of the more than 2.6 million net in-migrants to the South in the first half of the 1970s, more than 1.8 million of them were in Florida and Texas. Were it not for these two states, the South would have ranked behind the West in both overall population increase and population increase due to net migration.

Prior to 1970 most southern states were characterized by net out-migration. The South as a whole between 1950 and 1960 experienced a net loss of more than 1.4 million persons through migration. Only the large numbers of persons migrating into Florida, Texas, Virginia, Maryland, and Delaware during the 1950s (these states realized a net gain through migration of more than 2.1 million persons) prevented population losses in the South from being even more severe (U.S. Bureau of the Census, 1963a:12). During the 1960s the large numbers of persons migrating into these same few southern states more than made up for the net out-migration from most of the other states in the region (U.S. Bureau of the Census, 1976d:14).

The migration experiences of the South during the first half of the 1970s are in sharp contrast with those of previous decades. During the 1970s all southern states except the District of Columbia and Louisiana were characterized by net in-migration. The high levels of net out-migration during the 1950s in the majority of southern states were reduced significantly during the 1960s and then changed direction completely during the first half of the 1970s.

In less than one generation, the South has moved from a situation of substantial net out-migration to one of substantial net in-migration. However, this is not the striking feature of the dynamics of demographic change in the region. The net in-migration experiences of Florida, Texas, and a few other states during this period are no different in direction (although different in magnitude) from their net migration experiences during the 1950s and the 1960s. The singularly striking feature of the migration trends in the South during the first half of the 1970s is the extensive population gains through net migration in precisely those southern states which lost so heavily in the 1950s and the 1960s (U.S. Bureau of the Census, 1976b:1–2). These general points are embellished in later chapters by Poston and by Serow.

A PREVIEW

In the preface Price traced the intellectual heritage which has fostered the growth and development of southern demography. In this chapter we presented a general description of demographic developments and behavior in the South relative to those in the remainder of the nation. The next three chapters provide a much more detailed examination and focus on the three demographic variables of fertility, mortality, and migration. Rindfuss reports in chapter 2 that the South had higher fertility than the non-South until 1950. However, a convergence and reversal in fertility levels took place during the 1950s, when the increase in fertility was substantially greater in the non-South (64 percent) than in the South (41 percent). Indeed, during this interval older, less educated white women living in rural areas of the South actually experienced a decrease in fertility—a decrease that was not shared by their non-southern counterparts. By 1970 southern fertility was actually lower than nonsouthern fertility. Moreover, this lower fertility does not result from compositional factors in differentials in unwanted fertility. It exists because southerners *prefer* fewer children than nonsoutherners—and act accordingly. Rindfuss concludes that scholars interested in fertility will have to contend with region in the future.

In chapter 3 Rosenberg and Burnham demonstrate a marked convergence between mortality rates and morbidity in the South and the rest of the country. However, this convergence is still incomplete. Although the South experienced improvements in infant mortality, expectation of life at birth, and age-adjusted death rates that were greater than improvements in national levels since

1940, the South still had a lower health status in 1975 than the rest of the country. And this remains true even when specific causes of death are examined. Moreover, racial differentials in mortality are not always the same in the South as they are in the rest of the country. Although homicide rates for all races are higher in the South, the white-black differential is only half as large in the South as in the non-South. These differences may be compositional in nature, but Rosenberg and Burnham do not have the data necessary to test this hypothesis. After reviewing the results, they conclude that "the epidemiological transition of the nation is continuing and, with it, the transition of the South."

Sly analyzes the process of migration in chapter 4 and documents the reversal in patterns that has occurred. After a century of net out-migration, the South has become the recipient of net in-migration. The characteristics of the in-migrants differ from those of the out-migrants. Sly believes that current trends will continue and that the South will receive an even heavier volume of in-migration in the future.

In line with the social demographic emphasis of this volume, in chapter 5 Poston draws on the human ecological perspective and develops an interpretation for the migration patterns that have occurred in the South since 1970. He views migration as a mechanism of social change and adaptability for areas undergoing alterations in their sustenance activities. His analysis suggests that the construction component of sustenance organization, along with large-scale agricultural productivity, provided the principal influences on southern net migration patterns between 1970 and 1975. Like Sly, he also believes that net in-migration into the South will continue.

In chapter 6 Galle and Stern examine changes between 1950 and 1970 in the system of metropolitan areas in the southern region. They document that the system is characterized by a great deal of inertia in that the ordering of the metropolitan areas over time has been remarkably stable. On the other hand, they note that the metropolitan system of the South, so apparently separated from the rest of the nation in 1950, has been showing signs of closer integration in 1970, so much so that the authors hint that the southern system may become even more indistinguishable from that of the nation in future years. At the same time, Galle and Stern echo Price's suggestion that the growing similarity of the South with the balance of the nation may simply be the juxtaposition of two crosscutting trends at the same time.

In his discussion of industrialization in chapter 7 Singelmann also points out that two crossing lines may also diverge again. However, he concludes that "the past trends and their rate of change point more to the similarities than discrepancies between the South and the non-South in the future."

Serow views southern population change from an economic perspective in chapter 8. He posits that demographic behavior in the South is consistent with a generalized model of the demographic transition. Unlike some other contributors, particularly Rindfuss, he attributes any differences in demographic behavior between the South and the rest of the country to compositional effects. Serow believes that a gradual cessation of national population growth and the increasing cost of energy will influence future population trends in the South. As the population ages, there will be an increased demand for travel and other recreational activities. Moreover, persons at or near retirement age could constitute a larger portion of the migration stream. With its generally moderate climate, an abundance of recreational resources, lower tax structure, and generally lower cost of living, the South should gain a comparative advantage over the rest of the nation from both these developments. Increased energy costs should also enhance the economic position of the South. However, Serow does not view the future of the South with unbounded optimism. Indeed, he believes that by the end of the century "some parts of the South could find themselves in a position similar to that now faced by large urban areas elsewhere in the nation."

Continuing the social demographic theme of preceding chapters, Clarke examines southern population change from a political perspective in chapter 9. She maintains that regional differences in political culture exist and will continue to persist, although there remains a considerable amount of heterogeneity within the South. Clarke demonstrates that an assessment of the political impact of increased migration into the South should take into account the large volume of persons who are return migrants, or who are intraregional migrants.

In the concluding chapter, Myers emphasizes again the considerable demographic heterogeneity that exists within the South and casts a somewhat jaundiced eye upon continued efforts to write about "the" population of the South as though it were some monolithic entity. Yet, he believes this demographic diversity, combined with the fact that the timing and pace of demographic change in the South differ substantially from the patterns present in other sections of the country, provides unique opportunities for demographic scholars to test and expand their theoretical concepts. He also suggests several important dimensions of changing demographic conditions in the South that are likely to concern us in the future.

Thus, there is not complete consensus among the contributors concerning whether the characteristics of the South's population are becoming "merged" with those of the rest of the nation. However, the majority seem to believe that the South will continue to be different in several demographic dimensions. Several rationales for this expectation are presented. The nice thing about speculating about the future is that we can wait for it to happen and then compare it with our expectations.

This volume was organized after the 1976 annual meeting of the Southern Regional Demographic Group (SRDG), a professional group in which we have all been actively involved and which fosters the study of population by southern demographers. The opening and closing plenary sessions at the 1976 SRDG meeting were devoted to population change in the South. The 1978 annual meeting of the Population Association of America contained a panel discussion of "the Demography of the South." The 1979 SRDG annual meeting also contained a session on the same topic, and it is not unlikely that future meetings of SRDG and other professional societies will be dedicated to an in-depth examination of the basic issue: to what extent should southern region of residence continue to be included in demographic analyses?

2
Fertility

RONALD R. RINDFUSS

Regional fertility differences in the United States have long been recognized, and region has routinely been used as a control variable in examining various aspects of fertility.[1] Regional differences have also resulted in some researchers restricting themselves to collecting survey data for one geographical area in order to avoid the effects of regional variation (e.g., Masnick and McFalls, 1976).

Yet, contemporary sociologists have given little direct attention to regional differences in fertility (or to regional differences in other social phenomena as well). Region is controlled for, but rarely examined in its own right. Perhaps this lack of concern is because the regional fertility question is such a perplexing one: why is there or should there be a regional fertility differential? In many ways the question goes to the heart of the sociology of fertility because it asks for the social reasons for differences in fertility between two aggregates. This chapter examines the trend in the most prominent of the regional fertility differentials—the difference between the South and the remainder of the country. However, before addressing this more specific question, the general issue of possible causes of regional fertility differences needs to be further examined.

The two reasons generally given for differential behavior are: (1) aggregates differ with respect to their composition and (2) aggregates are distinct groups holding distinct values and norms. Although a mix of both explanations operates in most cases, it is generally clear which explanation is the predominant one. For example, with respect to the Catholic/non-Catholic fertility differential, it seems evident that Catholics and non-Catholics are two distinct groups holding different values and norms with respect to fertility and such related matters as contraception and abortion. (See Ryder and Westoff, 1971; or Whelpton, Campbell, and Patterson, 1966.) An example of compositional differences would be the relatively low crude birth rates in states such as Florida which are a function of the age composition of the population in those states.

Two approaches are usually taken to distinguish between these two types of explanations: (1) controlling empirically for compositional differences and (2) determining theoretically plausible reasons for the existence of group differences with respect to values and norms. Ideally, both types of evidence are needed before we can accept a difference in fertility as a sociological differential deriving from group membership. In the case of regional fertility differences, it is the latter evidence which is most problematic; i.e., the specific theoretical reasons for the differences. There are a number of theoretical possibilities, but they tend to be the type of explanation that stresses the continuing effect of a unique event or series of events. (One example is the opening of a family planning clinic in a given area—perhaps accompanied by an active campaign promoting the value of effective contraceptive use. The locating of a factory employing large numbers of women in a particular region provides a second example because the ready access of employment opportunities for women could provide alternative roles to the bearing and raising of children.)

With respect to the regions being considered here: why might the South be considered a social group and—if it can be so considered—why should membership involve distinct fertility values and norms, or the ability to achieve those values and norms? Certainly there are a number of distinct differences between the South and the remainder of the country, ranging from climate to the historical experiences of the Civil War and Reconstruction. Furthermore, Reed (1972) has presented evidence for considering the South as an ethnic group with respect to such factors as religion and outlook toward violence. Yet, I can find no a priori reason why Southerners, as Southerners, should hold or ever have held distinctive values and norms for fertility.

This chapter takes the approach of controlling for compositional differences and examines empirically the trend in the southern/nonsouthern fertility differential, with particular emphasis on the period since World War II. It is found that there has been a reversal in the differential: the South now has lower fertility. This new differential persists after controlling for potentially confounding factors,[2] and it is not the product of differential success in avoiding unplanned fertility. The concluding portion of this chapter returns to the theoretical question of why this regional fertility differential exists.

THE LONG VIEW

Historically the South has been the region of highest fertility within the United States (Whelpton, 1936; Vance, 1941, 1945; Grabill, Kiser, and Whelpton, 1958; Kiser, Grabill, and Campbell, 1968; Hathaway, Beegle, and Bryant, 1968; Cho, Grabill, and Bogue, 1970). Table 2.1 shows the child-woman ratio for each of the nine census divisions from 1800 to 1950. (The child-woman ratio is used despite its well-known methodological limitations because it is the only measure available for this period. Later in this paper, more refined measures are used for the post-World War II era.) During this entire period (1800–1950), the three southern divisions tended to have the highest fertility. The principal exceptions were on the frontier—the East North Central and West North Central Divisions during the first part of the nineteenth century. The high fertility in frontier regions is often attributed to the availability of inexpensive land and other resources (e.g., see Forster and Tucker, 1972).

After the passing of the frontier,[3] the South stood out as the area of highest fertility. Even when the frontier was being developed, the South tended to have higher fertility than the other settled regions along the Eastern Seaboard. After the Civil War, the fertility differences between the South and rest of the nation increased because fertility did not decline as fast in the South during this period as it did in the remainder of the country.

The historical reasons for "the South's extra fertility"—as Vance (1941) termed it—are difficult to disentangle given available data. The rural-urban, occupational, and religious composition of the South, relative to the remainder of the country, certainly played a part (Whelpton, 1936). Vance (1941) attributed part of the South's higher fertility to delays in the adoption of family planning methods. Data are not available to confirm or deny this hypothesis. However, it is worth noting that by the time of the 1960 Growth of American Families Study (Whelpton, Campbell, and Patterson, 1966) the proportion of couples that had ever used contraception was higher in the South than in any other region. Although the data are difficult to obtain, racial differences between the South

TABLE 2.1   Number of Children under 5 Years Old per 1,00

				White	
Year	United States	New England	Middle Atlantic	East North Central	West North Central
1800	1,342	1,164	1,334	1,918	a
1810	1,358	1,111	1,365	1,777	1,915
1820	1,295	980	1,244	1,683	1,768
1830	1,145	826	1,044	1,473	1,685
1840	1,085	770	951	1,280	1,446
1850	892	636	776	1,037	1,122
1860	905	639	784	1,016	1,118
1870	814	564	702	892	1,012
1880	780	520	648	781	930
1890	685	456	563	668	797
1900	666	497	567	620	731
1910	631	505	554	576	650
1920	604	543	562	570	605
1930	506	467	447	482	520
1940	419	365	337	407	452
1950	587	552	507	586	642

Source: Wilson H. Grabill, Clyde V. Kiser, and Pascal K
John Wiley and Sons, 1959), table E.
[a] Data not available.

omen 20 to 44 Years Old by Race, by Divisions, 1800-1950

South Atlantic	East South Central	West South Central	Mountain	Pacific	Negro Total
1,402	1,875	a	a	a	a
1,382	1,794	1,446	a	a	a
1,330	1,708	1,483	a	a	a
1,189	1,530	1,369	a	a	a
1,162	1,424	1,310	a	a	a
957	1,115	1,061	875	896	1,087
940	1,056	1,103	1,054	1,035	1,072
833	922	953	982	916	997
879	952	1,066	892	808	1,090
802	873	994	770	600	930
802	855	942	742	532	845
780	836	861	680	478	736
720	760	706	686	447	608
618	680	586	582	357	554
480	556	492	546	358	513
601	666	644	699	576	706

elpton, The Fertility of American Women (New York:

and the rest of the country undoubtedly also contributed to the fertility differences. Finally, the Civil War itself and the subsequent period of Reconstruction may have had the effect of slowing down the process of fertility declines (Grabill, Kiser, and Whelpton, 1958).

TRENDS SINCE WORLD WAR II

From the end of World War II through the end of the 1960s, it is possible to examine southern and nonsouthern fertility trends in greater detail. To do so, annual age-specific fertility rates have been constructed for the South and non-South (and for various groups within these two regions) by using own children data available from the 1960 and 1970 1 percent Census Public Use Tapes. The own children technique is described in detail elsewhere (Grabill and Cho, 1965; Cho, 1968; Cho, Grabill, and Bogue, 1970; Cho, 1971; Retherford and Cho, 1974). It is used because it permits construction of annual age-specific fertility rates and, thus, more detailed trend analysis than would be possible with children ever born data. In other work we have reported some limitations of own children data when used in the study of differential fertility (Rindfuss and Sweet, 1977). These limitations will not be repeated here, but in general we find that, even though the levels may be misspecified, own children data accurately estimate trends. Appendix A reports an investigation of the limitations of using own children data when such changeable characteristics as region and size of place of residence are used. Appendix A shows, in detail, that own children data produce reliable trend estimates even with such changeable characteristics.

Total fertility rates[4] for 1945–1969 are shown in figure 2.1 for South and non-South, defined in terms of the usual census classification.[5] It is clear from this figure that both regions of the country experienced the dominant trends of the period—the baby boom and the subsequent decline. This is consistent with the pervasiveness of fertility trends found for other social, economic, and racial groups within the country (Rindfuss and Sweet, 1977). It is also clear from figure 2.1 that there was considerable convergence between the two regions during the period, and apparently[6] a reversal in the long-standing regional differential has taken place. The convergence and apparent reversal occurred during the baby boom of the 1950s *and not* during the decline in fertility of the 1960s. The convergence occurred because the increase in fertility during the 1950s was substantially greater in the non-South (a 64 percent increase between 1945 and 1957) than in the South (a 41 percent increase). This also can be seen by looking at table 2.2. During the 1960s both the South and the non-South had similar rates of decline (33 and 31 percent respectively). Furthermore, the convergence did not occur during the two-year period of very rapid increases in fertility immediately after World War II, when pregnancies postponed during depression and war were occurring. During this period, 1945–1947, both the South and the non-South had similar rates of fertility increase (31 and 35 percent respectively). Rather, the convergence took place during the 1950s—a period of slower but more sustained growth in fertility levels.[7]

To examine this convergence further, we have calculated rates of fertility increase and decrease within educational groups and for younger (age 15–29) and older (30–44) women.[8] These are shown in table 2.2. First, it can be seen that the pattern of more rapid in-

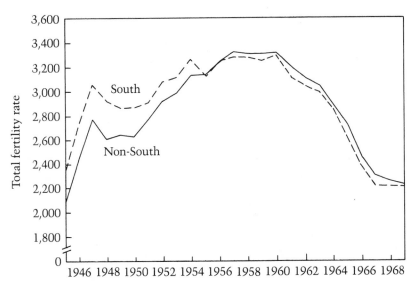

Figure 2.1. Total fertility rates for southern and nonsouthern women, 1945–1969

TABLE 2.2 Percentage Change in Fertility by Region of Residence and Education

Period and Years of Education	Total Fertility		Fertility 15-29		Fertility 30-44	
	Southern	Nonsouthern	Southern	Nonsouthern	Southern	Nonsouthern
1945-1957						
Total[a]	+41	+63	+62	+89	+5	+21
5-8 years	+33	+58	+50	+76	+1	+21
9-11 years	+51	+64	+75	+86	+5	+20
12 years	+66	+73	+95	+106	+16	+22
13+ years	+69	+55	+86	+86	+43	+19
1957-1967						
Total[a]	-33	-31	-31	-29	-38	-32
5-8 years	-23	-15	-20	-12	-30	-24
9-11 years	-31	-31	-29	-31	-37	-33
12 years	-31	-30	-28	-28	-38	-34
13+ years	-36	-32	-33	-32	-42	-32

[a]Total includes women with 0-4 years of education.

creases in total fertility rates during the 1950s in the non-South is found for all the educational groups shown, with the exception of those with some college education. Southern women who had attended college had a higher rate of increase during the 1950s than did comparable northern women. During the 1960s women in the various educational groups had remarkably similar rates of fertility decline in both the South and the rest of the country. The only exception here is the grade school category, and in this group convergence continued because Southerners experienced a somewhat faster rate of decrease than non-Southerners. Furthermore, it should again be noted that the convergence took place primarily during the 1950s and not during the immediate post-World War II rise in fertility. This can be seen comparing the following percentage of increase in fertility during 1945–1947:

Years of Education	South	Non-South
5–8	24	32
9–11	36	39
12	44	40
13+	39	30

The pattern of more rapid increase in fertility during the 1950s in the non-South is found for both younger and older women (see table 2.2). The contrast is especially striking among older women with a grade school education and among older women who dropped out of high school.

The convergence between the total South and total non-South during the 1950s (figure 2.1) occurred because it had taken place within many of the constituent groups within the South and non-South (see table 2.2, also tables 2.4 and 2.5) and because the educational attainment of southern women was rising faster than that of nonsouthern women. Using women aged 20–24 as an example, the proportion with only a grade school education in the period 1945–1957 decreased from 17 percent to 11 percent in the non-South and from 31 percent to 19 percent in the South.

In order to guard against the possibility that the critical factor in regional differentials is socialization rather than current place of residence, we calculated a set of annual age-specific fertility rates by place of birth rather than place of residence. Place of birth is being used here as an imperfect surrogate for place of socialization. Rates of fertility increase and decrease by place of birth are shown in table 2.3. Exact patterns emerge, as was the case with current

TABLE 2.3 Percentage Change in Fertility by Region of Birth and Education

Period and Years of Education	Total Fertility		Fertility 15-29		Fertility 30-44	
	Southern	Nonsouthern	Southern	Nonsouthern	Southern	Nonsouthern
1945-1957						
Total[a]	+42	+63	+64	+89	+6	+21
5-8 years	+40	+53	+57	+72	+6	+15
9-11 years	+58	+63	+70	+87	+12	+17
12 years	+66	+74	+94	+105	+18	+24
13+ years	+55	+59	+80	+86	+21	+26
1957-1967						
Total[a]	-32	-31	-30	-30	-39	-34
5-8 years	-20	-18	-16	-14	-33	-28
9-11 years	-32	-32	-30	-31	-38	-36
12 years	-29	-29	-26	-26	-39	-36
13+ years	-31	-33	-29	-33	-35	-34

[a]Total includes women with 0-4 years of education.

place of residence: non-Southerners had higher rates of increase in fertility during the 1950s than Southerners. During the 1960s the rates of fertility decline were very similar.

It might be argued that place of birth is too imperfect an indicator of place of socialization because some women may have changed places of residence at a very young age. So, in order to complete this portion of the analysis, we calculated annual age-specific fertility rates for women who were born in the South and were living in the South at the time of the census, as well as for women who were born in the non-South and were living in the non-South at the time of the census (figure 2.2). As figure 2.2 shows, this "pure" comparison has exactly the same trend as was evident for place of birth or place of residence: there was substantial convergence between the two regions during the 1950s and both regions experienced similar rates of decrease during the 1960s. The same patterns emerge whether place of residence or place of birth are used; therefore, in the remainder of this chapter, we will only refer to trends by place of residence.

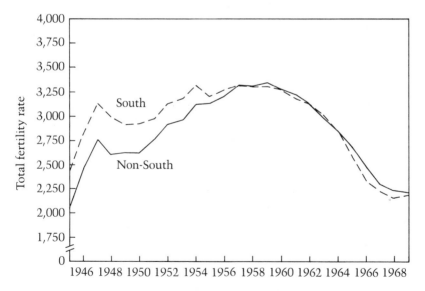

Figure 2.2. Total fertility rates for women born in the South and residing in the South at the time of the census and for women born in the non-South and residing in the non-South at the time of the census, 1945–1969

TABLE 2.4 Percentage Change in Fertility for Whites, by Education and Region of Residence

Period and Years of Education	Total Fertility		Fertility 15-29		Fertility 30-44	
	Southern	Nonsouthern	Southern	Nonsouthern	Southern	Nonsouthern
1945-1957						
Total[a]	+40	+61	+63	+87	0	+18
5-8 years	+27	+53	+47	+71	-12	+17
9-11 years	+47	+61	+70	+85	-1	+17
12 years	+66	+73	+94	+105	+16	+22
13+ years	+67	+56	+85	+86	+40	+20
1957-1967						
Total[a]	-34	-31	-33	-31	-38	-32
5-8 years	-21	-14	-19	-11	-27	-21
9-11 years	-40	-35	-33	-31	-38	-32
12 years	-32	-30	-30	-29	-39	-35
13+ years	-38	-32	-34	-32	-44	-32

[a]Total includes women with 0-4 years of education.

TRENDS WITHIN RACIAL GROUPS

Until World War II, the overwhelming majority of blacks lived in the South. Since that time large numbers of blacks have migrated to the North. For this reason and given the segregation between blacks and whites, it is necessary to see if this pattern in fertility trends found for the total for the two regions is also found within the two racial groups. Table 2.4 shows rates of increase in 1945– 1957 and rates of decrease in the period 1957–1967 for whites by place of residence and by education. The same patterns of convergence or nonconvergence are found for whites as was the case for the total group. The non-South experienced larger increases in fertility during the baby boom than did the South except for the college educated group. During the 1960s both regions experienced similar rates of fertility decline.

A surprising feature of table 2.4, however, is the finding that white southern women aged 40–44 did not participate in the pervasive fertility increases of the 1950s. In fact, among older white southern women who did not graduate from high school, there was an actual decrease in fertility during the 1950s. This represents an exception to the generalized baby boom, and, as shown in the next section, this decrease in fertility among older, less educated white women is found only in the rural South.

Unfortunately, it is not possible to examine post-World War II fertility trends within the black population in as detailed a manner as was the case for whites, for the simple reason that in many of the categories there is an insufficient number of blacks.[9] Within the South there was an insufficient number of blacks in the higher educational classifications to construct reliable rates, and within the non-South there was an insufficient number in the lower educational classification. However, for the total black populations of the South and non-South, it is possible to construct reliable rates. Table 2.5 shows rates of fertility increase during the 1950s and decrease during the 1960s for blacks for the two regions. Again, the same pattern is evident as was found for the total population: during the 1950s the increase in fertility was substantially greater among nonsouthern blacks than among southern blacks. During the 1960s both regions experienced similar declines in fertility.

TABLE 2.5 Percentage Change in Fertility for Blacks, by Region of Residence

Fertility Measure	1945-1957		1957-1969	
	Southern	Nonsouthern	Southern	Nonsouthern
Total Fertility	+45	+111	-38	-35
Fertility 15-29	+58	+123	-36	-34
Fertility 30-44	+25	+83	-42	-37

TRENDS WITHIN WHITE RURAL AND URBAN AREAS

A further compositional difference between the South and the remainder of the country is the urban and rural distribution of the population. While the South historically has been more rural than the remainder of the nation, this relationship has been changing since World War II as the South has been urbanizing more rapidly than the remainder of the nation (see Hamilton, 1970). Fertility traditionally has been higher in rural areas than in urban areas. Thus, it is mandatory to see whether the pattern of converging fertility occurred within both the rural and urban sectors of the two regions. Because there is an insufficient number of blacks in the sample to construct reliable rates for the various place of residence and region classifications, this section will be limited to the white population.

Table 2.6 shows increases and decreases in fertility during the 1950s and the 1960s for the urban and rural sectors of both South and non-South. The contrast in trends between the South and the rest of the country is substantially different in the urban sector versus the rural sector. Within the urban sector, there are quite similar rates of increase in fertility during the baby boom years for the two geographic regions. During the period of fertility decline, the decreases in fertility are remarkably similar for the urban sectors of both regions.

This suggests that there has been very little regional difference in urban fertility trends since World War II. Thus, whatever factors have been responsible for the dominant fertility trends since World War II have been operating within both the urban South and the urban non-South. Although estimates of fertility *levels* from own children data can be misleading (Rindfuss, 1976), it is worth noting that the fertility levels for the urban South and the urban non-South have also been very close throughout the entire period (levels are not shown in the table).

The similarity in trends is not found in the rural areas of the two regions (see the lower panel of table 2.6). During the period of declining fertility in the 1960s, the rural sectors of both regions experienced similar rates of decline. However, during the baby boom years between 1945 and 1957, there was a substantially smaller increase in fertility in the rural South than in the rural non-South. This is true of every educational category except college educated women.

Table 2.6 contains the only exception found to the pervasive increase in fertility which occurred within the United States between 1945 and 1957 (see Rindfuss and Sweet, 1977, for a discussion of the pervasiveness of postwar fertility trends). Among older, rural, southern white women, there was an actual 15 percent decline in fertility between 1945 and 1957. In an earlier publication (Rindfuss and Sweet, 1977), we noted that among all older, rural white women there was no net change in fertility between 1945 and 1957 and that among older, less-educated, rural white women there was an actual decline in fertility during the period. The data shown in table 2.6 specify that exception further: the decline in fertility during the baby boom only occurred among older, rural white Southerners and not among their nonsouthern counterparts.

A probable explanation for this exception to the generalized baby boom is that older, rural white southern women with limited education probably were an isolated group (geographically and socially) within American society prior to World War II, and they probably did not have access to moderately effective methods of contraception or knowledge of these methods. As we speculated earlier, it is possible that "among these women there was increased awareness and utilization of contraception—especially the con-

TABLE 2.6 Percentage Change in Fertility for Whites by Residence

Period and Years of Education	Total Fertility	
	Southern	Nonsouthern
1945-1957		
Total[a]	+60	+66
5-8 years	+55	+68
9-11 years	+60	+69
12 years	+74	+76
13+ years	+61	+54
1957-1967		
Total[a]	-32	-31
5-8 years	-10	-18
9-11 years	-36	-31
12 years	-31	-29
13+ years	-32	-32
1945-1957		
Total[a]	+27	+50
5-8 years	+13	+36
9-11 years	+27	+47
12 years	+47	+65
13+ years	+78	+66
1957-1967		
Total[a]	-31	-31
5-8 years	-25	-20
9-11 years	-31	-34
12 years	-29	-29
13+ years	-33	-34

[a]Total includes women with 0-4 years of education.

Education, Region of Residence and Size of Place of

Fertility 15-29		Fertility 30-44	
Southern	Nonsouthern	Southern	Nonsouthern
URBAN			
+81	+94	+20	+22
+76	+94	+8	+19
+80	+96	+14	+17
+104	+109	+24	+26
+73	+81	+42	+21
-31	-30	-36	-32
-6	-15	-20	-23
-35	-30	-41	-36
-28	-26	-41	-35
-29	-33	-37	-31
RURAL			
+40	+73	-15	+11
+29	+48	-16	+10
+51	+64	-16	+9
+74	+92	+2	+18
+119	+105	+22	+22
-27	-28	-41	-39
-21	-13	-35	-39
-26	-34	-45	-33
-26	-24	-38	-41
-33	-30	-33	-42

dom—as a result of education about prophylaxis during World War II" (Rindfuss and Sweet, 1977). Thus, the public health measures to combat venereal disease which took place in the armed forces probably had the effect of increasing awareness of certain contraceptive methods among those who did not have this knowledge. That this decline in fertility is found only in the rural South—a more isolated rural population than is found in non-South rural areas—further supports this possibility that it was brought about by increased awareness of contraception following World War II. Unfortunately, for reasons of diminishing sample sizes, it is not possible to construct the rates for subregions within the South. If it were possible, we would expect the rural fertility decline during the 1950s to be most concentrated in the more isolated areas of the rural South. The fertility decline during the 1950s found by DeJong (1968) for the southern Appalachians suggests that this is the case.

There is also another possibility. Even though the rural South experienced net out-migration in the decade following World War II, there may have been some movement of middle-class families into these areas—particularly the rural areas of the Piedmont region. This also might have contributed to the decline in fertility among older, rural white Southerners during the baby boom. Unfortunately, the appropriate data to test this possibility are not available.

WANTED AND UNWANTED FERTILITY COMPONENTS

It is possible to decompose the regional fertility differential into its wanted and unwanted components for the latter part of the period when the South had lower fertility than the non-South. To do so, we used data from the 1970 National Fertility Study (NFS) to examine regional differences in both the number of children wanted and in the number of unwanted births. The 1970 NFS is a multipurpose study based on a national probability sample of 6,752 ever-married women under 45 years of age residing in the continental United States (Westoff and Ryder, 1977). Details regarding the measurement of wanted and unwanted fertility are found in Ryder and Westoff (1972), but it should be noted that "wanted fertility" is the sum of the number of wanted births that have already occurred plus the additional number of births the respondent intends to have. "Unwanted fertility" is simply the number of unwanted births already born.

In order to control for such potentially confounding factors as age, race, religion, wife's education, number of times married, farm background, and age at marriage, a multiple regression approach was used. The findings are that Southerners want significantly fewer children than non-Southerners. (The tabular results are not shown here, but are available upon request from the author.) Southerners also have fewer unwanted children than non-Southerners; however, the differences are quite small and are not statistically significant. That Southerners want fewer children than non-Southerners suggests that the lower fertility found in the South will continue at least in the short run.

REGIONAL DIFFERENCES SINCE THE 1970 CENSUS

Detailed examination of trends in regional fertility differentials requires very large samples—the kinds which can be obtained only from censuses. However, it is possible to obtain at least a general notion of the trend in regional fertility differences since the late 1960s without waiting for the 1980 census. To do so, we have used data from the 1976 *Survey of Income and Education* (*SIE*) and from the various March *Current Population Surveys* (*CPS*) through 1977. By conventional standards these surveys have a large number of cases, but they are not sufficiently large to permit the types of detailed analyses reported earlier in this chapter. Instead we have examined the number of own children under three years of age for women currently married and under age 40 at the time of the census. This measure gives fairly reliable results for smaller samples (Rindfuss and Sweet, 1977).

Both the *CPS* and the *SIE* data yield the same results: the South has lower levels of current fertility than the rest of the country. Thus, the lower southern fertility that began in the 1950s has persisted through the mid-1970s.

SUMMARY AND CONCLUSIONS

To summarize, the long-standing higher fertility of the South relative to the non-South has ceased. The convergence and reversal in fertility levels occurred during the 1950s. In 1970 we found that southern fertility is lower than nonsouthern fertility and not because of compositional differences or differences in unwanted fertility. Rather, southern fertility is lower because Southerners *prefer* fewer children than non-Southerners. Thus, we must return to the question posed at the beginning of this chapter: why should *region of residence* be a sociological variable producing distinct fertility norms and values? For the present it is only possible to speculate about the various reasons why region might produce such an effect.[10] It is always possible that we have failed to control for all the appropriate compositional variables. However, the fact that the South-North regional fertility differential has existed for two centuries argues against this possibility and suggests that it is something about region itself that is producing the difference. The exact factors are unknown at present. It is implausible that the cause is longitude and latitude. Rather, the source of this regional difference is probably the same as the source of fertility differences across developed nations—differences in historical and cultural backgrounds.

From colonial times, through the Civil War, and to the present, the South and the non-South have had different historical experiences, and it is most likely that these different sets of experiences have produced different values and norms. The Civil War and Reconstruction serve as the most prominent examples, but there are many others as well.

Elsewhere, we have shown that the South and the rest of the country had a different fertility reaction to the 1954 desegregation ruling (Rindfuss, Reed, and St. John, 1978). It is beyond the scope of this chapter to examine all the differences in experience between the South and the rest of the country that could produce this regional difference in fertility. However, it is apparent that region is a variable that sociologists interested in fertility will have to contend with in the future. As Reed (1972) and others have shown, sociologists interested in other social phenomena will also have to contend with region.

Because the precise set of factors responsible for the regional fertility differential are presently unknown, it is difficult to predict the future of this differential. Currently, the South is a region of substantial net in-migration. The "new Southerners" bring with them a set of historical and cultural backgrounds that differ from those of long-term residents. The temptation is strong to suggest that the eventual outcome of the new migration will be a diminution of the regional fertility differential. However, the persistence of this regional differential over time tempers the urge to predict its decline.

METHODOLOGICAL APPENDIX A: STABILITY OF
THE FERTILITY RATE ESTIMATES

The fertility trend estimates presented here for the period since
World War II have been constructed by using own children data
from the 1960 and 1970 census Public Use Tapes. As shown elsewhere (Rindfuss, 1976), fertility rates obtained from these own
children data accurately estimate fertility *trends* (even though the
levels are misspecified) provided: (1) the characteristics of women
at the time of the census are applicable (or adjustable) to each of
the 15 years preceding the census and (2) error introduced by age
misstatement, mortality, children not living with their mothers,
and underenumeration are approximately constant over time. Typically, departures from this second assumption do not seriously
distort trend estimates, but departures from the first do (Rindfuss,
1977). Since this chapter used such changeable characteristics as
region of residence and size of place of residence, it is possible that
changes in characteristics of women might distort the trends. The
purpose of this appendix is to investigate that possibility.

With own children data in the United States, it is possible to estimate fertility rates for each 15 years preceding the census. Since
two successive decennial censuses are being used, there is a 5-year
period (1955–1959) for which two estimates are available for each
group and rate. This overlap period provides an internal check on
the consistency of the estimates.

The characteristic that is our central focus, region of residence,
is subject to change. In fact, it is well known that there have been
fairly large-scale transfers of population between the South and the
remainder of the country. Table 2.7 shows the ratio of the 1960
census estimates to the 1970 census estimates for the 5-year overlap period for southern and nonsouthern women for age and educational groups. By first examining the bottom panel of table 2.7, it
can be seen that the two sets of estimates are remarkably close for
all age groups of both the total southern group and the total nonsouthern group—suggesting that whatever change in region of residence that did occur was not sufficient to affect the estimates of
southern and nonsouthern fertility. The rest of the table shows the
effect of changes in educational status. For women aged 20 or
more, the ratio of the two estimates tends to be close to unity in
each category. For teenagers, however, changes in educational status influence the ratios between the two rates, and this effect is the
same in both the southern and nonsouthern groups.

TABLE 2.7 Ratio of 1960 Census Estimates to 1970 Census Estimates c
Overlap (1955-1959) by Education and Age Group

Comparisons of Age-Specific

Education Group and Years	15-19		20-24		25-29	
	Southern	Non-southern	Southern	Non-southern	Southern	Non-southern
5-8 years						
1959	.69	.75	1.07	1.04	.99	1.10
1958	.81	1.00	1.08	1.09	1.12	1.04
1957	.88	1.10	1.02	1.09	.85	1.09
1956	.98	.97	1.08	1.11	1.13	1.00
1955	1.04	1.30	1.08	1.09	1.07	1.05
9-11 years						
1959	.51	.42	1.04	1.02	1.08	1.05
1958	.56	.48	1.09	1.08	1.05	1.03
1957	.66	.61	1.04	1.08	1.04	1.02
1956	.88	.84	1.04	1.03	.99	1.02
1955	.89	.99	.98	1.03	1.01	.98
12 years						
1959	1.77	1.73	1.06	1.04	1.05	1.04
1958	1.32	1.22	1.05	1.03	1.05	1.02
1957	1.04	.96	.99	1.04	1.05	1.00
1956	.94	.79	1.02	.99	.98	1.03
1955	.83	.88	1.05	1.04	.95	1.03
13+ years						
1959	2.29	1.87	.95	1.04	1.09	1.03
1958	1.10	1.37	.91	1.00	1.00	1.01
1957	.95	.76	.92	.99	1.05	1.03
1956	.74	.70	.95	.99	.98	1.02
1955	.49	.60	.94	.97	.99	1.00
Total[a]						
1959	.99	.97	1.05	1.04	1.06	1.04
1958	.98	.97	1.05	1.05	1.05	1.02
1957	.97	.96	1.01	1.06	1.01	1.02
1956	1.02	.91	1.04	1.02	1.01	1.02
1955	.98	1.02	1.03	1.04	1.01	1.01

[a]Includes women with 0-4 years of education.

Fertility Rates among Southern and Nonsouthern Women for **Five-Year**

rtility Rates						Comparisons of Total Fertility Rates	
30–34		35–39		40–44			
	Non-		Non-		Non-		Non-
uthern	southern	Southern	southern	Southern	southern	Southern	southern
.01	1.12	1.15	.98	.91	.88	.96	1.00
.13	1.10	1.12	.96	1.07	1.01	1.03	1.05
.00	.97	1.09	.92	.98	.84	.95	1.05
.94	.95	1.11	.89	1.04	.89	1.05	1.01
.00	.98	1.03	1.06	.92	.83	1.05	1.09
.04	1.04	.97	.93	1.04	1.32	.92	.90
.09	1.08	1.29	1.03	.91	.94	.96	.93
.10	.96	1.00	1.04	.83	1.05	.95	.95
.90	1.00	.95	.95	.90	.88	.96	.97
.16	1.09	.88	.99	.73	.95	.98	1.01
.99	1.02	1.06	1.09	1.18	1.03	1.12	1.10
.08	1.05	1.09	1.03	1.37	1.11	1.09	1.05
.02	1.02	1.03	1.02	1.49	.91	1.03	1.01
.03	1.03	.96	1.07	1.00	.99	1.00	1.00
.99	1.05	1.13	1.04	1.12	1.13	1.00	1.03
.01	1.07	1.18	1.06	.96	1.23	1.08	1.07
.99	1.04	.94	1.09	.99	.96	.97	1.03
.07	1.02	1.09	.99	1.25	.78	1.02	1.00
.04	.99	.91	1.07	1.13	.90	.97	.99
.05	1.00	1.09	.97	1.01	1.06	.97	.92
.04	1.04	1.09	1.03	1.02	1.08	1.04	1.04
.08	1.06	1.14	1.02	1.08	1.02	1.05	1.03
.05	1.00	1.07	1.00	1.13	.91	1.02	1.02
.03	1.00	1.03	1.01	1.03	.93	1.02	1.00
.03	1.03	1.05	1.02	.96	.98	1.02	1.02

This lack of agreement between the two sets of rates for younger women by education has been discussed elsewhere (Rindfuss and Sweet, 1977: chapter 3). In order to minimize the effect of these educational change biases, whenever fertility rates for women aged 15–19 have been examined, the same procedures that have been used earlier (Rindfuss and Sweet, 1977) were used here: (1) the rates for the 2 years closest to the census (i.e., 1968–1969 for the 1970 census and 1958–1959 for the 1960 census) have been eliminated and (2) for the 3-year period when there are two estimates available (1955–1957), the estimates from the 1960 and 1970 censuses have been averaged. This has the unfortunate disadvantage of truncating the series at 1967 instead of 1969. Whenever fertility rates for women aged 15–19 are not being examined, the series has been extended the full 25 years and for the 5-year overlap period the two estimates have been averaged.

Furthermore, it should be noted that occasionally for the older age groups the ratio between the two estimates departs substantially from unity. For example, the ratio for age group 40–44 for nonsouthern women with 9–11 years of education for 1959 is 1.32. There is essentially no pattern to these large departures from unity at the older age groups, and they are the result of sampling error. Even though large samples have been employed in making these estimates, the very low level of fertility in the oldest age group (10–30 births per 1,000 women per year) produces fairly high sampling errors for this age group. However, the low level of fertility of this age group insures that their contribution to the total fertility rate for fertility 30–44 is minimal; hence, the high level of sampling variability can be ignored.

A characteristic that ought to remain constant is place of birth. Table 2.8 shows the ratio of the 1960 census estimates to the 1970 census estimates for the 5-year overlap period for women born in the South and women born outside the South for age and educational groups. The bottom panel of table 2.8 shows that the two sets of estimates are very close for the totals in each place of birth group. Thus, as expected, accurate fertility trend estimates can be obtained for place of birth group by using own children data.

Table 2.9 examines the ratio between the two census estimates for the situation where three characteristics can be changing simultaneously: region of residence, size of place of residence, and education. By first looking at the totals for the region of residence and size of place of residence categories, it can be seen that these ratios are generally close to unity. This suggests that whatever changes in region of residence or size of place of residence which have occurred have not been sufficient to affect the fertility estimates. However, within each of the four region of residence–size of place of residence groups, there is the characteristic distortion produced by changes in educational status.

NOTES

1. Portions of this chapter have appeared in *Social Forces* 57 (December 1978) and are reprinted here with its permission. The analysis was supported in part by a National Institutes of Health grant, no. HD07682; by a "Center for Population Research" grant, no. HD05876, to the Center for Demography and Ecology from the Center for Population Research of the National Institute of Child Health and Human Development; by funds granted to the Institute for Research on Poverty of the University of Wisconsin, Madison, by the Department of Health, Education, and Welfare pursuant to the Economic Opportunity Act of 1964; and by a "Center for Population Research" grant, no. HD05798, to the Carolina Population Center from the Center for Population Research of the National Institute of Child Health and Human Development. The programming assistance of Barbara Witt and bibliographic assistance of Craig St. John are gratefully acknowledged.

2. Whenever one examines the possible relationship between two variables by controlling for a set of potentially confounding variables, the implicit assumption being made is that all potentially confounding variables are being controlled. The embarrassingly low R^2s obtained in predicting fertility in developed nations suggest that this will not be the case. Thus, with respect to fertility as well as many other social phenomena, it is important not only to establish empirical relationships but also to establish the theoretical reasons for those relationships.

3. The Mountain states in the most recent years are also an exception, perhaps reflecting the growing influence of Mormons during these years.

4. The total fertility rate can be thought of as an estimate of the number of children that would be born to a cohort of 1,000 women if they went through the reproductive years exposed to the same age-specific fertility rates as were in effect during the particular period. For a more exact definition, see Shryock and Siegel (1973).

5. The following states, plus the District of Columbia, comprise the South: Alabama, Arkansas, Delaware, Florida, Georgia, Kentucky, Louisiana, Maryland, Mississippi, North Carolina, Oklahoma, South Carolina, Tennessee, Texas, Virginia, and West Virginia. The remainder of the states comprise the non-South.

6. The word "apparently" is used because the use of fertility estimates based on own children data to determine *levels* is often inappropriate (see Rindfuss, 1976). However, other indicators examined, but not reported here, also suggest

TABLE 2.8   Ratio of 1960 Census Estimates to 1970 Census Estimates (
Five-Year Overlap (1955-1959) by Education and Age Group

Education Group and Years	Comparisons of Age-Specific					
	15-19		20-24		25-29	
	South	Non-South	South	Non-South	South	Non-South
5-8 years						
1959	.63	.73	.98	1.11	1.01	1.06
1958	.86	1.00	1.00	1.11	1.12	1.03
1957	.91	1.04	.99	1.13	.98	1.00
1956	1.00	1.14	1.06	1.17	.98	1.02
1955	1.02	1.24	1.07	1.02	1.02	1.04
9-11 years						
1959	.48	.42	.99	1.02	1.10	1.10
1958	.56	.48	1.03	1.13	.97	1.13
1957	.64	.60	1.05	1.03	1.06	1.01
1956	.80	.83	1.03	1.07	.98	1.10
1955	.85	1.00	.97	1.00	.90	.98
12 years						
1959	1.45	1.76	.99	1.06	1.02	1.02
1958	1.26	1.21	1.07	1.03	1.08	1.03
1957	1.02	1.01	1.02	1.05	1.01	1.00
1956	.92	.84	1.02	1.02	.98	1.04
1955	.90	.87	1.02	1.07	.98	1.06
13+ years						
1959	1.87	1.93	.92	.97	.99	1.06
1958	.99	1.60	.99	.99	.95	1.02
1957	.94	.79	.98	1.00	1.03	1.06
1956	.70	.72	.89	1.01	1.07	1.03
1955	.54	.51	.94	.99	.85	.99
Total[a]						
1959	.86	.99	.99	1.05	1.03	1.04
1958	.94	.99	1.04	1.06	1.03	1.04
1957	.94	.98	1.03	1.05	1.02	1.01
1956	.97	.96	1.02	1.05	1.02	1.01
1955	.97	1.00	1.02	1.05	.97	1.02

[a] Includes women with 0-4 years of education.

rtility Rates for Women Born in the South and in the Non-South for

rtility Rates						Comparisons of Total Fertility Rates	
30-34		35-39		40-44			
uth Non-South	South	Non-South	South	Non-South	South	Non-South	
08	1.05	1.08	.99	.81	.92	.92	1.00
04	1.11	.95	1.08	.97	1.09	.99	1.07
98	1.01	.89	.99	1.02	1.14	.96	1.05
89	1.07	.96	.99	.93	.93	.91	1.09
00	1.05	.86	.97	.80	.83	1.01	1.06
99	.95	1.05	1.00	.85	1.10	.89	.90
06	1.08	1.00	1.02	.97	1.04	.90	.97
02	.98	.95	1.05	.94	1.08	.94	.93
90	1.09	.98	.95	1.22	.99	.95	1.02
07	1.08	.94	.97	.80	.98	.93	1.00
05	1.05	1.00	1.07	.82	1.01	1.06	1.10
08	1.08	1.02	1.06	.86	.97	1.09	1.06
98	1.01	.91	.99	1.06	.95	1.00	1.02
07	1.02	1.02	1.01	.66	.95	.99	1.01
01	1.07	1.16	.97	1.04	1.18	1.01	1.05
05	1.05	1.15	1.13	1.07	.93	1.03	1.05
99	1.05	.93	1.07	.76	1.08	.96	1.04
21	.99	1.11	.97	1.42	.74	1.06	1.00
06	1.00	1.24	.97	1.02	1.02	1.01	1.00
02	.98	1.29	.95	1.25	1.01	.94	.97
06	1.03	1.07	1.05	.85	.99	.99	1.03
07	1.07	1.00	1.06	.97	1.03	1.02	1.05
04	1.00	.96	1.00	1.05	.97	1.01	1.02
04	1.00	.96	1.00	1.05	.97	1.01	1.02
03	1.04	1.00	.98	.96	.99	1.00	1.03

TABLE 2.9   Ratio of 1960 Census Estimates to 1970 Census Estimates
Year Overlap (1955-1959) by Education, Rural/Urban Residence and Ag

| | \multicolumn{6}{c}{Comparisons of Age-Specif} |
| Education Group and Years | \multicolumn{2}{c}{15-19} | \multicolumn{2}{c}{20-24} | \multicolumn{2}{c}{25-29} |
	South	Non-South	South	Non-South	South	Non-South
					\multicolumn{2}{c}{URBAN}	
5-8 years						
1959	.81	.90	1.19	1.10	1.08	1.10
1958	1.23	1.07	1.13	1.11	1.16	1.05
1957	1.31	1.21	1.16	1.17	.84	1.05
1956	1.36	1.04	1.09	1.17	1.04	1.02
1955	1.02	1.33	1.17	1.12	.97	1.15
9-11 years						
1959	.50	.45	1.00	1.03	1.13	1.04
1958	.62	.47	-.18	1.11	.92	1.08
1957	.78	.58	1.09	1.03	1.11	.99
1956	.95	.81	1.15	1.05	1.02	1.06
1955	1.01	.98	.94	1.01	.94	.96
12 years						
1959	1.95	1.76	1.02	1.05	1.02	1.03
1958	1.45	1.19	1.05	1.03	1.11	1.01
1957	1.06	.98	1.06	1.06	.99	1.00
1956	.84	.82	1.03	.99	.93	1.04
1955	.84	.91	1.05	1.04	.97	1.07
13+ years						
1959	2.44	2.09	.93	.94	.95	1.03
1958	1.32	1.70	.99	.95	.98	.98
1957	.88	.69	.97	.98	1.01	1.06
1956	.55	.69	1.03	.92	.98	1.05
1955	.53	.62	1.00	.96	.91	.97
Total[a]						
1959	1.14	1.07	1.03	1.03	1.03	1.03
1958	1.19	.98	1.09	1.05	1.04	1.02
1957	1.14	1.00	1.07	1.06	1.00	1.02
1956	1.05	.93	1.07	1.01	.99	1.03
1955	.97	1.04	1.04	1.03	.95	1.03

ertility Rates among Southern and Nonsouthern White Women For Five-
roup.

ertility Rates						Comparisons of Total Fertility Rates	
30-34		35-39		40-44			
th	Non-South	South	Non-South	South	Non-South	South	Non-South
.02	1.00	1.33	1.04	.60	.88	1.05	1.04
.07	1.06	1.09	.87	1.08	1.00	1.15	1.06
.90	.95	1.04	.96	.76	1.00	1.03	1.09
.99	.99	1.02	.94	1.08	.81	1.11	1.05
.96	.98	.82	1.02	.93	.71	1.03	1.12
.06	.94	1.15	.96	.69	1.45	.91	.91
.99	1.08	1.38	1.02	1.00	1.00	.97	.96
.92	.96	1.15	1.04	1.13	.93	1.00	.92
.89	1.08	.76	1.02	1.23	1.09	1.01	1.00
.11	1.02	.71	.96	1.00	1.00	.95	.99
.01	1.06	1.18	1.07	.86	.88	1.11	1.09
.09	1.06	1.04	1.06	.88	1.00	1.11	1.04
.02	1.03	.96	.98	1.27	.88	1.03	1.02
.00	1.04	.89	1.02	.92	.81	.96	1.00
.01	1.09	1.08	.96	1.00	1.23	1.00	1.05
.08	1.05	1.10	1.09	.94	.89	1.03	1.03
.04	1.05	1.06	1.07	.82	.90	1.01	1.01
14	.95	1.06	.85	1.42	.67	1.04	.97
05	.97	1.00	.96	.69	1.00	.99	.98
14	.90	1.06	1.00	1.17	1.06	.99	.95
05	1.02	1.17	1.04	.81	.98	1.05	1.03
06	1.06	1.13	1.00	.98	1.00	1.08	1.03
01	.98	1.04	.96	1.08	.93	1.05	1.01
98	1.02	.92	.98	.85	.87	1.01	1.01
06	1.01	.96	.98	1.00	1.00	1.00	1.02

(continued)

Education Group and Years	15-19		20-24		25-29	
	South	Non-South	South	Non-South	South	Non-South
					RURAL	
5-8 years						
1959	.71	.51	1.01	.97	.88	1.03
1958	.89	.81	.92	1.02	1.19	.87
1957	.90	.82	1.02	.87	.94	.96
1956	.96	1.17	1.08	1.11	1.01	.90
1955	1.08	.97	.95	.91	.94	.97
9-11 years						
1959	.45	.37	1.06	.92	1.03	1.18
1958	.55	.45	1.00	1.11	1.05	1.18
1957	.56	.62	1.05	1.05	.95	1.13
1956	.74	.96	1.08	1.07	1.12	1.04
1955	.92	1.08	.94	1.08	.95	1.03
12 years						
1959	1.60	1.78	1.07	1.05	.99	.99
1958	1.30	1.27	1.16	1.01	1.04	1.04
1957	1.09	1.18	1.03	1.08	1.02	1.02
1956	1.25	.99	1.00	1.02	1.19	1.02
1955	1.04	.95	1.18	1.09	.96	1.04
13+ years						
1959	1.81	2.26	1.06	1.18	.97	1.11
1958	.83	2.12	1.11	1.10	1.04	1.01
1957	2.19	1.08	1.03	1.08	1.06	1.04
1956	1.42	1.00	.97	1.16	1.16	1.04
1955	.53	.63	.80	1.08	.76	.95
Total[a]						
1959	.82	.81	1.06	1.03	.97	1.04
1958	.92	.88	1.06	1.06	1.06	1.04
1957	.92	1.02	.98	1.05	.99	1.03
1956	1.04	1.14	1.04	1.07	1.11	1.01
1955	1.05	1.08	1.02	1.07	.94	1.01

Comparisons of Age-Specifi[c]

[a]Includes women with 0-4 years of education.

rtility Rates						Comparisons of Total Fertility Rates	
30-34		35-39		40-44			
uth	Non-South	South	Non-South	South	Non-South	South	Non-South
.15	1.14	.88	.87	.83	.84	.91	.89
.07	1.03	1.02	1.36	.92	1.29	1.00	.97
.88	.95	.96	.94	1.18	1.10	.95	.91
.93	1.10	1.00	.87	1.25	1.00	1.01	1.04
.02	.97	.81	.93	.79	.85	.97	.94
.05	.91	1.33	1.03	1.29	.70	.91	.84
.15	1.06	1.07	.98	1.00	1.41	.93	.96
.11	1.03	.91	1.12	.72	.89	.89	.96
.80	1.15	1.20	.97	1.21	.76	.97	1.03
.14	1.13	1.07	1.11	.76	.75	.97	1.07
.09	1.03	1.22	.84	1.00	1.27	1.14	1.09
.09	.98	.81	.95	1.14	.83	1.11	1.03
.08	1.01	1.00	.96	1.13	.90	1.04	1.04
.06	.93	1.20	.94	.59	1.09	1.08	1.00
.14	1.00	1.30	.99	1.07	1.05	1.11	1.04
.08	1.05	1.46	1.03	.81	1.04	1.08	1.15
.94	.94	.71	1.10	.83	1.38	.99	1.07
.22	1.13	1.53	1.15	.64	.90	1.15	1.08
.31	1.03	1.29	1.16	.88	1.21	1.14	1.09
.98	1.06	.75	1.09	.90	.75	.80	1.00
.12	1.03	1.13	.91	.89	.95	1.01	.99
.09	1.02	.96	1.05	1.11	1.18	1.04	1.03
.07	1.02	1.05	1.00	1.05	1.00	1.01	1.03
.00	1.01	1.15	.96	1.11	1.05	1.06	1.04
.09	1.02	1.00	1.02	.91	.91	1.01	1.04

a reversal. The only exception is the crude birth rates reported in the annual vital statistics. These crude rates show the South as having slightly higher fertility than the non-South, but the reason is the age structure of the South, which, partly as a legacy of the South's earlier high fertility rates, positively influences the crude birth rates.

7. The most marked period of convergence is between 1954 and 1955. As reported elsewhere (Rindfuss, Reed, and St. John, 1978), this appears to have been the result of the 1954 Supreme Court school desegregation decision.

8. Fertility 15–29 and fertility 30–44 are calculated in the same manner as a conventional total fertility rate, except that the age limits are 15–29 or 30–44, instead of 15–44. The sum of the fertility rate for women aged 15–29 and the fertility rate for women aged 30–44 is equal to the conventional total fertility rate.

9. In order to construct reliable annual age-specific fertility rate estimates from own children data, very large samples are needed (Retherford and Bennett, 1977).

10. It can be noted that one potential hypothesis can be ruled out: there is no statistically significant difference between the South and the rest of the country with respect to coital frequency. This conclusion is based on a multiple regression analysis with 1970 NFS data in which the following variables were included: age of wife, race, religion, education of wife, marital history, farm residence, farm background, age at first marriage, age of husband, parity, future fertility intentions, and most recent method of contraception used. Coital frequency is obtained from the following question:

Q.241: In the past four weeks, how many times have you had intercourse? The quality of the responses to this question is discussed in Westoff (1974).

3
Mortality

HARRY M. ROSENBERG AND DRUSILLA BURNHAM

Population change for any geographic area results from the dynamic interplay of three demographic factors: (1) fertility—the increment that results from the number of children born to residents of an area; (2) net migration—the additions or subtractions that result when persons move into or out of an area; and (3) mortality—the decrement that results from deaths to residents of an area. This chapter, which is principally descriptive and demographic in character, discusses mortality in the Southern Region focusing on the trends, differentials, and patterns of causes of death.

For the South an examination of mortality has an intrinsic interest because of the light that it may shed on what Vance called the "vitality" of the people; i.e. the "persistence of the spark of life—an inherent tendency to live and survive in the face of all the ills that life is heir to." He noted that

> the battle for life and survival can best be thought of in forms of an offense and a defense. If the harmful elements of the environment comprise the offense, the inherent force of vitality musters the defense, bolstered at every point by the forces of medical care and technique which must be regarded as part of our complex social environment. . . . We can measure the outcome of this conflict only in terms of performance, as in death rates, morbidity rates, and length of life (Vance, 1945 : 335).

Our judgment, therefore, of the vitality, or conversely, the health problems of the South is based upon several measures of mortality. We recognize, as have others, that the principle virtue of mortality data as indexes of health status is that they are objective, readily available, of good quality, and uniform in coverage. However, as Horace Hamilton has noted, "they are neither a sensitive nor a complete measure of health levels" (Hamilton, 1962:219). They reflect broad differences in health but not the variation in minor illnesses that may seriously impair the quality of life. Therefore, data on mortality as presented here should be regarded as only a partial view of what Vance called the South's "vitality."

In this chapter we make comparisons between the South and the nation as a whole.[1] In all of these comparisons, figures for the nation include those of the South. Thus, mortality differences between the two areas are somewhat more attenuated than they would have been had we compared the South with the rest of the nation. Thus, in 1940 the crude death rate in the South was 1,024.6 deaths per 100,000 population; the crude death rate for the nation as a whole was 1,076.4; and the crude death rate for the remainder of the nation was 1,100.0 per 100,000 population. The principal reason for comparing data for the South with that of the nation as a whole is that these data are more readily available.

DEATH RATES

In 1940 the crude death rate in the South was 1,024.6 deaths per 100,000 population or nearly 5 percent *below* the crude rate of 1,076.4 of the entire United States. By 1975 the crude death rate in the South had declined 12.5 percent to 896.0 per 100,000 population, while the rate in the United States had declined 17.5 percent to 888.5 (figure 3.1 and table 3.1).

Many factors influence both the observed trend and observed differential in mortality between the region and the nation. These factors include the demographic characteristics of populations such as age, race, and sex composition; the distribution of causes of death; socioeconomic characteristics that influence utilization of health care services; the availability and quality of health care services; cultural patterns of the population; and the quality and completeness of the data.

This chapter restricts itself to a largely descriptive analysis of the demographic factors associated with the comparative mortality patterns between the South and the United States and changes in these patterns during 1940–1975. By carefully examining the influence of demographic factors, one can get a better understanding of the comparative risk of death in the South and how this has changed over time.

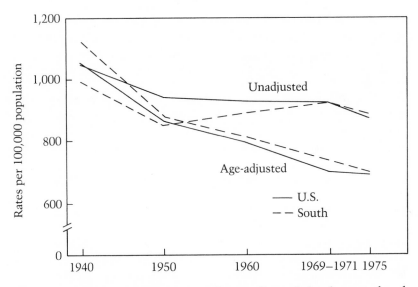

Figure 3.1. Crude death rates and age-adjusted death rates for the South and the United States, selected years, 1940–1975

Quality and Completeness of Data

The death statistics used in this chapter are based on data from the vital statistics registration system. In 1933 the geographic coverage of the death registration system in the U.S. included all states for the first time. Completeness of death registration, however, can be questioned as late as 1940 or 1950 for particular areas or particular segments of the population. Although there is no solid substantiating evidence, the relatively low death rates reported for white and nonwhite population in the South in 1940 suggest that there may have been some underregistration of deaths in this area. In general, the analysis in this chapter covers 1940–1975. However, in the discussion using data by race, we are limited to 1940 through 1969–1971 because the requisite population data for the construction of age-adjusted death rates by race are not available for the postcensal years after 1970.

Age Composition

One of the major factors that affects comparative indexes of mortality is the age composition of the population. Generally, an area with a "young" population tends to have a low crude death rate be-

TABLE 3.1   Death Rates and Age-Adjusted Death Rates

| Year | United States | | South | | So⟍ |
	Unadjusted	Age-Adjusted	Unadjusted	Age-Adjusted	Unadjus
1940	1,076.4	1,077.2	1,024.6	1,150.3	1,059
1950	963.8	881.5	878.2	899.1	885
1960	954.7	811.5	907.2	833.6	908
1969-71	946.5	716.9	944.2	751.0	943
1975	888.5	690.7	896.0	713.8	892

Note: Rates are per 100,000 population. Data are by pla
years.   Computational procedures for age adjustment of
appendix.

cause it has proportionately more young people who are subject to
a lower risk. In 1940 the South was demographically "younger"
than the United States as a whole; nearly 40 percent of the southern population in 1940 was under 20 years of age, compared with
only about 35 percent of the nation's population. As a result some
indexes of mortality for the South would tend to be biased downward if no correction were made for the effect of its young population. The distorting impact of differences in age composition on
comparative mortality levels can be eliminated by "adjusting"
death rates to a standard population. This has been done in this
chapter through age standardization of death rates by the Direct
Method, a procedure described in detail in the appendix to this
chapter.

While on an unadjusted basis, the death rate in the South in 1940
was nearly 5 percent *below* the corresponding rate for the United
States; on an age-adjusted basis, the death rate in the South was

lantic	East South Central		West South Central	
Age-justed	Unadjusted	Age-Adjusted	Unadjusted	Age-Adjusted
200.5	1,042.1	1,163.7	961.9	1,070.9
928.8	914.0	922.1	839.0	837.8
852.7	953.6	851.5	873.0	791.6
762.8	1,003.9	773.4	905.1	717.3
704.7	946.5	745.3	868.2	707.0

occurrence for 1940; by place of residence for other
ath rates and sources of the data are described in the

about 7 percent above that of the nation as a whole. This indicates
that when the effect of the South's age structure is taken into account the aggregate risk of death in the region was higher than in
the United States as a whole in 1940.

In general, data reported in table 3.1 and figure 3.1 show that on
an age-adjusted basis mortality trends for the region and the U.S.
were strikingly similar during the 36-year period. Age-adjusted
death rates for both areas declined by over one-third, from 1,150.3
deaths per 100,000 population to 713.8 in the South and from
1,077.2 to 690.7 per 100,000 population in the United States. The
trend for both areas was consistently downward with the greatest
proportionate reductions occurring during the first ten years. During these years the age-adjusted rates in both the U.S. and the
South dropped by 2 percent per year, compared with about 1 percent annual decline during 1950–1975. The overall differential between region and nation in the age-adjusted rate was reduced by

more than half during the period because the decline for the South was greater than that for the entire nation, 37.9 percent to 35.9 percent. By 1975 the South's age-adjusted death rate was only 3 percent higher than that of the nation.

Racial Composition

Another factor influencing overall comparative mortality levels is the racial composition of the population. Because the nonwhite population, generally, has higher death rates than the white population, areas with proportionately more nonwhites tend to have overall death rates that are higher. In relative terms in 1940, the South had 2.4 times as many nonwhites as did the nation, and nonwhites constituted almost one-quarter of the South's population. By 1970, however, this proportion had been reduced to less than one-fifth. During the same period, the nonwhite population accounted for a growing share of U.S. population—increasing from approximately 10 percent to 12 percent. Thus, even with unchanging risks of death for each color group, the changes in the racial composition of the South and the nation would have contributed to a reduction in mortality in the South and to a more favorable comparison of the South with the U.S.

To what extent are the patterns and trends of mortality change in the South since 1940 associated with the actual differential mortality between the white and nonwhite populations of the region? While the level of mortality in the South in 1940, measured by the age-adjusted death rate, was almost 7 percent higher than that of the U.S., the reported corresponding rates for both major color groups were *below* those of the U.S. as a whole. For southern whites the age-adjusted rate was 1,015.1 deaths per 100,000 population in 1940, while for the entire white population the rate was 1,018.2. For the southern nonwhite population, the rate was 1,610.4, compared with 1,633.4 for all nonwhites. The relatively low rate for southern nonwhites leads us to suspect that there may have been some underreporting of deaths in the South in 1940 and possibly for earlier years as well.

If the color-specific death rates in 1940 are accepted as reliable, one can examine relative improvements in mortality between the two groups over the ensuing three decades. From 1940 to 1969–1971, age-adjusted death rates for both major color groups declined by about one-third, with improvements being slightly greater for the population of other races than for the whites. During this same period, substantial improvements in mortality occurred for both color groups for the U.S. as a whole. Indeed, improvements in mortality for both color groups were measurably greater than the improvements for these groups within the South. The reported figures indicate that this is particularly true for the nonwhite population. For this group age-adjusted death rates declined by 35 percent in the region and by 39 percent in the U.S. By 1969–1971 the overall death rate for the South, on an age-adjusted basis, was almost 5 percent higher than the rate for the nation. For white Southerners the risk of death was about 1 percent higher (687.2 compared with 681.2), and for nonwhite Southerners the age-adjusted death rate was almost 6 percent higher than the rate for the comparable group in the nation (1,053.7 compared with 996.7).

Sex Composition
Comparison of overall mortality levels between two areas can also be influenced by the sex composition of the population of the respective areas if the relative risk of death differs between males and females. In general in the United States, females at each age have a lower risk of death than males. Thus, areas with proportionately more females would tend to have a lower overall mortality rate.

The sex composition of a population is customarily expressed as the ratio of males to females, or the "sex ratio." In 1940 in the United States the sex ratio was 100.7 males per 100 females; in the South there were 99.6 males per 100 females. This means that there were an almost equal number of males and females in each area. In 1970 the ratio for the U.S. had declined to 94.8 males per 100 females, and in the South, to 95.0 males per 100 females or 5 percent more females than males in each area. Thus, for the region and the nation, there were parallel changes in the sex composition of the population—from a situation of near parity in sex composition to one in which females measurably outnumbered males.

In terms of comparative mortality levels for white males and females between the U.S. and the South, in 1940 in the United States, the age-adjusted death rate for white males was 1.29 times the rate for white females (1,147.6 deaths per 100,000 compared with 887.8, respectively). In the South, however, the age-adjusted death rate for white males was 1.33 times the rate for white females (1,158.2 compared with 870.5). Between 1940 and 1969–1971, age-adjusted death rates for white males and females declined, but they declined more rapidly for white females. The net effect was to increase the sex differential in mortality between white males and females; the ratio increased to 1.78 for the nation and 1.88 for the

South. For the nonwhite population, the ratio of male to female mortality was the same in the South and the nation at both times. In 1940 the ratio was 1.16, while in 1969–1971 it was 1.60. Thus, there was a marked increase in the sex differential in mortality between nonwhite males and females in both areas. However, neither the sex composition of the South's population nor the comparative risk of death between males and females appears to have important bearing on the relative mortality of the areas or on changes in their relationship since 1940. In the South and the U.S., there were parallel increases in the proportion of the female population and in the mortality "advantage" of females over males.

In summary, between the South and the U.S. as a whole, comparative levels of mortality can be influenced by the demographic composition of the respective populations of each area. Thus, the aggregate level of mortality, measured by the death rate, may reflect in large measure the sex, age, and racial composition of the population. Between the South and the U.S., comparisons have not been affected by the sex composition of the population but have been markedly affected by changes in both the age structure of the population and its racial composition.

The relatively "young" population at the beginning of the period tended to bias downward the death rate of the South, while, in contrast, the large nonwhite population of the area tended to push the overall rate in the opposite direction, upward. Only by taking these two factors into account simultaneously (by looking at the age-adjusted death rate separately for each color group) is it possible to see that the relative risk of death in the region continues to be higher than for the nation as a whole and that the major source of the convergence in the mortality pattern for the region and the nation has been due to growing similarity in the age structure and the racial composition of the South and the U.S. since 1940.

GEOGRAPHIC VARIATION IN THE SOUTH

Census Divisions

Within the South the considerable diversity in mortality patterns is a reflection of local differences in economy, environment, degree of urbanization, and demographic composition of the population. In 1940 among the three census divisions that comprise the South, those states in the South Atlantic Division had the highest relative mortality. Their age-adjusted death rate was 1,200.5 deaths per

100,000 population or more than 4 percent above that of the Southern Region. The rate of 1,163.7 for the East South Central states was only slightly higher than that of the entire South, and the states in the West South Central Division had a rate of 1,070.9, nearly 7 percent lower than that of the South. These differential rates reflect the racial composition of the divisions. The division with the highest risk of death, the South Atlantic Division also had the highest proportion of nonwhites, 26.5 percent. The East South Central Division, which had a risk of death only slightly higher than that of the entire region, had a proportion of nonwhites (25.8 percent) which was only slightly higher than that of the region. The West South Central Division had both the lowest risk of death and the lowest proportion of nonwhites, 19.1 percent. In 1940 the heterogeneity of health status in the South was reflected in the range of nearly 11 percent between the census division with the highest age-adjusted rate and that with the lowest. This range was 1.6 times as great as the percentage difference in the level of mortality between the South and the U.S. in the same year.

During 1940–1975 the relative reductions in mortality for the U.S., the South, and the divisions within the South led to a narrowing of differentials among the areas. Thus, the South, with higher initial mortality, showed more rapid reductions in age-adjusted death rates during the period than did the U.S. as a whole—37.9 percent compared with 35.9 percent. Within the South the census division with the highest rate in 1940, the South Atlantic Division, showed the greatest relative decline—41.3 percent compared with 35.9 percent and 34.0 percent for the East South Central and the West South Central Divisions respectively. Thus, geographic differences in mortality both between the South and the U.S. and within the South narrowed considerably during 1940–1975. Some of the narrowing of differences in mortality within the South as well as between the South and the U.S. can be explained by changes in the racial composition of these areas.

States
Even among states within the same census division, there was considerable variation in mortality levels because of differences in urbanization, industrial and occupational structures, racial composition, socioeconomic status of the population, and other factors. Figure 3.2 shows the variation among the southern states according to the level of their age-adjusted mortality rates in 1969–1971.

The southern states and the District of Columbia are ranked in

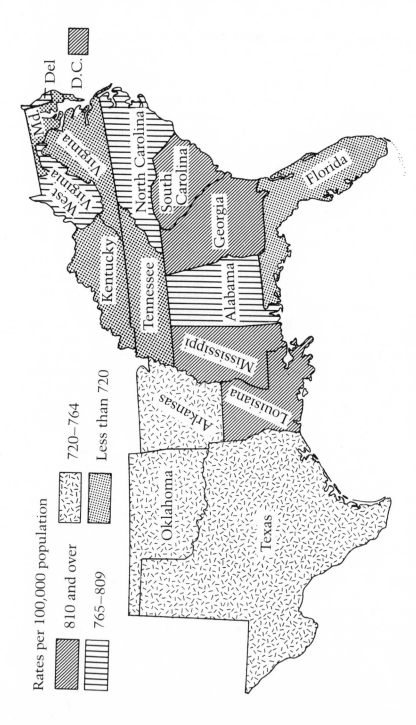

Rates per 100,000 population

810 and over

720–764

765–809

Less than 720

Figure 3.2. Age-adjusted death rates for all causes, total population: South, 1969–1971

TABLE 3.2 Age-Adjusted Death Rates, Rank, and Mortality Index for the Total Population

		Age-Adjusted Death Rate 1969-1971	Index	
			South Equals 1.00	U.S. Equals 1.00
Rank	State			
1	Oklahoma	679.7	.91	.95
2	Texas	699.0	.93	.98
3	Florida	701.3	.93	.98
4	Arkansas	710.8	.95	.99
--	United States	716.9	.95	1.00
5	Tennessee	745.0	.99	1.04
6	Maryland	750.2	1.00	1.05
--	South	751.0	1.00	1.05
7	Virginia	751.5	1.00	1.05
8	Kentucky	754.3	1.00	1.05
9	Delaware	766.0	1.02	1.07
10	North Carolina	781.6	1.04	1.09
11	West Virginia	786.5	1.05	1.10
12	Alabama	786.8	1.05	1.10
13	Louisiana	810.3	1.08	1.13
14	Georgia	819.7	1.09	1.14
15	Mississippi	830.0	1.11	1.16
16	South Carolina	850.2	1.13	1.19
17	District of Columbia	963.9	1.28	1.34

Note: Rates are per 100,000 population. Computational procedures for age adjustment of death rates and sources of the data are described in the appendix.

table 3.2 by their age-adjusted death rates for all causes in 1969–1971. Also, ratios of each state's mortality to the mortality of the U.S. and of the South are presented. The rates range from 679.7 deaths per 100,000 population in Oklahoma to 963.9 in the District of Columbia, a difference of 284.2 deaths. This difference may be compared with a difference of 34.1 deaths between the South and the U.S. for the same period. Because mortality variations among southern states reflect to a large degree differences in the racial composition of the respective areas, it is useful to examine the state patterns separately for white and nonwhite populations.

Figure 3.3 and table 3.3 show age-adjusted death rates for the white population in states of the South during 1969–1971. In addition, states are ranked in terms of these rates in table 3.3. For

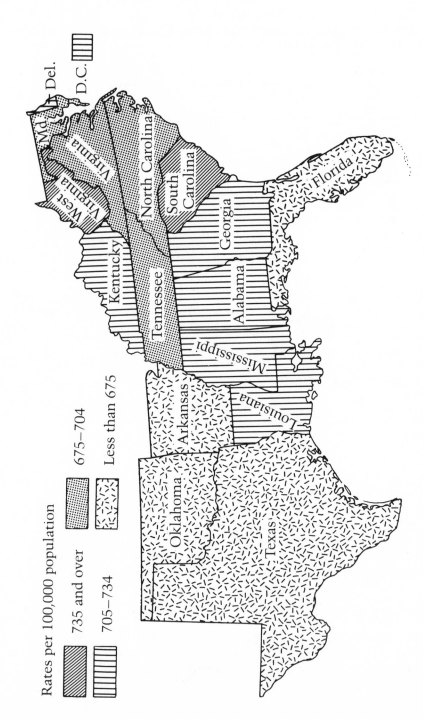

Rates per 100,000 population

735 and over

705–734

675–704

Less than 675

Figure 3.3. Age-adjusted death rates for all causes, white population: South, 1969–1971

TABLE 3.3 Age-Adjusted Death Rates, Rank, and Mortality Index for the White Population

			Index	
	Age-Adjusted		South	U.S.
		Death Rate	Equals	Equals
Rank	State	1969-1971	1.00	1.00
1	Florida	639.6	.93	.94
2	Oklahoma	662.6	.96	.97
3	Texas	664.4	.97	.98
4	Arkansas	667.7	.97	.98
--	United States	681.2	.99	1.00
5	Virginia	682.7	.99	1.00
--	South	687.2	1.00	1.01
6	Maryland	693.9	1.01	1.02
7	Tennessee	695.1	1.01	1.02
8	North Carolina	700.3	1.02	1.03
9	Delaware	705.9	1.03	1.04
10	Alabama	707.3	1.03	1.04
11	Louisiana	724.6	1.05	1.06
12	Kentucky	727.2	1.06	1.07
13	Georgia	727.3	1.06	1.07
14	Mississippi	730.1	1.06	1.07
15	District of Columbia	734.0	1.07	1.08
16	South Carolina	746.3	1.09	1.10
17	West Virginia	771.7	1.12	1.13

Note: Rates are per 100,000 population. Computational procedures for age adjustment of death rates and sources of the data are described in the appendix.

the white population, age-adjusted death rates ranged from 639.6 deaths per 100,000 population in Florida to 771.7 in West Virginia, a difference of 132.1 deaths. Again the variation within the South as measured by the range in death rates is considerably greater than between the South and the U.S., differences of 132.1 compared with 6.0.

Age-adjusted death rates for the nonwhite population of each state in the South are shown in figure 3.4 and table 3.4. For the nonwhite population, the range of rates was considerably greater than for the white population. These rates ranged from 839.2 deaths per 100,000 population in Oklahoma to 1,166.0 in Delaware, a difference of 326.8 deaths. This compares with the variation between the South and the U.S. of 57.0 deaths. However, it should also be noted that for the nonwhite population the difference between the South and the U.S. is greater than the comparable dif-

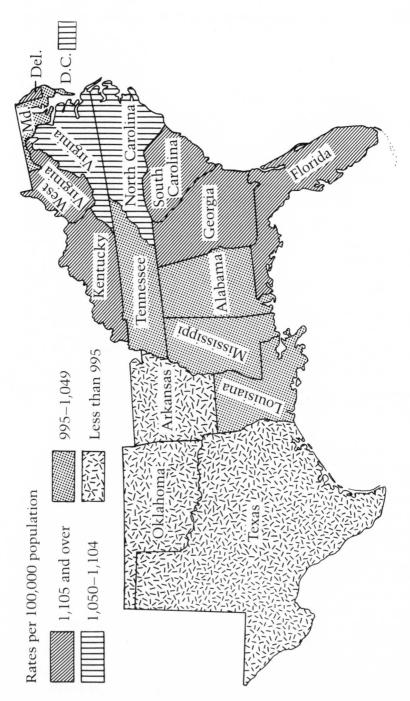

Figure 3.4. Age-adjusted death rates for all causes, all other population: South, 1969–1971

TABLE 3.4 Age-Adjusted Death Rates, Rank, and Mortality Index for the All Other Population

Rank	State	Age-Adjusted Death Rate 1969-1971	Index South Equals 1.00	U.S. Equals 1.00
1	Oklahoma	839.2	.80	.84
2	Arkansas	939.0	.89	.94
3	Texas	957.4	.91	.96
--	United States	996.7	.95	1.00
4	Mississippi	1,029.5	.98	1.03
5	Maryland	1,033.5	.98	1.04
6	Louisiana	1,037.7	.98	1.04
7	Alabama	1,040.8	.99	1.04
8	Tennessee	1,042.3	.99	1.05
--	South	1,053.7	1.00	1.06
9	Virginia	1,069.5	1.01	1.07
10	North Carolina	1,092.6	1.04	1.10
11	District of Columbia	1,102.0	1.05	1.11
12	Florida	1,112.3	1.06	1.12
13	Georgia	1,120.9	1.06	1.12
14	Kentucky	1,124.0	1.07	1.13
15	South Carolina	1,130.6	1.07	1.13
16	West Virginia	1,154.9	1.10	1.16
17	Delaware	1,166.0	1.11	1.17

Note: Rates are per 100,000 population. Computational procedures for age adjustment of death rates and sources of the data are described in the appendix.

ference for the white population, differences of 5 percent and 1 percent, respectively. The relatively high rank of Oklahoma and Texas for the nonwhite population may reflect the large proportion of American Indians classified within this color group.

The greater variation in mortality within the South, as compared to the variation in mortality between the South and the U.S., may partially reflect the diversity within the South in the environment, degree of urbanization, economic structure, etc., as well as the variation in racial composition.

INFANT MORTALITY

An important aspect of epidemiological change both in the United States and in the South are trends in infant mortality; i.e. deaths

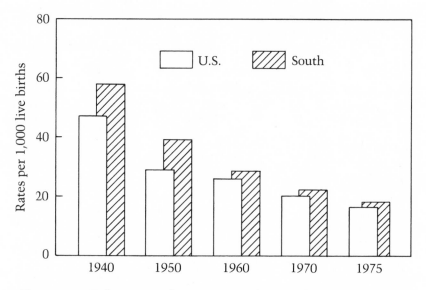

Figure 3.5. Infant mortality rates in the South and the United States, selected years, 1940–1975

among children under one year of age. Because of its apparent sensitivity to socioeconomic status, infant mortality rates have often served as proxy measures or indicators of social and economic conditions. Infant mortality rates for the U.S. and the South are shown in figures 3.5 and 3.6 and in table 3.5 for selected years from 1940 to 1975.

The infant mortality rate for the South in 1940 was 58 deaths per 1,000 live births; this means that almost 6 percent of the children born in the region died before their first birthday. The corresponding figure for the United States was 47 infant deaths per 1,000 live births, or almost 5 percent of children in the U.S. died before their first birthdays. During 1940–1975 infant mortality declined dramatically in the United States; at the end of the period, it was one-third the level it was at the beginning of the period, 16.1 per 1,000 live births. In other words, the infant mortality rate declined almost twice as fast as the age-adjusted death rate for the nation as a whole. For the South the decline in infant mortality during the period (from 58.0 per 1,000 live births to 17.8) was more impressive than that for the United States, a decline of 69 percent compared with 66 percent.

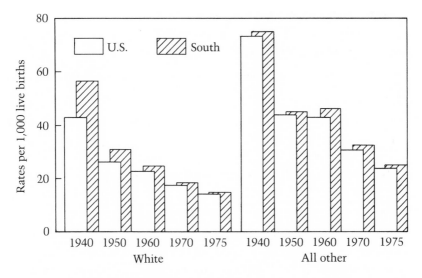

Figure 3.6. Infant mortality rates by color in the South and the United States, selected years, 1940–1975

The more rapid improvement in the southern versus national rates is partially a reflection of changes in the racial composition of the population at risk. Generally, for infant mortality, the population at risk is considered to be live births. Because the nonwhite population generally experiences higher infant mortality rates, those areas with a greater proportion of nonwhite live births would be expected to have higher overall infant mortality rates. During 1940–1975 nonwhite live births as a proportion of all births in the South remained virtually the same, 26.4 and 26.6 percent, while, in the nation as a whole, the proportion of nonwhite live births increased from 12.6 percent in 1940 to 18.8 percent in 1975.

The improvement of southern infant mortality rates in comparison to U.S. rates may also be a reflection of the dramatic increases in the proportion of live births occurring in hospitals. In 1940, 55.8 percent of live births in the United States occurred in hospitals compared with 31.2 percent in the South. By 1975, the comparative figures were 98.5 and 98.7 percent respectively. Thus, in 1975, there was very little difference between the South and the United States in the percentage of live births occurring in hospitals.

Infant mortality rates for both color groups in the South as well

TABLE 3.5   Infant Mortality Rates by Color

Color and Region	1940	1950	1960	1970	1975
All Races					
United States	47.0	29.2	26.0	20.0	16.1
South	58.0	34.6	29.0	22.3	17.8
South Atlantic	57.1	33.7	30.6	22.1	18.2
East South Central	55.9	36.2	32.3	23.0	18.1
West South Central	61.1	34.6	29.0	22.0	17.0
White					
United States	43.2	26.8	22.9	17.8	14.2
South	51.9	30.8	24.5	18.7	14.9
South Atlantic	48.2	28.1	23.6	18.0	14.9
East South Central	50.6	32.5	25.6	18.7	14.7
West South Central	56.7	32.4	24.9	19.6	15.0
All Other					
United States	73.8	44.5	43.2	30.9	24.2
South	75.9	45.3	46.8	32.9	25.7
South Atlantic	77.5	46.5	47.2	32.6	25.9
East South Central	69.1	44.8	48.4	35.2	27.1
West South Central	79.8	43.1	44.3	31.4	24.1

Note: Data are by place of occurrence for 1940; by place of residence for other years.   Rates are per 1,000 live births.   Sources are described in the appendix.

as the nation showed similar improvements. In 1940 the South was 51.7. By 1975 the rate in the nation had dropped over 67 percent to 14.2; in the South the drop was slightly greater, about 71 percent to 14.9 per 1,000 live births. For nonwhites in 1940, the infant mortality rates in both the U.S. and South were considerably higher than comparable rates for whites. In the U.S. the nonwhite rate was 73.8 per 1,000 live births. In the South the comparable figure was 75.6 per 1,000 live births. During 1940–1975, the decline in nonwhite infant mortality in the U.S. was the same as the decline in white infant mortality; both declines were approximately 67 percent. In the South, however, the decline for nonwhites was less than for white, 66 percent compared to 71 percent. Thus, the converging infant mortality patterns between the South and the nation reflect the changing racial composition of births in the South and the more rapid reductions in white infant mortality in the region than in the U.S. as a whole.

Trends in infant mortality by color since 1940 may reflect in part registration incompleteness, particularly in the earlier years of the period. This may be especially true for nonwhite infant deaths and births. For this population a relatively large proportion of children in the South were born outside hospitals. In 1950, the earliest year for which we have southern data by color and hospital status, over 42 percent of nonwhite children in the United States were born outside hospitals, compared with about 7 percent of white children. Comparable figures for the South were about 58 and 17 percent. By 1975 estimates for the United States were 1.9 percent of nonwhite children and 1 percent of white children; for the South these estimates were 2.7 percent and 1 percent, respectively.

An association between out-of-hospital births and underreporting of infant deaths may account in part for an anomalous 3.3 percent increase in infant mortality for the nonwhite population between 1950 and 1960 (figure 3.6). The rapidly increasing proportion of in-hospital births may have resulted in improved reporting of infant deaths and, thus, in increases in nonwhite infant mortality during the period. If southern nonwhite infant deaths, however, had been registered more completely in 1950, the apparent regional excess may have been greater than the reported 2.8 percent.

Similar to infant mortality patterns are those for neonatal and postneonatal mortality as shown in table 3.6. Neonatal deaths are infant deaths occurring within the first twenty-eight days of life, and postneonatal deaths are deaths occurring between the twenty-eighth day and one year of age. Epidemiologically, neonatal and postneonatal deaths are assumed to be influenced by somewhat different factors. Neonatal deaths are believed to be affected more by conditions prior to birth, such as maternal nutrition and genetic or biological factors. Postneonatal deaths, on the other hand, are assumed to be more closely associated with physical, social, and environmental factors to which the young infant is exposed. These factors would include nutrition, sanitation, the infant's health environment at birth, and those conditions conducive to early growth and survival. One indicator of the conditions conducive to early growth and survival could be the proportion of in-hospital births. As we indicated earlier, in the South in 1940, proportionately more births occurred outside hospitals than in hospitals. By 1975, however, this situation had changed so that virtually all births were in hospitals.

In 1940 the neonatal and postneonatal mortality rates for the United States were 28.8 and 18.3 per 1,000 live births; for the South they were 32.9 and 25.1, respectively. The relatively high postneonatal mortality rate compared with the neonatal mortality rate in both the South and the U.S. seems to reflect the relatively unfavorable environmental factors surrounding infancy at that time.

During 1940–1975 in the United States, postneonatal mortality rates declined by 75 percent, and neonatal mortality rates declined by about 60 percent. The comparable declines for the South were 81 and 61 percent (table 3.6). For the white population in the South, there were greater reductions in postneonatal and neonatal mortality rates than in the nation as a whole. These reductions contributed to the convergence in the rates between the region and the nation. For the nonwhite population, on the other hand, the reductions in the neonatal and postneonatal rates in the South were less than the corresponding declines in the United States.

From the above discussion, it can be seen that the risk of death for infants of both color groups, white and nonwhite, or both geographic areas, the country as a whole and the South, declined dramatically. Many factors are believed to be involved in this decline, including improvements in the care of the newborn infant as indicated by the increased proportion of in-hospital births.

EXPECTATION OF LIFE AT BIRTH

The expectation of life at birth is a hypothetical mortality index that indicates how many years an infant could expect to live if throughout its lifetime the infant were exposed to the mortality conditions prevailing at a particular time. Estimated values for the expectation of life at birth are shown in table 3.7 and figure 3.7 for selected years, 1939 through 1969–1971, by color and sex for the South and the nation.

In 1939 the estimated average life expectancy in the United States was 63.7 years. During the next 30 years, over 7 years were added to the average expected length of life in the United States. By comparison, at the beginning of the period in the South, life expectancy was about 2 years less than that for the nation, but by 1970 more than 8 years had been added to the index. Because of the South's relatively greater reductions in mortality during the period, the gap in life expectancy between the South and the United States was reduced from about 2 years in 1939 to 1 year by 1969–1971.

In 1939 life expectancy differences between the color groups were almost 11 years at the national level. While white infants could expect to live an average of 64.7 years, infants of other races could expect to live only 53.9 years. By 1969–1971 life expectancy in the United States had increased 6.9 years for the white population and 11.1 years for nonwhites. The respective increases in the South exceeded those at the national level for whites but not for nonwhites. Despite improvements in life expectancy for the nonwhite population, most of whom are black in the South, life expectancy in 1969–1971 was only about the level that the white population had attained 30 years earlier.

An important factor in examining differentials and trends in life expectancy is sex. As we saw earlier, females tend to have lower death rates than males. A similar differential can also be seen in terms of life expectancy. In 1939 in the U.S., female infants could expect to live 65.6 years, or 3.9 years longer than their male counterparts. White female infants could expect to live 66.8 years, or 4.1 years longer than white male infants, and nonwhite female infants could expect to live 55.2 years, or 2.7 years longer than nonwhite males. In the South in 1939, similar differentials prevailed. White females could expect to live about 66.3 years, or about a half year less than their counterparts in the nation and about 4.3 years more than their male counterparts in the South. Nonwhite females, however, could expect to live only 55.4 years, or approximately 0.2 years longer than nonwhite females in the country and 2.5 years longer than nonwhite males.

In the ensuing 30 years, life expectancy increased dramatically

TABLE 3.6 Infant, Neonatal, and Postneonatal Mortality Rates

Color and Region	Infant Mortality			Neonatal Mortality			Postneonatal Mortality		
	1940	1975	% Change	1940	1975	% Change	1940	1975	% Change
All Races									
United States	47.0	16.1	-65.7	28.8	11.6	-59.7	18.3	4.5	-75.4
South	58.0	17.8	-69.3	32.4	12.8	-61.1	25.1	4.9	-80.5
South Atlantic	57.1	18.2	-68.1	33.6	13.2	-60.7	23.5	5.0	-78.7
East South Central	55.9	18.1	-67.1	32.6	13.1	-59.8	23.3	5.0	-78.5
West South Central	61.1	17.0	-72.2	32.3	12.2	-62.2	28.8	4.7	-83.7
White									
United States	43.2	14.2	-67.1	27.2	10.4	-61.8	16.0	3.8	-76.3
South	51.7	14.9	-71.2	30.2	11.0	-63.6	21.5	3.9	-81.9

South Atlantic	48.2	14.9	-69.1	29.9	11.1	-62.9	18.3	3.8	-79.2
East South Central	50.8	14.7	-71.1	30.8	10.9	-64.6	20.0	3.8	-81.0
West South Central	56.6	15.0	-73.5	30.0	11.0	-63.3	26.6	4.0	-85.0

All Other

United States	73.8	24.2	-67.2	39.7	16.8	-57.7	34.1	7.5	-78.0
South	75.6	25.7	-66.0	40.6	17.8	-56.2	35.0	7.8	-77.7
South Atlantic	77.5	25.9	-66.6	42.0	18.1	-56.9	35.5	7.8	-78.0
East South Central	69.2	27.1	-60.8	37.3	18.8	-49.6	31.9	8.3	-74.0
West South Central	79.7	24.1	-69.8	41.8	16.7	-60.0	37.9	7.3	-80.7

Note: Rates are per 1,000 live births. Data are by place of occurrence for 1940; by place of residence for 1975. Sources are described in the appendix.

TABLE 3.7 Estimated Life Expectancy at Birth, by Color and Sex: United States and the South, Selected Years, 1939 to 1969-71

Year and Area	Total			White			All Other		
	Both Sexes	Male	Female	Both Sexes	Male	Female	Both Sexes	Male	Female
1939									
United States	63.7	61.7	65.6	64.7	62.7	66.8	53.9	52.5	55.2
South	61.7	59.9	63.6	64.1	62.0	66.3	54.2	52.9	55.4
Difference[a]	-2.0	-1.8	-2.0	-.6	-.7	-.5	+.3	+.4	+.2
1949-1951									
United States	68.3	65.6	71.0	69.2	66.3	72.0	60.9	58.9	62.9
South	67.3	64.4	70.1	69.2	66.1	72.4	60.5	58.5	62.4
Difference[a]	-1.0	-1.2	0.9	0.0	-.2	+.4	-.4	-.4	-.5
1959-1961									
United States	69.9	66.8	73.2	70.7	67.6	74.2	63.9	61.5	66.5
South	69.0	65.9	72.8	71.0	67.3	74.7	62.2	59.6	64.7
Difference[a]	-.9	-.9	-.4	+.3	-.3	+.5	-1.7	-1.9	-1.8
1969-1971									
United States	70.8	67.0	74.6	71.6	67.9	75.5	65.0	61.0	69.1
South	69.8	65.8	74.1	71.3	67.2	75.6	64.0	60.0	68.1
Difference[a]	-1.0	-1.2	-.5	-.3	-.7	+.1	-1.0	-1.0	-1.0

[a] Difference is expectation of life for South minus that for U.S.

Note: Data for 1939 are by place of occurrence; by place of residence for other years. Computational procedures and sources of the data are described in the appendix.

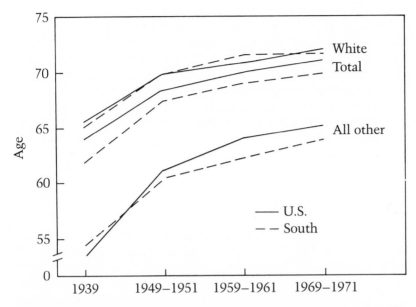

Figure 3.7. Estimated life expectancy at birth by color for the South and the United States, selected years, 1939 to 1969–1971

for all groups. In 1969–1971 in the nation as a whole, female infants could expect to live 74.6 years or nearly 8 years longer than male infants. Eight years is nearly twice the differential in 1939. Increases in life expectancy for both white females and all other females were greater than the increases for their male counterparts. Similar trends occurred in the South. In fact, the increase of 10.5 years in life expectancy for females was almost double the increase of 5.9 years for males. Again, the increases for both white and all other females were greater than the increases for white and all other males.

A number of explanations exist for the phenomenon of longer female life expectancy. Traditionally, it was thought that females lived longer because they did not work outside the home and therefore were subject to less stress. However, in recent years more and more females are working in the labor force; yet the differential in life expectancy between males and females has continued to increase, suggesting that such environmental explanations are incorrect or inadequate. Perhaps other environmental or biological factors may account for the widening differential.

Among the southern states, variations in life expectancy shown in table 3.8 portray essentially the same geographic variation in mortality risk as those portrayed in figures and tables 3.2, 3.3, and 3.4. Oklahoma has the best mortality conditions for both color groups combined. Florida seems to have the most favorable mortality conditions for the white population and very unfavorable conditions for nonwhites. Again, considerable variability in life expectancy remains within the South. Oklahoma's relatively favorable conditions for nonwhites may reflect the large proportion of American Indians classified as nonwhites.

CAUSE-OF-DEATH PATTERNS

Improvements in the health status of the South as measured by greater average life expectancy, lower infant mortality rates, and lower age-adjusted death rates have been accompanied by major changes in cause of death patterns. This is true for both the South and for the nation. Since 1940 infectious and parasitic diseases, as well as certain diseases of early infancy, have declined in terms of prevalence and as cause of death. While their proportionate importance has diminished, the influence of other diseases, mainly chronic and degenerative diseases, has risen. Chronic and degenerative diseases have gradually assumed preeminence as major causes of death.

Comparisons of cause-specific death rates between time periods or different geographic areas could be affected by several factors. The trends in cause-specific death rates during 1940–1975 have been influenced by three revisions in the International Classification of Diseases (see appendix to this chapter). The impact of changes, while statistically measureable, does not alter the general ranking of major disease categories as causes of death nor does it significantly modify broad trends in mortality depicted in table 3.9.

Trends in cause-specific mortality may also be affected by the presence or absence of influenza epidemics. Years in which epidemics occur have more deaths from chronic diseases, such as diseases of heart and tuberculosis, as well as more deaths from influenza and pneumonia. It has been suggested that the increase in chronic disease mortality associated with epidemics is because a person with a chronic disease, such as ischemic heart disease, is an

TABLE 3.8 Estimated Life Expectancy at Birth

	Total			White			All Other[a]	
Rank	State	Life Expectation at Birth	Rank	State	Life Expectation at Birth	Rank	State	Life Expectation at Birth
1	Oklahoma	71.4	1	Florida	72.2	1	Oklahoma	67.8
2	Texas	70.9	2	Oklahoma	71.9	2	Arkansas	65.9
–	United States	70.8	3	Texas	71.7	3	Texas	65.5
3	Arkansas	70.7	4	Arkansas	71.7	–	United States	65.0
4	Florida	70.7	–	United States	71.6	4	Maryland	64.6
5	Maryland	70.2	5	Virginia	71.6	5	Tennessee	64.5
6	Tennessee	70.1	6	Maryland	71.6	6	Louisiana	64.4
7	Kentucky	70.1	7	Delaware	71.4	7	Virginia	64.1
8	Virginia	70.1	–	South	71.3	8	Mississippi	64.0
9	Delaware	70.1	8	Tennessee	71.2	–	South	64.0
–	South	69.8	9	North Carolina	71.1	9	Alabama	63.9
10	West Virginia	69.5	10	Alabama	70.9	10	Kentucky	63.6
11	North Carolina	69.2	11	Louisiana	70.7	11	District of Columbia	63.6
12	Alabama	69.1	12	Kentucky	70.7	12	North Carolina	63.2
13	Louisiana	68.8	13	District of Columbia	70.6	13	Florida	62.9
14	Georgia	68.5	14	Georgia	70.6	14	Georgia	62.9
15	Mississippi	68.1	15	Mississippi	70.5	15	South Carolina	62.6
16	South Carolina	68.0	16	South Carolina	70.3			
17	District of Columbia	65.7	17	West Virginia	69.8			

[a]Life expectancy figures for Delaware and West Virginia for the All Other population are unavailable. The estimated figure for the South excludes these two states.

Note: Sources of the data are described in the appendix.

TABLE 3.9 Major Causes of Death in the South, 1940 and 1975

Rank	Cause	Death Rate per 100,000	% of All Deaths
	Major Causes in 1975		
	All causes	896.0	100.0
1	Diseases of heart	321.9	35.9
2	Malignant neoplasms	164.4	18.3
3	Cerebrovascular disease	98.2	11.0
4	Motor vehicle accidents	25.9	2.9
5	Influenza and pneumonia	25.7	2.9
	All other causes	252.4	29.0
	Major Causes in 1940		
	All causes	1,024.6	100.0
1	Diseases of heart	206.9	20.2
2	Influenza and pneumonia	89.5	8.7
3	Nephritis, all forms	89.0	8.7
4	Vascular lesions of the central nervous system	87.5	8.5
5	Malignant neoplasms	78.7	7.7
	All other causes	473.0	46.2

Note: Rates are per 100,000 population. Data are by place of occurrence for 1940, by place of residence for 1975. Sources are described in the appendix.

easy victim for influenza and pneumonia and that the death would be attributed to the chronic disease because of the underlying cause of death principle (Collins, 1953). During 1940–1975 there were several epidemics. While the death rate for a specific cause may be elevated for a particular year, the overall trend may also be adversely affected. We have not attempted to adjust any of the data for the effects of influenza epidemics because information on these epidemics is not readily available for the southern states.

Comparison of cause-specific death rates between the South and the U.S. may also be attenuated somewhat by the inclusion of data on the South in the figures for the U.S. Comparisons between the South and the U.S. may also be influenced by some unmeasurable factors such as regional differences in diagnosis.

Rankings of the causes of death in 1975 seen in table 3.9 show important similarities as well as differences when compared with those in 1940. As a group the major causes accounted for proportionately more deaths in 1975 than they did in 1940. Thus, in 1975 they accounted for over seven of every ten deaths. In 1975 over one-third of the deaths in the South were from heart diseases, while in 1940 only about one-fifth of the deaths in the South were from this cause. The second most prevalent cause of death was malignant neoplasms, which accounted for almost two of every ten deaths in the South in 1975, and less than one of every ten deaths in the South in 1940. Cerebrovascular diseases, or stroke, accounted for 11 percent of all southern deaths in 1975 and 8.5 percent in 1950. In terms of their proportionate impact, the other causes of death are far behind these three major causes—heart disease, cancer, and stroke.

The relative increase of deaths from chronic diseases between 1940 and 1975 provides evidence of what one scholar has characterized as the "epidemiologic transition" (Omran, 1977). The transition experienced in the 35-year period in the South and in the nation was one in which infectious diseases, such as influenza and pneumonia, tuberculosis, and diarrhea-enteritis, as well as deficiency diseases, such as pellagra, were replaced as major causes of death by the chronic diseases: heart disease, cancer, and stroke. These three causes of death accounted for less than half the annual deaths in the South in 1940; their share had increased to almost two-thirds in 1975.

Trends in mortality for selected causes of death since 1940 are shown in tables 3.10 and 3.11. These particular causes were selected because they were among the five major causes of death in the South in 1940 or in 1975 (ischemic heart disease—a major component of heart disease—malignant neoplasms, cerebrovascular disease, motor vehicle accidents, influenza and pneumonia, and nephritis), because they represent an earlier public health problem (tuberculosis), or because they represent a notable, emerging health problem in the South (homicide and cirrhosis of liver). An additional consideration was the availability of comparable cause of death data for the South and the nation during the period under study. Together all of the census examined in this chapter accounted for 71 percent of the age-adjusted death rate for all causes in 1975.

Data in table 3.10 extend for the entire 35-year period of 1940–1975. However, those in table 3.11 which show mortality for selected causes by color and sex end with 1969–1971. The requisite

TABLE 3.10 Age-Adjusted Death Rates for Selected Causes: United States and the South, Selected Years, 1940 to 1969-1971

Cause and Area	1940	1950	1960	1969-1971	1975
All causes					
U.S.	1,077.2	881.5	811.5	716.9	690.7
South	1,150.3	899.1	833.6	751.0	713.8
Ischemic heart disease					
U.S.	NA	190.0	225.5	230.3	220.1
South	NA	149.6	197.5	224.2	211.3
Malignant neoplasms					
U.S.	120.3	127.7	129.1	129.9	135.7
South	93.9	111.7	118.4	126.1	133.2
Malignant neoplasms of respiratory system					
U.S.	7.2	13.0	19.5	28.4	32.9
South	4.8	11.3	18.7	29.9	35.0
Cerebrovascular disease					
U.S.	91.1	91.6	85.7	67.0	64.2
South	106.1	101.5	99.1	76.8	70.5
Chronic nephritis					
U.S.	79.1	14.8	5.9	3.0	2.4
South	102.2	20.2	7.7	3.7	2.9

Influenza and pneumonia					
U.S.	70.2	28.9	31.6	22.0	19.3
South	96.4	36.9	36.0	23.7	19.4
Tuberculosis					
U.S.	45.8	21.6	5.5	2.1	1.3
South	60.3	27.7	6.8	2.6	1.6
Motor vehicle accidents					
U.S.	26.1	22.6	20.9	27.5	21.7
South	26.7	26.2	24.9	33.2	26.0
Homicide					
U.S.	6.2	5.2	4.9	9.3	10.6
South	13.3	10.1	8.6	13.8	14.7
Cirrhosis of liver					
U.S.	8.5	8.6	10.6	14.5	13.6
South	6.4	6.3	7.5	12.0	12.0

Note: Rates are per 100,000 population. Data are by place of occurrence for 1940; by place of residence for other years. Computational procedures for age adjustment and sources of the data are described in the appendix.

TABLE 3.11 Age-Adjusted Death Rates for Selected Causes

Cause, Color, and Sex	United States 1940	United States 1969-1971	United States % Change	South 1940	South 1969-1971	South % Change
All causes	1,077.2	716.9	-33.4	1,150.3	751.0	-34.7
White	1,018.2	681.2	-33.1	1,015.1	687.2	-32.3
White male	1,147.6	896.9	-21.8	1,158.2	922.9	-20.3
White female	887.8	502.6	-43.4	870.5	489.9	-43.7
All other	1,633.4	996.7	-39.0	1,610.4	1,053.7	-34.6
All other male	1,755.3	1,249.5	-28.8	1,730.3	1,322.1	-23.6
All other female	1,509.8	781.3	-48.8	1,491.8	830.5	-44.3
Ischemic heart disease	190.0[a]	230.3	21.2	149.6[a]	224.2	49.9
White	193.8[a]	228.2	17.8	157.2[a]	218.3	38.9
White male	264.1[a]	323.5	22.5	222.0[a]	316.0	42.3
White female	126.8[a]	149.9	18.2	95.6[a]	137.7	44.0
All other	137.5[a]	244.2	77.6	118.0[a]	254.6	115.4
All other male	162.9[a]	300.2	84.3	141.1[a]	312.2	121.3
All other female	112.4[a]	197.2	75.4	96.0[a]	207.3	115.9
Malignant neoplasms	120.3	129.9	8.0	93.9	126.1	34.3
White	121.5	127.5	4.9	96.0	121.6	26.7
White male	117.4	154.4	31.5	89.7	151.1	68.5
White female	126.0	107.1	-15.0	102.5	98.7	-3.7
All other	100.6	151.2	50.3	85.6	149.0	74.1
All other male	82.8	187.5	126.4	65.0	185.1	184.8
all other female	118.7	131.2	2.1	106.0	120.2	12.4

Malignant neoplasms of respiratory system	7.2	28.4	294.4	4.8	29.9	522.9
White	7.5	27.9	272.0	5.3	29.8	462.3
White male	11.5	49.7	332.2	8.0	53.8	572.5
White female	3.4	10.1	197.1	2.4	10.1	320.8
All other	4.2	31.9	659.5	2.9	30.4	941.4
All other male	6.2	57.0	819.4	4.0	55.1	1,277.5
All other female	2.2	10.7	386.4	1.7	9.7	470.6
Cerebrovascular disease	91.1	67.0	-26.5	106.1	76.8	-27.6
White	85.8	62.4	-27.3	91.1	66.7	-26.8
White male	87.0	69.9	-19.7	97.9	76.5	-21.9
White female	84.6	56.6	-33.1	84.4	59.0	-30.1
All other	150.5	108.4	-28.0	162.2	128.9	-20.5
All other male	140.0	115.6	-17.4	153.7	140.5	-8.6
All other female	161.6	102.2	-36.8	170.8	119.4	-30.1
Chronic nephritis	79.1	3.0	-96.2	102.2	3.7	-96.4
White	72.3	2.3	-96.8	85.1	2.5	-97.1
White male	78.1	2.9	-96.3	97.2	3.0	-96.9
White female	66.7	1.9	-97.2	73.0	2.0	-97.3
All other	137.5	8.8	-94.4	164.7	10.1	-93.9
All other male	165.2	10.1	-93.9	175.5	11.4	-93.5
All other female	149.1	7.8	-94.8	153.2	8.9	-94.2

[a] Data for Ischemic heart disease are for 1950. Data for 1940 are not available.

Cause, Color, and Sex	United States		%	South		%
	1940	1969–1971	Change	1940	1969–1971	Change
Influenza and pneumonia	70.2	22.0	-68.7	96.4	23.7	-75.4
White	62.9	19.8	-68.5	82.4	20.3	-75.4
White male	69.4	26.0	-62.5	87.2	26.4	-69.7
White female	56.2	15.2	-73.0	77.4	15.5	-80.0
All other	139.0	37.6	-72.9	142.9	38.7	-72.9
All other male	154.5	49.7	-67.8	156.2	50.9	-67.4
All other female	123.6	27.5	-77.8	130.1	28.6	-78.0
Tuberculosis	45.8	2.1	-95.4	60.3	2.6	-95.7
White	36.1	1.5	-95.8	44.3	1.9	-95.7
White male	44.0	2.5	-94.3	50.0	3.0	-94.0
White female	27.9	.8	-97.1	38.5	.9	-97.7
All other	131.3	7.0	-94.7	111.4	6.6	-94.1
All other male	146.2	10.6	-92.7	119.6	10.3	-91.4
All other female	115.8	3.9	-96.6	103.0	3.7	-96.4
Motor vehicle accidents	26.1	27.5	5.4	26.7	33.2	24.3
White	26.2	27.0	3.1	27.7	32.1	15.9
White male	40.1	40.2	.2	43.3	47.9	10.6
White female	12.2	14.5	18.9	11.9	16.8	41.2
All other	25.3	31.7	25.3	23.7	38.9	64.1
All other male	40.9	51.0	24.7	39.0	64.1	64.4
All other female	10.0	14.9	49.0	8.9	17.0	91.0

Homicide	6.2	9.3	50.0	13.3	13.8	3.8
White	3.1	4.7	51.6	5.9	6.9	16.9
White male	4.9	7.3	49.0	10.1	11.0	10.0
White female	1.3	2.2	69.2	1.7	2.9	70.6
All other	33.7	42.9	27.3	36.9	46.0	24.7
All other male	55.9	75.7	35.4	62.9	81.5	29.6
All other female	12.5	14.3	14.4	12.6	15.7	24.6
Cirrhosis of liver	8.5	14.5	70.6	6.4	12.0	87.5
White	8.6	13.3	54.7	6.5	11.1	70.8
White male	11.6	18.6	60.3	9.4	15.4	63.8
White female	5.6	8.7	55.4	3.6	7.4	105.6
All other	7.1	23.6	232.4	6.0	16.4	173.4
All other male	9.1	31.2	242.9	8.1	20.4	151.9
All other female	4.9	17.2	251.0	4.0	13.0	225.0

Note: Rates are per 100,000 population. Data for 1940 are by place of occurrence and by place of residence for 1969–1971. Computational procedures for age adjustment and sources of the data are described in the appendix.

population data for the construction of age-adjusted death rates for the South (and other regions) are not available for individual years after the most recent decennial census—in this case the 1970 *Census of Population*.

Diseases of Heart and Ischemic Heart Disease
The leading cause of death—a broad category called diseases of heart—maintained its number one rank through 1940–1975 and also increased in relative importance as a cause of death. In 1940 over one out of five deaths in the South were ascribed to diseases of heart; by 1975 the proportion had risen to one out of three. Furthermore, the death rate for diseases of heart increased during the period from 206.9 to 321.9 deaths per 100,000 population.

Diseases of heart is a broad category of which a major component is ischemic heart disease, previously identified as coronary heart disease and arteriosclerotic heart disease including coronary disease. In 1975 ischemic heart disease constituted nearly 90 percent of all deaths in the United States ascribed to diseases of heart. Between 1950[2] and 1969–1971 age-adjusted death rates in the nation increased from 190.0 to 230.3 deaths per 100,000 population (table 3.10). However, between 1969–1971 and 1975, an important reversal occurred in the trend. After years of increase in fatalities due to ischemic heart disease, the rate dropped below the national level that prevailed 15 years earlier. A similar pattern of long-term increase and subsequent decrease was also experienced by the population of the South. Historically, death rates from this cause have been lower in the South than in the U.S. In 1950 age-adjusted death rates for ischemic heart disease in the South were 21.3 percent below national levels. In 1975, however, they were only 4 percent below the U.S. level.

Trends in mortality by color and sex are shown in table 3.11 and figure 3.8 for 1950 and 1969–1971. For these years the requisite decennial census data are available for the computation of age-adjusted death rates by color for the United States and the South. The nonwhite population in 1950 exhibited lower age-adjusted death rates from ischemic heart disease than those of the white population, but, during the ensuing 20-year period, their mortality rates crossed over the rates for the white population. That is, increases in death rates from ischemic heart disease for the nonwhite population were so much greater than those of the white population during the period—77.6 percent compared with 17.8 percent—that their death rates increased from 29 percent below the

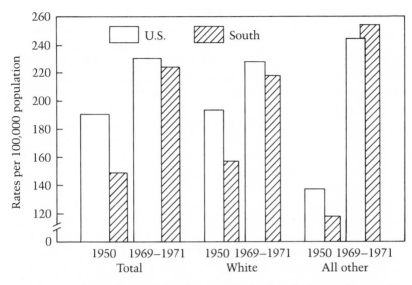

Figure 3.8. Age-adjusted death rates for ischemic heart disease by color for the South and the United States, 1950 and 1969–1971

rate of the white population in 1950 to 7 percent above the corresponding rate in 1969–1971.

In the South the same general pattern occurred during the period. The rate for the nonwhite population more than doubled (from 118.0 per 100,000 population in 1950 to 254.6 in 1969–1971); while the rate for the white population increased by less than 50 percent (from 157.2 per 100,000 population in 1950 to 218.3 in 1969–1971). In fact, the increase in ischemic heart disease for southern nonwhites was so large, 115.4 percent, that by 1969–1971, this rate exceeded the national rate by 4 percent.

In general, white males both in the South and the U.S. had the greatest risk of dying from ischemic heart disease in 1950, followed by all other males, white females, and all other females. While all four color-sex groups showed increases in ischemic heart disease between 1950 and 1969–1971, white males in both the South and the nation still exhibited the greatest risk of death from this cause at the end of the period.

Malignant Neoplasms
From 1940 to 1975, malignant neoplasms, more commonly known as cancer, accounted for an increasing share of southern deaths. The

percentage of all deaths in the South ascribed to cancer increased from 8 to 18 percent during the 35-year period. The sustained southern and national increase in the risk of dying from malignant neoplasms is illustrated in figure 3.9 which shows age-adjusted death rates by color for selected years, 1940 through 1975, for all malignant neoplasms as well as for malignant neoplasms of the respiratory system. Respiratory cancer is the most rapidly increasing component within the broader category of malignant neoplasms. During the 35-year period, age-adjusted rates for cancer (all components) increased nearly 42 percent for the South, compared with only 13 percent for the United States. In 1940 the South's rate was almost 25 percent below the national level. However, by 1975 the level of cancer mortality in the South was virtually the same as that in the nation because of the more rapid increases in the southern rates during 1940–1975. In 1975 the age-adjusted death rate for malignant neoplasms in the South was 133.2 deaths per 100,000 population, compared with 135.7 for the nation; the comparable rates in 1940 were 93.9 and 120.3, respectively (table 3.10).

At the beginning of the 35-year period, white Southerners were at a greater risk than other Southerners to die of cancer. In 1940 the color differential in age-adjusted death rates from this cause was more than 10 percent in the South and 22 percent in the nation. Between 1940 and 1969–1971, the nonwhite population experienced greater increases than the white population. During this period in the South, nonwhite age-adjusted death rates increased almost three times as fast as the comparable rates for the white population (table 3.11). Because of the more rapid increase in cancer death rates for the nonwhite population, the level of their mortality, which in 1940 was below that of the white population, was about 22 percent higher than that of the white population in 1969–1971. Nationally, the 1969–1971 rates for nonwhites also exceeded those of the white population by about 18 percent.

In 1940 white females both in the South and in the U.S. had the greatest risk of dying from cancer followed by all other females, white males, and all other males. During the 30-year period, 1940–1971, white females showed a decline in the age-adjusted rate in both the South and the U.S. The other three color-sex groups showed increases, with nonwhite males showing the greatest increases in both the South and the U.S. By 1969–1971 the highest cancer death rates were for nonwhite males, followed by white males, nonwhite females, and white females.

Also illustrated in figure 3.9 are trends in respiratory cancer.

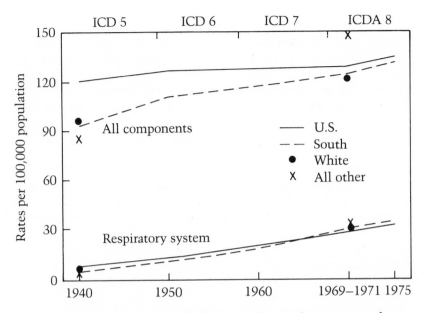

Figure 3.9. Age-adjusted death rates for malignant neoplasms by color for the South and the United States, selected years, 1940–1975

Data on this specific cause are presented because the rapid increase in fatalities from this disease has given an upward thrust to general cancer mortality in the South and in the nation. Death rates for cancer (all sites) increased more than 34 percent between 1940 and 1969–1971 in the South. However, death rates for cancer of the respiratory system increased more than 500 percent during the same period. The southern increases for respiratory cancer were almost twice those that occurred nationally. Proportionately, the southern age-adjusted death rate in 1940 for respiratory cancer comprised about 5 percent of the rate for all cancers, 4.8 deaths per 100,000 population compared with 96.9. By 1975 its proportionate share of the rate had grown to over 26 percent. Indeed, if one were to subtract death rates attributed to respiratory cancer from death rates for all sites of cancer, the southern death rates for the other sites would have increased by about 10 percent during 1940–1975, rather than the 42 percent reported for all sites.

In 1940 in the United States, death rates from respiratory cancer were lower among persons of other races, 4.2 per 100,000 popula-

tion, than for the white population, 7.5. The same general relationship also existed in the South in 1940, although Southerners had a
slightly lower risk than the U.S. By 1969–1971, however, rates for
both whites and nonwhites in the South were higher than comparable rates in the U.S. For nonwhites the rates had increased
about twice as fast as those for whites so that in the region and the
nation as a whole by 1969–1971 nonwhite population experienced
a greater risk of death due to respiratory cancer than the white
population.

In 1940 white males had the greatest risk of dying from respiratory cancer in the U.S., 11.5 per 100,000 population and 8.0 in the
South. Nonwhite males had the next greatest risk, 6.2 in the nation and 4.0 in the South, followed by white females and nonwhite
females. In 1969–1971, however, nonwhite males in the U.S. and in
the South showed the greatest risk of dying. Nonwhite males
showed the greatest increase in the age-adjusted rate from 6.2 in
1940 to 57.0 in 1969–1971 for the U.S., or an increase of over 800
percent. In the South the increase was even greater from 4.0 in
1940 to 55.1 per 100,000 population in 1969–1971, an increase of
over 1,200 percent.

Cerebrovascular Disease
Cerebrovascular disease, popularly known as stroke, is the third
major cause of death in the South today. In 1940 the comparable
category of diseases (called "vascular lesions of the central nervous
system") was the fourth leading cause of death (table 3.9). In 1940
this disease accounted for nearly 9 percent of deaths in the South;
by 1975 it accounted for 11 percent.

While the relative importance of cerebrovascular disease as an
underlying cause of death has increased in terms of both its rank
among the major causes and its share of all deaths annually, the
relative "risk" of dying from this cause has actually declined since
1940, as measured by the age-adjusted death rate. The age-adjusted
death rate for cerebrovascular disease declined one-third during
this period both nationally and in the South. Mortality rates due to
stroke have been consistently higher in the South than in the nation for both whites and nonwhites, as shown in figure 3.10. In
1940 and during 1969–1971, the death rate from stroke for Southerners was about 12 percent above the national figure. In 1969–
1971 the rates were 76.8 deaths per 100,000 population in the South
and 67.0 in the United States. Rates for southern whites in 1969–
1971 were about 7 percent above the nation, while rates for non-

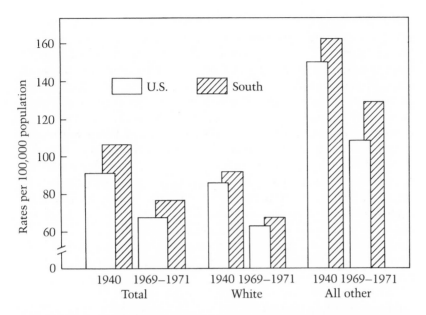

Figure 3.10. Age-adjusted death rates for cerebrovascular disease by color for the South and the United States, 1940 and 1969–1971

whites in the South were almost 19 percent higher than the rates for this group in the nation.

Stroke is a much more serious problem as a cause of death for the nonwhite than for the white population. In 1940 the age-adjusted rates for the nonwhite population in the South were about 80 percent above those of the white population. Thirty years later the color differential was over 90 percent.

In 1940 in the United States, nonwhite females had the greatest risk of dying from cerebrovascular disease, 161.6 per 100,000 population, followed by nonwhite males, white males, and white females. Nonwhite females in the South had even a greater risk, 170.8 per 100,000 population. During the ensuing 30 years, nonwhite females in the South and in the U.S. showed the greatest declines, such decreases that in 1969–1971 they had lower age-adjusted rates than their male counterparts.

Nephritis
The third major cause of death among Southerners in 1940 was nephritis (all forms), a disease affecting the kidneys. This cause ac-

counted for nearly 9 percent of all deaths. Chronic nephritis, the major component of nephritis (all forms), accounted for 40 percent of all nephritis deaths. In the South the age-adjusted death rate for chronic nephritis stood at 102.2 deaths per 100,000 population in 1940, 29 percent above the national figure (table 3.10). During the 35-year period, 1940–1975, death rates from this cause declined by over 96 percent in the U.S. and in the South. In 1975 the rate stood at only 2.4 and 2.9 deaths for the respective areas. While both color groups shared in the 90 percent reduction in mortality from this cause, differentials persisted in 1969–1971, the most recent date for which data are available. The rate in 1969–1971 for nonwhites in the South was 10.1, compared with 2.5 for the white population, or a ratio of 4 to 1. National mortality differentials by color for chronic nephritis were about the same magnitude.

All four color-sex groups participated in this decline. Similar reductions for these groups occurred both in the South and in the nation.

Influenza and Pneumonia
The general reduction in mortality from influenza and pneumonia during nonepidemic years reflected substantial advances in both the standard of living in the United States and the adoption and widespread use of antibiotics during the period. In 1940 influenza and pneumonia accounted for nearly 9 percent of all southern deaths. In 1975 they accounted for only about 3 percent.

The general trend in mortality from these causes, shown in table 3.10, was a reduction of more than 50 percent between 1940–1950 in the age-adjusted rates, followed by a more gradual reduction of about one-third during the next 25 years. This general pattern was shared by the South and the nation during the 35-year period. In 1940 age-adjusted death rates from influenza and pneumonia in the South were about 40 percent above those of the U.S. By 1975 the age-adjusted rates had declined by 79.9 and 72.5 percent, respectively. They now stood at virtually the same level for the South and the nation. Death rates for the nonwhite population at the national level were more than double those of the white population in 1940 (table 3.10). In the South in 1940, the white population had death rates above those of the white population in the nation, and death rates for nonwhites in the South exceeded those of the whites by about 70 percent. In 1969–1971 the rates in the South and in the U.S. were very similar. The excess of nonwhite mortality compared with white mortality, however, had increased to about 90 percent nationally and in the South.

Nonwhite males in both periods had the greatest risk of dying from influenza and pneumonia in the nation as a whole and in the region. All four color-sex groups showed sharp declines during the 30-year period.

Tuberculosis

Tuberculosis was still a serious public health concern in the South in 1940 because it accounted for about 1 in 20 deaths annually. It was also the seventh leading cause of death in the United States. The southern rate of 60.3 deaths per 100,000 population was almost one-third greater than the national figure for 1940. During the next 35 years, mortality from this cause declined by over 97 percent in the United States and in the South. By 1975 the rates for the nation and the region stood at 1.3 and 1.6, respectively (table 3.10).

Historically, there were and still remain substantial differences between color groups in the risk of dying from tuberculosis. In 1940 age-adjusted rates for nonwhites were about three times those of whites. While both color groups shared in the precipitous reductions in mortality from this cause during the 1950s and 1960s, the 3 to 1 excess of mortality among the nonwhite population persisted in 1969–1971 (table 3.11). At that time rates in the South were 6.6 and 1.9 deaths for nonwhite and white populations, respectively. Comparable national figures were 7.0 and 1.5.

The four color-sex groups shared equally in the reductions in mortality from tuberculosis. Nonwhite males in the South and in the nation, however, still had the greatest risk of dying from tuberculosis in both 1940 and in 1969–1971.

Motor Vehicle Accidents

By 1975 deaths due to accidents, the major component of which is motor vehicle accidents, had become a major cause of death in the South (table 3.9). Its relative importance as a cause of death increased not because of major increases in the risk of dying from motor vehicle accidents during 1940–1975 but rather because of reductions in death rates for other major causes during the period. Between 1940 and 1975, the age-adjusted death rate for motor vehicle accidents in the South fluctuated in the range of 20 to 33 deaths per 100,000 population (table 3.10). Southern death rates for motor vehicle accidents tended to be about 25 percent above the national rates during the 35-year period. The rate for the nonwhite population, which in 1940 was slightly below the rate for the white population, crossed over the rate for the white population by 1969–1971. At that time the nonwhite rate exceeded the white rate by 21 percent in the South and by 14 percent in the nation (table 3.11).

Males generally have a higher risk of dying from motor vehicle accidents than females. This was true in 1940 and in 1969–1971 for both white and nonwhite males in the South and in the nation. Both white and nonwhite females, however, showed greater increases during the 30-year period for both region and nation.

Homicide
The South has been portrayed as one of the more violent regions of the nation, especially in terms of the incidence of homicide. To what extent do our statistics bear this out? In 1940 southern death rates for homicide, on an age-adjusted basis, were more than twice as high as those of the United States. This differential exceeds by a wide margin that for any of the other causes of death previously discussed. The next highest differential representing an excess for the South of about 40 percent was for influenza and pneumonia. Mortality from homicide in the South in 1940 stood at 13.6 deaths per 100,000 population on an age-adjusted basis (table 3.10). By 1975 the southern rate had increased by more than 10 percent, a gain, however, less than the nation's of 71 percent during the same 35-year period. Because of the rapid national increase in death rates for homicide, the national/regional differential in mortality narrowed. In 1940 the southern rate was more than double the national rate, but by 1975 it was only one-third greater.

Is the convergence of southern homicide rates with national ones a reflection of the changing racial composition of the South and the U.S.? In the discussion of overall mortality in the South, we saw that the proportion of nonwhites in the South decreased between 1940 and 1970, while the proportion in the nation increased. Homicide rates are higher among nonwhites than among whites. Thus, even with unchanging risks of death for each color group, the changes in racial composition would have contributed to a relative reduction of homicide in the South and to an increase in the nation.

By 1969–1971 the nonwhite population of the South had a homicide rate of 46 deaths per 100,000 population, more than six times the rate for the white population (table 3.11 and figure 3.11). The

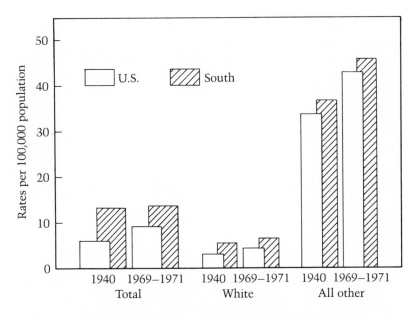

Figure 3.11. Age-adjusted death rates for homicide by color for the South and the United States, 1940 and 1969–1971

national differential was slightly greater, and the rates are comparable in magnitude. The serious nature of homicide as a cause of death among "other races" in the South is reflected in its relative rank among the important causes we have discussed. In terms of the age-adjusted death rate, the homicide rate for the nonwhite population in 1969–1971 exceeded the rate for motor vehicle accidents, cirrhosis of liver, influenza and pneumonia, and malignant neoplasms of the respiratory system. For the white population, death rates from homicide were lower than the rates for all of these causes.

Homicide rates for nonwhite males in 1969–1971 were greater than rates for other color-sex groups in the United States and in the South. Between 1940 and 1969–1971, white females, however, showed the greatest increase, almost 70 percent in both the South and the nation.

Cirrhosis of Liver
In 1940 death rates from cirrhosis of liver were 6.4 deaths per 100,000 population in the South and 8.5 nationally. During the

next 35 years, death rates from this cause increased very rapidly, by 60 percent nationally and by 88 percent in the South. Historically, death rates for this cause have been lower in the South than in the nation. They remained so in 1975, although the southern rate was converging with that of the U.S. (table 3.10). The national age-adjusted rate in 1975 was 13.6, compared with the regional rate of 12.0—a difference of 13 percent compared to a 1940 difference of 31 percent. As with a number of other causes, death rates for the non-white population crossed over the level of the rate for the white population during the period after 1940 (table 3.11). Although the rate for the nonwhite population was slightly below that of the white population in 1940, by 1969–1971 it exceeded the rate for whites by about 50 percent in the South and by 77 percent nationally.

Both white and nonwhite males show a higher risk of dying from cirrhosis of liver for both periods and both areas. Both white and nonwhite females, however, had greater percentage increases in their rates during 1940 to 1969–1971 nationally and in the South.

FURTHER DIFFERENCES IN MORTALITY BETWEEN WHITE AND NONWHITE POPULATIONS

The burden of low health status has fallen particularly heavily on the nonwhite population of the South. In 1940 there were a few major causes of death for which the nonwhite population had a lower death rate than the white. These causes included malignant neoplasms, ischemic heart disease, cirrhosis of liver, and motor vehicle accidents. By 1969–1971, however, the death rate for the non-white population in the South for even these categories exceeded the rate for whites. Sometime between 1940 and 1969–1971, the level of nonwhite mortality for these causes too had crossed over the white level. Thus, death rates of the nonwhite population exceeded those of the white in 1969–1971 for each of the causes discussed previously. The extent of the color differentials by cause is summarized in table 3.12 as a ratio of the age-adjusted death rate for whites divided by the age-adjusted death rate for nonwhites. Ratios are shown for both the United States and the South in 1969–1971.

For all causes, mortality of the nonwhite population exceeded that of the white population by 46 percent in the nation and by 53 percent in the South. In other words, in 1969–1971 the mortality

TABLE 3.12 Nonwhite-white Ratio of Age-Adjusted Death Rates
for Selected Causes

Cause	U.S.	South
All Causes	1.46	1.53
Ischemic heart disease	1.07	1.16
Malignant neoplasms (all components)	1.19	1.23
Malignant neoplasms of respiratory system	1.14	1.01
Cerebrovascular disease	1.74	1.93
Chronic nephritis	3.83	4.04
Influenza and pneumonia	1.90	1.91
Tuberculosis	4.67	3.47
Motor vehicle accidents	1.17	1.21
Homicide	9.13	6.67
Cirrhosis of liver	1.77	1.48

Note: Based on data in table 3.11.

rate of the nonwhite population was still half again the rate of the
whites and this differential was even greater in the South. By
cause, the differential in the South is greater for heart disease
(ischemic), cancer, and stroke than in the nation. For stroke—cerebrovascular disease—the rate for nonwhites in the South is almost
twice that of whites.

Excess deaths among the nonwhite population still exist for
some infective diseases. For example, mortality due to tuberculosis in 1969–1971 was about five times greater among the nonwhite population than among whites in the U.S. In the South,
however, it was three times greater for nonwhites. Also, mortality
due to influenza and pneumonia was almost twice as great nationally for nonwhites; in the South it was a third as great for nonwhites (table 3.12). The most prominent difference in the risk of
death was, as we noted earlier, for homicide. Nationally, the likeli-

hood of being killed by another person was nine times greater among nonwhites than among whites in 1969–1971, compared with seven times greater in the South.

In his study of human resources in the South written in 1945, Vance commented on the much higher rates of mortality in the black population. He noted that "the problem of Negro health, serious as it is in its economic and social aspects, is nothing of a medical mystery. Excess Negro mortality is made of the elements that cause excess deaths everywhere. It is related to occupational factors found in rough, heavy work, to poor housing, heating, and sanitation, to inadequate nutrition and poor medical care" (Vance, 1945:349).

The health status of blacks was vastly better in 1975 than in 1940. Gains in expectation of life at the national level, in infant mortality, and in general mortality have exceeded those of the white population. However, although important gains have been made in the South, improvement of nonwhite mortality has not been as rapid as gains outside the South. In summary, while both the nonwhite population of the South and the nation have made substantial strides in health status, they both have substantially poorer health than the white population. Death continues to discriminate against the nonwhite population both nationally and in the South.

CONCLUSION

In 1940, according to almost every major mortality indicator, the health status of the South was below that of the nation. General mortality rates (adjusted for age composition), infant mortality, and expectation of life at birth reflected the relatively poorer health of Southerners. During 1940–1975 their health status improved considerably, generally paralleling and in some cases exceeding improvements in mortality for selected causes in the United States population. While regional improvements in infant mortality, expectations of life at birth, and age-adjusted death rates were greater than those of the United States, the South at the end of the 35-year period still had a somewhat lower health status than the United States.

One of the prominent aspects of mortality change in the South during 1940–1975 was a *convergence* with national patterns. This was true not only of the general indicators of health status but also of death rates for specific causes. For virtually every cause, death rates at the end of the 35-year period were more like those of the nation than at the beginning of the period. This happened both where southern age-adjusted death rates were initially lower than the U.S.—malignant neoplasms, ischemic heart disease, cirrhosis of liver—and where the age-adjusted rates were higher—cerebrovascular disease, tuberculosis, chronic nephritis, influenza and pneumonia, and homicide. While some of this convergence can be attributed to real changes in the risk of death, much of it is due to changes in racial compositions.

Data presented in this chapter show that the South has been undergoing rapid mortality change during 1940–1975. Only barely perceptible is an earlier stage of epidemiologic history for the region when infectious diseases such as tuberculosis ranked high among causes of death. The recent history of southern mortality shows the epidemiological transition to a greater proportion of deaths attributable to chronic and degenerative diseases. Heart disease, cancer, and stroke now account for almost two out of three annual deaths in the South. Moreover, the age distribution of deaths has changed. An increasingly larger share of deaths occur now to older persons. This is attributable only in part to changes in the mortality patterns toward chronic diseases. It also reflects the impact of substantial declines in fertility of southern women and changes in migration patterns, topics discussed in more detail in this volume by Rindfuss, Sly, and Poston. The population of the South appears to be sharing increasingly in the health attributes of the United States, as an industrialized society with a generally improving standard of living. The epidemiological transition of the nation is continuing and with it the transition of the South.

APPENDIX

Sources
The data in this chapter are based on published and unpublished figures from the Division of Vital Statistics, National Center for Health Statistics, U.S. Department of Health, Education, and Welfare. The principal published sources are:
1. *Vital Statistics of the United States, Volume II, Mortality*, published annually.
2. *Vital Statistics Rates in the United States, 1940–60*. The sources of specific tables are:

Table 3.1. Rates for 1940, 1950, and 1960 for the United States and the census divisions are from *Vital Statistics Rates in the United States, 1940–60,* tables 66 and 67. Rates for 1969–1971 and 1975 are unpublished data from the Division of Vital Statistics, National Center for Health Statistics. Rates for the South are unpublished data, estimated by methods described below.

Table 3.2. Age-adjusted rates for 1969–1971 are unpublished data from the Division of Vital Statistics, National Center for Health Statistics. Rates for the South are estimated by the methods described below.

Table 3.3. Same as table 3.2.

Table 3.4. Same as table 3.2.

Table 3.5. Rates for 1940, 1950, and 1960 for the United States and the census divisions are from *Vital Statistics Rates in the United States, 1940–60,* tables 42 and 43A. Rates for 1970 are from *Vital Statistics of the United States, Volume II, Mortality,* part A. Rates for the South, all years, and for 1975 are unpublished data from the Division of Vital Statistics, National Center for Health Statistics.

Table 3.6. Same sources as table 3.5.

Table 3.7. Figures for 1939 are derived from "United States Abridged Life Tables, 1939, Urban and Rural, by Region, Color, and Sex," *Vital Statistics—Special Reports,* vol. 23, no. 15, 1948; national figures for 1949–1951 and 1959–1961 are from *Vital Statistics Rates in the United States, 1940–60,* table 52; figures for 1969–1971, "State Life Tables, 1969–1971," *U.S. Decennial Life Tables for 1969–1971;* regional figures for 1949–1951, 1959–1961, and 1969–1971, see below for method of estimation.

Table 3.8. National Center for Health Statistics, U.S. Department of Health, Education, and Welfare, "State Life Tables, 1969–1971," *Decennial Life Tables, 1969–1971.*

Table 3.9. Rates for the South for 1940 and 1975 are published data from the Division of Vital Statistics, National Center for Health Statistics.

Table 3.10. Rates for 1940, 1950, and 1960 for the United States are from *Vital Statistics of the United States 1940–60,* table 67. Rates for 1969–1971 and 1975 are unpublished data from the Division of Vital Statistics, National Center for Health Statistics. Rates for the South are unpublished data estimated by methods described below.

Table 3.11. Same sources as table 3.10.

TABLE 3.13 Age-Adjusted Death Rates: Comparison of Use of
10-Year Age Groups and Broad Age Groups

Cause	1940	1960	1975
All causes			
U.S. 10-year	1,076.1	760.9	638.3
U.S. broad	1,077.2	811.5	690.7
Tuberculosis			
U.S. 10-year	45.9	5.4	1.2
U.S. broad	45.8	5.5	1.3
Malignant neoplasms			
U.S. 10-year	120.3	125.8	130.9
U.S. broad	120.3	129.1	135.7
Malignant neoplasms - respiratory			
U.S. 10-year	7.2	19.2	32.5
U.S. broad	7.2	19.5	32.9
Diabetes			
U.S. 10-year	26.6	13.6	11.6
U.S. broad	26.6	13.9	12.4
Ischemic heart disease			
U.S. 10-year	NA	214.6	196.1
U.S. broad	NA	225.5	220.1
Cerebrovascular disease			
U.S. 10-year	91.0	79.7	54.5
U.S. broad	91.1	85.7	64.2
Influenza and pneumonia			
U.S. 10-year	70.2	28.0	16.6
U.S. broad	70.2	31.6	19.3
Cirrhosis of liver			
U.S. 10-year	8.6	10.5	13.8
U.S. broad	8.5	10.6	13.6
Chronic nephritis			
U.S. 10-year	79.0	5.7	2.2
U.S. broad	79.1	5.9	2.4
Motor vehicle accidents			
U.S. 10-year	26.2	22.5	21.3
U.S. broad	26.1	20.9	21.7
Other accidents			
U.S. 10-year	46.2	27.4	23.5
U.S. broad	46.9	28.6	24.5
Homicide			
U.S. 10-year	6.3	5.2	10.5
U.S. broad	6.2	4.9	10.6

Note: Rates are per 100,000 population.

Age-Adjusted Death Rates
All age-adjusted rates in this chapter have been adjusted to the
Standard Population of the United States in 1940 by the Direct
Method. Age-adjusted rates for 1969–1971 and for 1975 differ computationally from rates for 1940, 1950, and 1960. Rates for 1969–
1971 are based on age-specific rates for the 3-year period and were
computed using 10-year age groups. Age-adjusted rates for 1940,
1950, and 1960 were computed using the four age groups, under 25
years, 25–44 years, 45–64, and 65 years and over. For 1975 the age
groups used were under 20 years, 20–44, 45–64, and 65 years and
over. An illustration of the effect of grouping ages on the age-
adjusted rates for selected causes in 1940, 1960, and 1975 is shown
in table 3.13. Age-adjusted rates for the total Southern Region for
1940, 1950, 1960, and 1969–1971 are based on a weighted average
of published rates for the three census divisions that comprise the
region. The weights are the divisions' proportionate share of the
total region's population in the year for which the rates are being
computed.

Life Expectancy
Expectation of life at birth for the South and for the United States
in 1939 is based on a weighted average of life expectancies for
places of 100,000 or more population, for places considered as other
urban, and as rural. Life expectancies for the South in 1949–1951
represent a weighted average of figures for the three census divisions that comprise the South. For 1959–1961 and 1969–1971 life
expectancies for the South are a weighted average of figures for
each state in the region. Life expectancies for the "all other" population are based on data for those states for which life expectancies
were available in 1959–1961 and 1969–1971, thus excluding West
Virginia and Delaware.

Place of Occurrence and Place of Residence
For the years other than 1940, death rates are based on deaths by
place of residence; for 1940, on deaths by place of occurrence. The
effect of the 1940 classification procedure is not likely to be great.
The percentage of resident deaths occurring outside the South in
1940 was less than 1 percent.

Comparability of Cause of Death Statistics
Since 1900 the International Classification of Diseases has been revised every 10 years to keep abreast of medical knowledge. Revi-

TABLE 3.14 Comparability Ratios for Selected Causes between
Four Revisions of the International Classification of
Diseases

Cause of Death	5th/6th Revision	6th/7th Revision	7th/8th Revision
Tuberculosis	.95	1.01	NA
Malignant neoplasms	.96[a]	.99	1.00
of respiratory system	.96	1.00	1.03
Ischemic heart disease[b]	NA	.98	1.15
Cerebrovascular disease	1.16	1.00	.99
Influenza and pneumonia	NA	.94	1.04
Cirrhosis of liver	.80	.99	1.00
Chronic nephritis	1.43	1.02	NA
Motor vehicle accidents	1.00	1.00	.99
Homicide	1.00	1.00	.99

[a]The category of malignant neoplasms of lymphatic and
hematopoietic tissues excluded leukemia and Hodgkins
disease during the fifth revision.

[b]The most nearly comparable category during the sixth and
seventh revisions was arteriosclerotic heart disease, including coronary disease.

sions covering the period in the chapter, 1940–1975, were in effect
during the following years:

Fifth Revision,   1940–48
Sixth Revision,   1949–57
Seventh Revision, 1958–67
Eighth Revision,   1968–75

The comparability ratios are based on coding the same deaths occurring in a given year by both the prior and the new revision.
Table 3.14 shows these ratios for the causes contained in this chapter. These ratios were based on the double coding of data for 1950
(fifth/sixth), 1958 (sixth/seventh), and 1966 (seventh/eighth). A
ratio of 1.00 indicates that the coding was completely comparable
between revisions.

From table 3.14 several comparability ratios stand out as very different from 1.00. For instance, between the fifth and sixth revisions, the ratios for cirrhosis of liver and chronic nephritis indicate for the former that approximately 20 percent fewer deaths were coded to cirrhosis under the sixth revision and for chronic nephritis that about 43 percent more deaths were coded to this cause under the sixth revision. Thus, between 1940 and 1950, the decrease in chronic nephritis was probably less than the rates indicate and for cirrhosis of liver the increase was probably greater. Several other causes also show breaks in comparability that could substantially affect trend comparisons.

NOTES

Note: This chapter is dedicated to William Kirkpatrick ("Pat") Reid, Jr.

1. The South in this discussion is a sixteen-state area along with the District of Columbia. By census division the areas are as follows: *South Atlantic Division*: Delaware, Maryland, District of Columbia, Virginia, West Virginia, North Carolina, South Carolina, Georgia, and Florida; *East South Central Division*: Kentucky, Tennessee, Alabama, and Mississippi; and *West South Central Division*: Arkansas, Louisiana, Oklahoma, and Texas.

2. Comparable national and regional data for this cause of death are not readily available for 1940.

4
Migration
DAVID F. SLY

As a purely demographic phenomenon or in relation to its social and economic causes and consequences, the study of migration is more complex than either the study of fertility or mortality. For instance, unlike fertility, which can only increase population and mortality which can only decrease population, migration is the only component of population change which can either increase or decrease population size. Similarly, with respect to population structure, all persons who enter a population at birth do so at the same age. And, while there is variation in the ages at which people leave a population through death, each person only dies once, and, in the whole population, this tends to occur at relatively predictable ages. In the case of migration, however, persons can enter a population at any age, and they may enter and leave the same population numerous times. Migration may also alter the social and economic structure of a population more rapidly than either fertility or mortality.

Finally, and perhaps most important for understanding the uniqueness of the migration phenomenon is that unlike other demographic behavior we can never study it by looking solely at the population within which the phenomenon is observed. That is, whereas it is common to seek the causes of fertility and mortality within the population where they occur, the very nature of the migration process dictates that its causes must be sought in at least two populations. In addition to these general problems, several other issues always emerge which are related to the areas studied and the types of data analyzed. In this chapter we will have occasion to outline these problems as they relate specifically to the issues at hand.

Two hundred years of migration in the South is, indeed, a simple phrase or title when one first hears it. Yet, upon reflection a number of perplexing issues emerge which social scientists should, perhaps, be nearly, but not quite, ashamed of. The first of these revolves around the issue of what is the South and how should one go about demarcating its boundaries? Should agricultural, cultural, political, geological, social, or economic criteria be applied; or is a single criterion sufficient to properly encapsulate this amoeba? Do its elusive boundaries coincide with county or state boundaries or with those of politically demarcated areas? As the reader is probably aware, these questions have been asked numerous times in the past, and the only major point of agreement which has emerged from some thirty-odd definitions is that seldom is the census-defined Southern Region accepted (Sly and Weller, 1972; McKinney and Bourque, 1971; Woodward, 1951; Odum, 1936; Vance, 1929).

Most researchers have rejected it because all areas within the census-defined region do not meet some specific criteria. To a substantial degree, this results from the time-bound nature of the criteria frequently selected by those advocating alternatives. For instance, several researchers have suggested at various times the use of a criterion intended to measure cotton production (Sly, 1972); however, if this criterion is applied today, it would virtually restrict the southern region to a relatively small number of counties not even forming a contiguous area. Indeed, there are few criteria that could be applied equally to all possible areas in 1776, 1876, and 1976 and be expected to yield a constantly defined area.

Nevertheless, some consistency in definition is needed, and, because of the span of time to be observed in this chapter, the use of states to construct a region is a necessity. Because trends have been reported and have become familiar within Census Bureau geographic units, the census-defined South will be used here as the major unit of analysis. However, in a number of places companion statistics will also be provided for a redefined Southern Region. The redefined Southern Region is made up of seven states (Alabama, Mississippi, Georgia, Kentucky, Tennessee, South Carolina, and North Carolina) which form a contiguous area and exclude nine of the states and the District of Columbia included in the census-defined region. To a substantial degree, these states make up the eastern portion of the Central and Eastern Upland Regions and the entire Southeast Coastal Plain Region described some years ago by Bogue and Beale (1959). When aggregated, these states also give the best fit in terms of corresponding to what many other researchers have referred to as the Cotton Belt, the Bible Belt, and the Old South, although they, in fact, do not correspond to any of these areas.

The second set of problems which adds to the complexity of this chapter's objective involves making some tentative decisions about "migration" in both conceptual and statistical terms. Conceptually, one must begin by acknowledging the differences between migration as individual and aggregate phenomena, as well as the analytical distinctions between migrations and migrants (Goldstein and Sly, 1975:143−200; Shryock and Siegel, 1971:616−672; Hawley, 1950:319−347). When conceptualized as an individual phenomenon, migration is one type of demographic behavior available to individuals; the central types of questions of greatest interest are those which help to predict why some people decide to move while others do not and why some migrants experience certain consequences after moving (Speare, Goldstein, and Frey, 1974; Lansing and Mueller, 1969). Similarly, when concern is with the individual, one may want to know why certain people move repeatedly (Morrison, 1967:553−561; Toney, 1976:297−310) or why certain migrants follow one specific route between two points while others take alternative routes.

Although the individual perspective is useful for understanding why people are mobile, the aggregate perspective provides considerably more information about the demographic conditions and consequences of migration for the group, since the unit of analysis is a populaton. From this latter perspective, migration is conceptualized as a component of areal population change, and, as such, the important questions relate to its role in increasing or decreasing population size—that the size of the change produced by migration is relative to other changes in the organization, environment, technology, and population structure of the aggregate, as well as the consequences of such changes.

This latter perspective is the primary one employed in this chapter, if for no other reason than it is the one we are restricted to for historical-statistical reasons. That is, we must rely upon census data which relate to place of residence or which allow us to estimate net migration employing residual techniques (Sly, 1972) to construct any historical picture of the South's migration patterns. In point of fact, data on individual migrants and individual migrations are simply not available in any historical series. In addition to these restrictions, the term "migration" will be used here in a generic sense to refer to all classes of geographic mobility, be they interregional, interstate, or intercounty; we trust that in each case, however, the referent will be clear.

Finally, any effort of this type must be selective in terms of coverage. In the first part of the chapter, we will discuss four important contextual consequences of migration to and within the South. In particular we will focus on changes in the regional distribution of the U.S. population, the urban-rural distribution of population within the South, as well as changes in its racial and age composition. It is important to bear in mind that these factors have social, economic, and political significance as well as demographic importance. We are referring to them as contextual consequences because, while they do indicate the changing conditions under which the region's migration has occurred, they are also strongly influenced by earlier patterns and volumes of migration. That is, what are conditions of migration at one point are to a considerable extent shaped as a consequence of earlier volumes and patterns of migration.

All of the data discussed here have been taken from various publications of the U.S. Bureau of the Census, including *Census of Population* volumes and special reports, *Current Population Reports*, and Historical Statistics, or from sources which have relied upon census data, such as Lee et al. (1957) and the volumes produced by Bowles and Tarver (1965).

CONTEXTUAL CONSEQUENCES OF MIGRATION: CHANGING REGIONAL, URBAN-RURAL, RACIAL, AND AGE COMPOSITION

Regional Distribution
Somewhat ironically, the Census South has always been one of the most heavily populated regions of the country. According to the census of 1790, the population of the U.S. was nearly equally divided between the regions now referred to as the South and the Northeast. As the populations of the North Central and Western Regions developed, they did so at the proportional expense of the Census South and the Northeast, although more so from the latter than the former. Indeed, during the period from 1800 to 1870 (see table 4.1), one of the most spectacular regional demographic events to occur was the rapid development of the North Central Region, which by 1870 contained about one-third of the nation's popula-

tion. During the period from 1880 to the turn of the present century, the westward movement was fully launched, and, although
the population of the region has grown rapidly ever since, its regional distributional impact has been mediated by the sheer size of
population in the other three regions. Thus, since the early part of
the century, the proportion of the nation's population in all regions
outside the West declined until 1970. But, interestingly enough,
the effect in the Census South has been less than the effect in both
the Northeast and the North Central Regions. For instance, between 1910 and 1970, the percentage of total population in the
Northeast declined by nearly four points and that in the North
Central by nearly five points while in the Census South the comparable decline was only one point.

Between 1970 and 1974, a marked turnaround in this sense has
occurred, and, by the end of this period, estimates indicate that the
Census South has not only begun to increase its share of the nation's population once again but also that it has recovered in the
short span of 4 years what it had lost, so to speak, in the preceding
60 years. That is, the percentage of the nation's population in the
Census South (31.9) in 1974 was identical to what it was in 1910.
This minor change of only 1 percent does not seem overly significant until we recall that a shift of this magnitude required a net
redistribution of about 2,120,000 persons. By 1980, population projections suggest that the South will contain 37.5 percent of the
country's population.

Finally, although there is considerable coincidence between the
secular trends in the percentage of the nation's population living in
the Census South, and in the redefined South, there are a few notable differences. First, although the percentage of the nation's population living in the Census South declined steadily after 1790, it
increased markedly through 1830 in the redefined South, after
which it began to decline. Second, after the decline in the redefined South set in, its pace was considerably more rapid than was
the decline in the Census South. For instance, from 1840 through
1970, the percentage of the nation's population living in the Census South declined by about 25 percent while over the same period
the percentage of the nation's population in the redefined South
decreased by over 50 percent. Similarly, from 1910 to 1970, when
this percentage declined by just one point in the Census South, it
declined by nearly four points in the redefined South. This, of
course, is an important signal, suggesting not merely that migra-

TABLE 4.1   Percent Distribution of U.S. Population

	1974	1970	1960	1950	1940	1930	1920	19
Total Population								
Northeast	23.2	24.1	24.9	26.1	27.2	27.9	28.0	28
North Central	27.2	27.8	28.8	29.4	30.4	31.3	32.1	32
West	17.6	17.2	15.6	13.3	10.9	10.0	8.7	7
Census South	31.9	30.9	30.7	31.2	31.5	30.7	31.2	31
Redefined South[a]	12.6	12.3	12.8	13.9	14.7	14.4	15.1	16
Urban Population								
Northeast		27.6	28.8	33.0	36.9	38.6	41.8	44
North Central		28.0	29.2	30.2	31.4	32.3	32.8	32
West		18.3	16.4	13.4	11.3	10.4	8.8	8
Census South		26.1	25.6	23.3	20.5	18.7	17.1	15
Redefined South[a]		9.1	8.6	7.9	7.6	7.0	6.5	6
Rural Population								
Northeast		17.3	18.3	15.6	14.6	14.3	14.0	14
North Central		27.2	28.1	28.3	29.1	30.1	31.4	32
West		14.9	14.3	13.3	10.4	9.5	8.6	7
Census South		40.6	39.3	42.8	45.9	46.0	46.0	45
Redefined South[a]		18.9	20.0	22.4	23.8	23.8	24.2	24

[a] Redefined South includes seven states: Alabama, Georgi
Carolina.

tion patterns between these two areal units are different but also
that examination of migration in only one will lead to inappropriate and misleading conclusions.

Rural-Urban Distribution
One of the most generalized indicators of the modernization of
areal units is their level of urbanization (Goldstein and Sly, 1977:
17–65; Davis, 1972). Throughout most of the history of this country, it generally has been true that population movements have
tended to gravitate toward urban areas and their more varied opportunities. Thus, from a regional perspective, one expects the in-

1890	1880	1870	1860	1850	1840	1830	1820	1810	1800	1790
27.6	28.9	31.7	33.7	37.2	39.6	43.1	45.2	48.2	49.7	50.1
35.6	34.6	33.6	28.9	23.3	19.7	12.5	8.9	4.0	.9	---
5.0	3.6	2.6	2.0	.8	---	---	---	---	---	---
31.8	32.9	31.8	35.4	38.7	40.7	44.4	45.9	47.8	49.4	49.9
17.5	19.0	19.1	21.6	25.0	25.0	28.5	27.7	26.7	24.9	21.2
46.4	52.2	55.0	60.9	64.6	67.9	69.7	69.3	72.4	76.1	78.7
33.6	29.7	27.3	20.3	11.1	7.0	3.6	.1	.4	---	---
5.3	3.9	2.6	1.6	.3	---	---	---	---	---	---
14.8	14.3	15.1	17.2	21.0	25.1	26.7	29.4	27.2	23.9	21.3
5.9	5.3	5.9	6.2	7.1	6.8	7.6	7.9	6.3	7.5	7.9
17.5	19.8	23.9	27.0	32.3	36.2	40.5	43.4	46.3	48.0	48.5
36.7	36.5	35.9	31.1	25.0	21.2	13.4	9.5	4.3	1.0	---
4.8	3.5	2.6	2.1	.9	---	---	---	---	---	---
43.5	40.2	37.7	39.9	41.8	42.6	46.1	47.1	49.4	51.0	41.5
23.8	24.3	23.7	25.3	28.3	29.5	30.4	29.3	28.3	26.0	21.9

sissippi, Kentucky, Tennessee, South Carolina, and North

terregional flow of migration to be from the least urban regions to the more urban regions, and within regions one expects urbanization to be achieved through a healthy contribution from rural to urban migration. In short, the level and the process of urbanization have important implications for various types of migration, including interregional and intraregional. Yet, for urbanization to occur, it is necessary for the urban population to grow faster than the rural population, and this frequently is a consequence of migration.

The data presented in table 4.2 show that the level of urbanization in the Census South has historically been lower than the level of urbanization in other regions of the country. During the period

TABLE 4.2   Level of Urbanization in the U.S.

	1970	1960	1950	1940	1930	1920	1910	190
United States	66.7	63.0	59.6	56.5	56.1	51.2	45.6	39.
Northeast	76.1	72.8	75.4	76.6	77.6	75.5	71.8	66.
North Central	67.4	63.9	61.1	58.4	57.9	52.3	45.1	38.
West	71.1	66.1	59.9	58.5	58.4	51.8	47.9	39.
Census South	56.2	52.7	44.6	36.7	34.1	28.1	22.5	18.
Redefined South	48.9	42.2	35.1	29.3	27.4	21.9	18.0	14.

prior to 1850, the level of urbanization in the South was remarkably low, and the tempo of urbanization in the region was also low when compared to that in the Northeast. For instance, by 1850 industrialization and commercialization had gained a strong foothold in the Northeast, and the level of urbanization in that region had already exceeded 26 percent. In the Census South, the dominant position of agriculture and rural ways of living are clearly reflected in its 8 percent level of urbanization. Even more remarkable is that in the redefined South the level of urbanization by 1850 had reached only about one-half the level of urbanization in the Census South.

By 1860 each of the other regions of the country had a level of urbanization clearly above that in the Census South, and by 1890, when the Census South was 16 percent urban, each of the other regions had a level of urbanization at least twice as high. Similarly, by 1920 each region outside the Census South was more urban than rural; yet, by this time the level of urbanization in the Census South had just passed 25 percent, while the level in the redefined South had just reached 22 percent. If we maintain the urban definition through 1970, it turns out that it was not until the late 1950s that the Census South became more urban than rural and that even as late as 1970 the redefined South had not attained this status.

The important point here is not merely that these figures reflect the relative lack of nonagricultural development in the Census South and the redefined South but that this was likely to create the conditions which would help allow both areas to facilitate urban-

1890	1880	1870	1860	1850	1840	1830	1820	1810	1800	1790
35.1	28.2	25.7	9.8	15.3	10.8	8.8	7.2	7.3	6.1	5.1
59.0	50.8	44.3	35.7	26.5	18.5	14.2	11.0	10.9	9.3	8.1
33.1	24.2	20.8	13.9	9.2	3.9	2.6	1.1	.9	.0	---
37.0	30.2	25.8	16.0	6.4	---	---	---	---	---	---
16.3	12.2	12.2	9.6	8.3	6.7	5.3	4.6	4.1	3.0	2.1
11.8	7.8	7.9	5.7	4.3	2.7	2.4	2.1	1.7	1.8	1.9

ization in the remaining regions of the country. The crucial consideration is that the pattern of population distribution within these areas relative to that in the other regions of the country by 1950 strongly suggests that the South represented at this time the last regional frontier.

Racial Composition
By the middle of the nineteenth century, over 90 percent of the nation's black population resided in the Census South, and, as late as 1910, this figure had not changed significantly (table 4.3). During each decade following 1910, with the exception of the Depression years from 1930–1940, substantial decreases in the percentage of the nation's black population in the Census South did occur. Given their magnitude, there can be little doubt that they were substantially contributed to by migration. Nevertheless, it is important to note that these figures represent both the direct contribution of migration to the regional redistribution of the black population and the cumulative indirect effects of the redistribution of black childbearing resulting from migration. Thus, if it is assumed that younger persons are particularly prone to migrate and that they are also childbearers, it is not surprising that the greatest decline in the percentage of blacks in the Census South did not occur until the 1960–1970 decade. That is, it is very likely that although the percentage of blacks living in the Census South declined substantially during later decades, migration had continuously less to do directly with this than did the changing distribution of births occurring to the black population. Latest available data indicate that

TABLE 4.3   Percentage of Total U.S. Black Population in Each Region

	1970	1960	1950	1940	1930	1920	1910	1900
Northeast	19.2	16.1	13.4	10.6	9.6	6.5	4.9	4.4
North Central	20.3	18.3	14.8	11.0	10.6	7.6	5.5	5.6
West	7.5	5.7	3.8	1.3	1.0	.8	.5	.3
Census South	53.0	60.0	68.0	77.0	78.7	85.2	89.0	89.7
Redefined South	27.9	32.1	37.4	42.9	44.3	50.6	58.3	65.0

by 1975 a clear majority of the nation's black population lived outside the Census South.

If the black population residing in the redefined South and the Census South had declined at the same rate, we would expect to find that the percentages reported in table 4.3 maintain a constant ratio. In fact, this does not happen. The percentage for the Census South declined by 68 percent over the entire period. The sharper decline in the redefined South reflects a substantially different pattern of change than that described for the Census South. For instance, between 1850 and 1910, the percentage of the nation's blacks in the Census South changed by just 3 percent, while that in the redefined South changed by almost thirty points. From 1910 through 1970, the decline in the redefined South still exceeded that in the Census South; however, during this period the declines in the two analytical units were considerably more comparable, equaling 30 percent in the former and 36 in the latter. What these observations, of course, suggest is that during the earlier period, there was a marked tendency for blacks residing in the redefined South to redistribute themselves, but this redistribution process was largely confined to the Census South. Similarly, during the latter period, blacks continued to redistribute themselves away from the redefined South; however, unlike the earlier period, this redistribution process became more dispersed and involved more than the census region.

Although data are not presented here, the above observations suggest that the racial composition of the Census South has undergone substantial changes. In 1870 the Census South was over 55

0-1970

▶0	1880	1870	1860	1850
6	3.5	3.3	3.5	4.1
8	5.9	5.1	4.1	3.7
4	.2	.1	.1	.1
0	90.5	91.5	92.2	92.1
5	75.4	73.1	83.8	87.4

percent black, and by 1900 it was slightly less than 50 percent black. Following 1910 the figure began to change more dramatically, and by 1970 the census region was less than 25 percent black. Again, however, it is important to note that these changes reflect the combined influences of white and black rates of population growth and that the change cannot be ascribed exclusively to the effect of migration.

Age Composition
The final contextual consequence of migration to be considered is the changing age composition of the southern population, and particularly, the role of aging of the population. As with other contextual consequences, it is important to keep in mind that many factors in addition to migration can cause changes in the age composition of the elderly population of regions; these include differences in mortality through time, in patterns of births, in mortality at the older ages, and the age-specific growth rates of other age groups.

With these limiting conditions in mind, we can examine the data in table 4.4 which show that before 1920 no region in the U.S. had more than 5 percent of its population in age group 65 and over. Between 1920 and 1950, however, the percentages of regional populations which were over 65 increased so much that by the end of the period the Census South had less than 8 percent of its inhabitants in this age group. Beginning with the 1940–1950 decade, the percentage of the Census South's population which was elderly began to increase more rapidly than comparable percentages in other

TABLE 4.4 Percentage of Population Within Each Region Age 65 & Over

	1975	1970	1960	1950	1940	1930	1920	1910	1900	1890	1880	1870
Northeast	11.2	10.6	10.1	8.7	7.2	5.7	4.0	4.8	4.8	5.0	4.8	4.2
North Central	10.6	10.1	9.8	8.9	7.7	6.3	5.3	4.9	4.3	3.2	2.3	2.4
West	9.5	8.9	8.6	7.9	7.3	5.8	4.6	3.8	3.6	2.5	1.8	1.2
Census South	10.5	9.6	8.3	6.9	5.5	4.3	3.8	3.3	3.1	2.5	2.8	2.6

	1970-1975	1960-1970	1950-1960	1940-1950
Northeast	6.6	15.6	30.5	32.8
North Central	6.8	12.8	27.8	28.9
West	15.9	28.9	50.2	53.2
Census South	18.3	31.9	40.8	50.1
U.S.	11.6	21.2	34.9	36.1

regions of the country. By 1970 the percentage of the Census South's population in this category exceeded that of the West; moreover, it was only one point less than that of the Northeast. This trend appears to have continued into the post-1970 period.

Despite these observations the data actually tend to mask the magnitude of the regional differential in the growth of the elderly and its resulting changing regional distribution. The bottom portion of table 4.4 presents data showing the percentage of increase in the population 65 and over in each region and the entire country. From 1940 to 1960, the pace of change in the elderly population of the South was exceeded only by that in the West, where the base population was small compared to that in the Census South. Since 1960, however, the pace of change in the elderly in the Census South clearly exceeded that in the remaining regions and was actually more than double the pace of change in the Northeast and North Central Regions. These marked contrasts in growth resulted in an increase in the proportion of the nation's elderly living in the Census South from 25 percent in 1940 to 32 percent in 1975. Indeed, by 1975 the South's elderly population (7.1 million) was twice that of the West and exceeded that in the other two regions by more than 1 million.

SOUTHERN MIGRATION PATTERNS

Net Migration
During the one hundred years from 1870–1970, the pattern of net migration differs depending upon which definition of the South is used (see table 4.5). The Census South experienced alternative decades of population increase resulting from migration and population decline resulting from migration from 1870 through 1900; thereafter, population losses from migration occurred each decade through 1960. With the exception of the Depression decade, the absolute and relative loss increased successively from 1900–1910 through 1940–1950. Despite the decline in net migration loss during the Depression decade, the volume still exceeded a half million, and the sharp increases in net migration decline during the two decades following the Depression reflect, in part, changes within the region as well as changes in the rest of the country. Within the Census South, a substantial amount of agricultural reorganization and modernization was occurring with no concomitant increase in the demand for unskilled and semiskilled la-

borers in other economic sectors. Moreover, the civil rights movement was helping to kindle a spark of independence and hope for many people in the region. Outside the region the nation was gearing up for a war economy and developing its industrial potential to meet the needs of a country and world at war. The war itself exposed many Southerners to opportunities, potentials, and attractions in other parts of the country. In short, the net migration loss of over 3 million people during the two decades from 1940 through 1960 undoubtedly reflects conditions indigenous as well as external to the region.

Beginning with the census decade of 1960, however, this pattern showed a dramatic reversal with nearly three-quarters of a million persons being added to the Census South's population through migration. How long this trend will continue is at present unknown, but all available data suggest that it is becoming more salient. For instance, although not shown in table 4.5, the Census Bureau has estimated that during the 4 years following the 1970 census the net migration gain to the Census South was nearly double what it had been in the previous 10 years. (For additional discussions see chapters 1, 5, and 8 in this volume.) During the earlier of these periods, migration accounted for only 11 percent of the total population increase in the region, while, in the period since 1970, migratory change has accounted for nearly 30 percent of the total Census South's population increase.

The redefined South, on the other hand, has had net out-migration during each census decade since 1870, and, with the exception of the war decade from 1940 to 1950, the volume of loss resulting from migration from these states was greater than the volume of loss or gain to the Census South. In fact, each state within the redefined South contributed to the net migration decline of the area during each decade from 1870 through 1970 with two exceptions: South Carolina during the first and Georgia during the last. The magnitude of the net migration decline to this area is suggested by the fact that, during the decade following 1940, nearly 5 million inhabitants of the area were lost through migration and this number actually exceeds the total number of people living in most states in the area in 1970.

Whereas the reversal of net migration loss to the Census South began during the 1960 decade, it did not begin in the redefined South until after 1970. The post-1970 period, thus, marks the first time in over 100 years that the redefined South has had net migration gains. With the single exception of Georgia, in the last census all states making up the redefined South had net losses resulting from migration during each census decade over the last 100 years; yet, in the post-1970 period, all these states reversed this trend and had net gains from migration. In fact, the only state in the Census South not to have net gains from migration during this period was Louisiana.

Within the Census South, but outside the redefined South, there are other states which deserve special attention since they represent exceptions to the general rule of net migration loss. The most consistent exceptions have been Florida, which over the entire 100-year period never had a decade of population loss resulting from migration, and Texas, which had net migration loss only during the Depression decade. In this sense the migratory increase to Florida has been particularly astounding, averaging 1.5 million during each of the two decades following 1950.

The important point, however, is that the pattern of population loss resulting from migration corresponds over the period with the changing percentage of the nation's population in both the Census South and the redefined South. During each decade when net out-migration occurred, the percentage of the nation's population in the Census South declined except during the Depression decade. When net in-migration to the region reemerged during the 1960s, the percentage of the nation's population in the region began to increase again. If current patterns of net migration continue, by 1980 nearly 37.5 percent of the U.S. population will live in the South.

In the lower portion of table 4.5, separate estimates of net migration are shown for the black population. These data highlight the important role which black mobility has played in the region's population loss resulting from migration, particularly in the decades following 1910. We have indicated earlier that after 1910 dramatic decreases began in the percentage of the region's population which was black and that this percentage declined from just under 50 percent after 1900 to only 25 percent by 1970. That migratory change made a significant contribution in this respect is suggested by the fact that following 1910 there had never been a decade during which the black population did not make up at least 53 percent of the total net migration loss to the region. Indeed, during the three decades following 1940, blacks have accounted for successively larger proportions of the decline resulting from migration, despite their decreasing proportion in the region's population. By 1960–1970, when the region had its first net migration increase since 1890, this resulted solely from the net migration increase of

TABLE 4.5 Volume of Total and Black Net Migration

	1870-1880	1880-1890	1890-1900	1900-1910	1910-1920	1920-1930	1930-1940	1940-1950	1950-1960	1960-1970
					TOTAL					
Alabama	-60,700	-11,500	-40,400	-47,800	-113,900	-149,200	-165,300	-271,000	-368,331	-229,681
Arkansas	84,000	75,100	-82,800	-27,200	-74,700	191,300	-128,800	-320,400	-432,463	-49,987
Delaware	-2,300	4,300	-1,200	2,700	5,100	-3,500	16,000	14,500	64,002	37,342
District of Columbia	18,100	36,100	34,300	41,000	97,000	27,300	157,800	78,500	-158,283	-99,907
Florida	12,100	51,100	36,900	103,500	101,600	297,600	280,300	510,900	1,616,790	1,331,093
Georgia	-40,000	-19,500	-56,100	-41,700	-98,100	-414,900	-134,100	-224,300	-213,570	67,604
Kentucky	-47,200	-96,800	-65,100	-177,800	-167,100	-206,100	-93,500	-319,200	-389,546	-154,026
Louisiana	-12,000	-3,000	1,400	10,600	-64,700	-23,200	5,700	-112,100	-49,686	-122,951
Maryland	-11,200	-10,700	8,200	-8,300	43,100	10,200	87,000	213,300	319,993	380,584
Mississippi	-5,600	-60,600	-44,500	-46,400	-199,300	-101,600	-90,300	-344,900	-433,455	-268,767
North Carolina	-14,400	-57,700	-88,800	-80,400	-74,300	-7,900	-85,400	-202,800	-327,838	-80,571
Oklahoma			501,300	491,500	62,400	-51,800	-269,400	-356,100	-218,436	15,532
South Carolina	25,700	-35,900	-75,500	-80,600	80,900	-256,900	-102,500	-172,400	-221,786	-132,444
Tennessee	-91,800	-77,700	-95,400	-156,900	-131,200	-113,800	-14,900	-102,800	-272,499	-45,018
Texas	308,500	151,200	147,700	131,100	114,300	243,500	-72,800	132,900	113,831	198,353
Virginia	-51,100	-80,900	-91,500	-73,700	-27,700	-231,600	200	15,200	2,202	155,526
West Virginia	24,000	-4,800	17,200	46,100	-1,700	-53,800	-73,600	-210,800	-446,711	-262,298
Census South	+136,100	-141,300	+105,700	-45,400	-724,400	-844,400	-683,600	-1,676,500	-1,415,786	+740,384
Redefined South	-285,400	-359,700	-465,800	-631,600	-864,800	-1,250,400	-686,000	-1,642,400	-2,227,025	-842,903

Alabama	-36,100	-5,800	-1,700	-22,100	-70,800	-80,700	-63,800	-165,500	-224,201	-227,648
Arkansas	25,400	44,700	-7,900	22,500	-1,000	-46,300	-33,300	-116,100	-432,463	-98,237
Delaware	-1,300	300	-700	-400	-600	500	2,300	2,400	5,999	4,639
District of Columbia	6,200	13,400	8,700	9,800	18,300	16,000	47,500	61,200	53,756	35,758
Florida	1,400	15,700	23,400	40,700	3,200	54,200	49,900	7,200	101,507	-20,980
Georgia	-20,300	12,300	-27,300	-16,200	-74,700	-260,000	-90,300	-191,200	-204,297	-137,991
Kentucky	-13,000	-22,400	-12,200	-22,300	-16,600	-16,600	-9,100	-22,800	-15,503	-6,913
Louisiana	-1,300	3,300	-21,600	-16,100	-51,200	-25,500	-8,400	-113,800	-92,279	-157,442
Maryland	-7,500	-7,600	6,500	11,400	7,000	5,000	10,700	19,900	35,999	87,789
Mississippi	17,600	-13,300	-10,500	-30,900	-129,600	-68,800	-58,200	-258,200	-323,326	-277,577
North Carolina	-7,900	-38,500	-48,700	-28,400	-28,900	-15,700	-60,000	-127,300	-206,897	-177,607
Oklahoma			79,300	54,800	800	1,900	13,000	-38,800	-26,050	-10,409
South Carolina	15,700	-18,600	-65,500	72,000	-74,500	-204,300	-94,300	-159,000	-217,784	-176,912
Tennessee	-24,500	-18,700	-19,000	-34,300	-29,300	-14,000	8,600	38,200	-56,898	-56,860
Texas	21,000	12,600	7,100	-10,200	5,200	9,700	4,900	-67,300	-26,765	-21,543
Virginia	-37,600	-53,400	-70,800	-49,300	-27,200	-117,200	-36,900	-30,600	-71,452	-67,116
West Virginia	2,100	3,600	5,800	15,300	15,500	12,800	-4,100	-16,700	-40,337	-24,489
Census South	-60,100	-72,400	-155,100	-3,700	-718,400	-749,000	-321,500	-1,178,400	-1,740,991	-1,269,354
Redefined South	-68,500	-105,000	-184,900	-164,400	-475,600	-660,100	-367,100	-885,800	-1,248,906	-1,061,508

the white population. In fact, white movement to the South actually exceeded white movement from the South a decade earlier.

In short, with the exception of few census decades since data have been gathered, the population losses resulting from migration have been disproportionately absorbed by the region's black population. Actually, during the census decades beginning in 1870, 1890, 1950, and 1960, as well as during the post-1970 period, the number of white migrants into the Census South exceeds the number of white migrants leaving the Census South. And from 1900 to 1930, the net loss of whites to the region was extremely insignificant. In those years when white net change due to migration was not positive, the percentage of total loss accounted for by blacks fluctuated from between just 8 percent during 1900–1910 to 99 percent during 1910–1920. Even during the war decade of 1940–1950, the net loss from migration by the black population of the Census South accounted for over 70 percent of the total population loss to the region from migration.

It is very interesting, however, to compare these observations with those for the redefined South. This area did sustain substantial losses resulting from migration of the white population during each decade from 1870 through 1960. Thus, from 1870 to 1910, white net migration loss accounted for between 75 percent and 60 percent of the total net loss resulting from migration. However, in the decades following 1910, blacks consistently accounted for about 55 percent of all population declines resulting from migration. To a substantial degree this pattern and its differences from that of the Census South reflect the greater diversity of the latter and the changes in agriculture particularly characteristic of the former, which we have already discussed.

Finally, a special note needs to be added on what will come to be the region's major social problem in the future. Before 1940 the Census South had a strong tendency to lose population through migration at all ages. After 1940, however, this pattern tended to change, and, at all ages above 60, minor population gains began to become manifest. These gains became more significant during the 1950s, but, even during this period, they seem to have had only minor impacts on the overall age composition of the population. Beginning in the 1960s, however, this influx of persons at or near retirement age began to skyrocket despite a continued net out-migration of persons in their 20s. Thus, during the 1960s, when net population gain through migration became a reality in the region, many observers concluded that it signaled a new day of boom to the region. Even a quick glance at the age composition of net migration quickly calls this perspective into question. For instance, from 1960 to 1970, when the region gained 740,000 persons through migration, 610,000 of these, or 82 percent, were over the age of 60; and 708,000 or 96 percent, were over 55. At the same time that gains are being registered at these ages, losses are continuing to occur at ages 0–9 and 20–29, further compounding the burden of an increasing dependent population. If Northerners could claim that migration was the mechanism which allowed Southerners to shift their burden on them during the 40s and 50s, Southerners should be able to make this claim of Northerners during the 70s and 80s.

Destinations
We need to take note of the relatively specific and unchanging destinations of migrants leaving the Census South. Although precise data on places of destination are not available, state of birth data are useful for depicting the pattern of settlement of persons born in the Census South and living outside the region at each census date. In 1870, 85 percent of whites born in the Census South and living outside the region lived in just five states (Missouri, Illinois, Indiana, Ohio, and Pennsylvania). Although the top five states changed and the percentage fluctuated from decade to decade, as late as 1970 five states (California, Ohio, Illinois, Indiana, and Michigan) contained 73 percent of the southern born white population living outside the region. Similarly, black streams to areas outside the Census South have been highly specific and for the most part have followed the same paths as white streams. The same five states, for instance, which housed 85 percent of the whites born in the Census South and living outside it in 1870 were also the top five states for blacks, housing 79 percent of them. The top five states in 1970 (the same as for whites except that Indiana is replaced by New York) contained 75 percent of U.S. blacks born in the South and living outside it at the time of the census.

What these data reflect is the overwhelming tendency for Southerners leaving the Census South, black and white alike, to go to those areas where the relatively unskilled can compete in the labor markets of the industrialized states of the Northeast and North Central Regions. Moreover, and more important for our purposes, these data also show the crucial role which southern migration played in helping mediate the pull which the West was having on the Northeast and North Central Regions. That is, from one perspective one can argue that migration from the South helped the region make its burden the responsibility of the industrialized North. Yet, from another perspective, one can argue that were it not for southern migration to these areas, their development would have been seriously jeopardized or the growth of the West considerably restricted. The important role which southern migration has played in the development of areas outside the Census South is suggested by the fact that in 1970 between 8 and 12 percent of the populations living in Ohio, Michigan, Illinois, and California were originally natives of the Census South.

Migrants arriving in the Census South, on the other hand, have shown similar degrees of origin concentration. By 1970, for instance, New York and Pennsylvania each had more than 800,000 of their natives in the Census South, and Ohio and Illinois each had about 500,000. Another 500,000 Southerners in 1970 had been born in Massachusetts and Indiana, while California was the only state in the West to have more than 150,000 of its natives living in the South. In short, migrants to the South have overwhelmingly come from the Northeast and the North Central Regions, and the states sending the most migrants to the South (New York, Ohio, and Pennsylvania) have not changed since 1870. Of particular interest in this respect, however, is that few blacks born outside the region have elected to move into it. By 1970 only two states (New York and Pennsylvania) had more than 30,000 of their native blacks living in the South, and no other state had even 10,000 in the region. Recent data, however, suggest that this trend may be changing and that in the post-1970 period more blacks may be moving into the region than are leaving it.

MIGRATION WITHIN THE SOUTHERN REGION

Interstate Migration
Our analysis of migration patterns within the Southern Region is restricted to examining the flows of migration between states in the Census South. While we have constructed matrices showing the flow of migration from and to every state in the region from all other states in the region, space requires that these results be summarized. Accordingly, table 4.6 shows the number of persons at each census for each state in the region, beginning in 1930, who were born in another state of the region and residing in the specified state, as well as the number of persons born in that state and residing in another state in the region. The former is frequently re-

ferred to as the lifetime migration to the state and the latter as the lifetime migration from the state. The difference between the two may be interpreted as the net effect of the lifetime migration, or the difference between the total number of persons living in a state who were born in another state in the region and the number of persons born in that state and living in another state in the region. Data are shown separately for white and nonwhite populations of each state.

Careful analyses of these data suggest that they be used only as an indicator of very general trends since they do not appear to be highly reliable. For instance, at any one date, the number of "in-migrants" should equal the number of "out-migrants." But in fact they do not, and the differences are larger than can be attributed solely to rounding. Second, estimates of intercensal net migration should indicate that the volume of net out-migration is equal to the volume of net in-migration and again a comparison of figures indicates this is not the case. There are a number of possible explanations for these inconsistencies, the most likely of which are (1) that a substantial number of Southerners move within the region prior to leaving it, (2) that a number of Southerners born in one state in the region die in another after having been counted as a migrant in the latter, and (3) that there is a considerable amount of return migration.

With these restrictions in mind, some guarded statements about interstate migration within the region may be made. Although it should be theoretically possible to estimate the intercensal net migration for each state from these data, we restrict our observations to the lifetime patterns at each census date. In this respect it appears that by 1930 the dominant patterns of interstate migration of the white population had already been established. At this time nine of the seventeen states within the region had net migration losses to the other states. With few exceptions, the areas of major decline resulting from migration are concentrated in the Old South (our redefined South for the most part), while with few exceptions the areas of increase resulting from migration are concentrated in the South's northeastern corridor, surrounding the District of Columbia, and in the Sunbelt states of Florida, Texas, and Louisiana. Indeed, the only exceptions are Virginia in the Washington, D.C., area, which had a net loss of lifetime migrants, and Oklahoma, which is not in the Sunbelt and which had a lifetime net gain from migration.

With few exceptions this pattern of lifetime migration has been

TABLE 4.6 Intraregional Estimates of Interstate Migration

White

	1970			1960			1950			1940			1930		
	To	From	Net	To	From	Net	To	From	Net	To	From	Net	To	From	Net
Alabama	3,703	6,330	-2,627	2,861	5,620	-2,759	2,255	4,662	-2,407	1,193	4,002	-2,809	1,309	3,693	-2,384
Georgia	5,880	6,443	-563	4,234	5,985	-1,751	2,767	4,700	-1,933	2,169	3,465	-1,296	1,877	2,939	-1,062
Kentucky	1,707	3,803	-2,096	1,535	3,301	-1,766	1,208	2,538	-1,330	1,127	2,345	-1,218	1,201	2,267	-1,066
Mississippi	2,046	4,243	-2,197	1,661	4,164	-2,503	1,366	3,231	-1,865	1,589	2,735	-1,146	1,162	2,533	-1,371
North Carolina	4,502	6,169	-1,667	3,564	5,404	-1,840	2,120	3,637	-1,517	1,932	2,565	-633	1,692	2,455	-763
South Carolina	3,844	3,127	717	2,362	2,786	-424	1,698	1,986	-288	1,269	1,579	-310	1,070	1,529	-459
Tennessee	4,747	5,915	-1,168	4,366	5,277	-911	3,649	4,144	-495	3,530	3,751	-221	2,622	4,341	-1,719
Arkansas	2,101	7,835	-5,734	1,735	4,427	-2,692	1,980	3,636	-1,656	2,029	3,543	-1,514	2,079	3,614	-1,535
Delaware	615	404	211	570	279	291	273	123	150	245	99	146	221	95	126
District of Columbia	380	3,589	-3,209	985	2,486	-1,501	1,062	1,317	-255	1,106	462	644	875	349	526
Florida	12,888	3,034	9,854	9,971	1,803	8,168	4,107	736	3,371	3,590	430	3,160	2,762	399	2,363
Louisiana	3,519	3,509	10	3,058	2,972	86	2,529	1,832	697	1,833	1,429	404	1,570	1,352	218
Oklahoma	2,662	4,506	-1,844	3,789	4,044	-255	3,654	2,666	988	4,275	1,991	2,284	5,207	1,504	3,709
Texas	10,996	5,737	5,261	10,266	4,598	5,668	7,974	3,751	4,223	13,879	3,140	10,739	6,883	6,038	845
Virginia	7,125	5,550	1,685	5,651	4,858	793	2,651	3,728	-1,077	2,273	3,378	-1,065	1,774	3,066	-1,292
West Virginia	1,119	4,058	-2,939	1,244	3,246	-2,002	1,382	1,914	-532	1,380	1,168	212	1,456	878	578
Maryland	6,279	2,255	4,024	5,023	1,838	3,185	2,592	1,124	1,468	1,569	950	619	1,226	877	349

Nonwhite

Alabama	316	1,406	-1,090	412	1,408	-996	446	1,294	-848	429	1,280	-851	580	1,228	-648
Georgia	705	2,153	-1,448	623	2,533	-1,910	636	2,209	-1,573	391	2,058	-1,667	707	1,968	-1,261
Kentucky	298	128	170	216	118	98	299	99	200	321	105	216	351	124	227
Mississippi	256	1,591	-1,335	352	1,828	-1,476	430	1,754	-1,324	556	1,648	-1,092	674	1,672	-998
North Carolina	858	1,744	-886	986	1,819	-833	982	1,610	-628	979	1,183	-204	1,063	1,768	-705
South Carolina	270	1,754	-1,484	227	2,102	-1,875	176	1,938	-1,762	177	1,777	-1,600	164	1,834	-1,670
Tennessee	1,039	385	654	1,228	314	914	1,307	430	877	1,164	496	668	1,077	542	535
Arkansas	350	424	-74	652	437	215	778	269	509	1,035	458	577	1,326	473	853
Delaware	171	38	133	178	27	151	140	12	128	105	10	95	92	9	83
District of Columbia	1,672	504	1,168	1,775	233	1,542	1,433	156	1,277	1,029	113	916	720	85	635
Florida	2,591	395	2,196	2,813	301	2,512	2,146	232	1,914	1,878	172	1,706	1,574	190	1,384
Louisiana	632	1,252	-620	711	1,226	-515	598	1,113	-515	599	1,110	-511	615	1,194	-579
Oklahoma	338	122	216	373	142	231	462	86	376	620	83	537	856	74	782
Texas	1,453	402	1,057	1,298	393	905	1,004	389	615	884	470	414	950	616	339
Virginia	1,032	1,183	-151	1,119	1,286	-167	1,002	1,183	-181	699	1,170	-471	661	1,241	-580
West Virginia	136	138	-2	258	128	130	426	101	325	542	57	485	624	56	568
Maryland	1,793	291	1,502	1,405	328	1,077	1,195	290	905	789	259	530	662	256	406

sustained from decade to decade since 1930. For instance, in 1950 all states with net migration losses in 1930 had net migration losses in 1950, and, in all these states except South Carolina and Tennessee, these net losses in 1950 exceeded the estimates in 1930, suggesting that they continued to lose whites during the period in their exchanges with other states in the region. Two areas, the District of Columbia and West Virginia, had net gains of whites from intraregional interstate migration in 1930 but net losses thereafter. The former undoubtedly reflects the massive suburbanization of the District of Columbia and the decentralization of the federal bureaucracy into the surrounding area, while the latter suggests the influence of the Appalachian economy.

Among the states which had net gains in 1930, there was a marked tendency (with the exceptions mentioned above) to have larger net gains by 1950. Oklahoma did not have this experience, but, in the other states, particularly Texas, Florida, Louisiana, and Maryland, the increases were substantial. While the flows into the former three states were fairly diffuse, coming from all over the region, those into the latter were heavily concentrated from the District of Columbia and surrounding states.

By 1970 the patterns established for white intraregional interstate migration had not changed substantially. Indeed, the only salient exceptions appear to be South Carolina, which by 1970 had a net gain of intraregional lifetime migration; Louisiana, which showed a net loss; and Virginia, which showed a larger net gain in 1970 than its net loss in 1950. Finally, Georgia showed a net loss in 1970, but the very substantial decline in its loss surely indicates that it has become a new pole, attracting many southern whites.

Separate data are shown for blacks in the lower portion of table 4.6. These data are interesting for the contrasts they provide. In some respects they indicate similarities between the patterns for blacks and whites, but they also suggest divergences. For instance, as with whites, the data for blacks show a considerable amount of stability to the pattern over time. Of the ten states showing net gains from lifetime migration in 1930, all but two (Arkansas and West Virginia) had net gains in 1970. As among whites major gains occurred over time in the Sunbelt states of Florida and Texas. But unlike whites, blacks also have moved into border states, such as Kentucky, Tennessee, and particularly the District of Columbia, in greater numbers than blacks born in these areas have moved to different southern states. Finally, some careful comparisons of the data for 1960 and 1970 suggest additional contrasts, the most salient of which are: (1) unlike the continuous white flow into Florida, by 1970 blacks appear to have begun to leave Florida for other southern states in greater numbers than they are entering and (2) like whites, there seems to be a substantial reversal of a long-term trend of net loss to Georgia in more recent years.

Rural-Urban Migration
One important manifestation of rural to urban migration for the Southern Region has been these interregional flows of migration just discussed. The vast majority of migrants leaving the South and heading North, whether the trip was made in one or a series of moves, settled permanently in urban areas outside the region. Over the period from roughly 1860 through 1960, this interregional rural and urban migration had a double-barreled effect on the urbanization gap between the South and other regions; migrants leaving the region were added to the numerators of other regions and not to the South.

During the early phase of this movement, migration from southern agricultural counties corresponds rather well with swings in the agricultural economy of the region. Following the reorganization of southern agriculture and the emergence of the new plantation system around the turn of the century, however, this migration became retarded, as a substantial part of the system had built into it the necessary mechanism to keep croppers and tenants on the land. As southern agriculture mechanized and diversified, landholdings were consolidated and increasing numbers of croppers and tenants were displaced to become either migrants or farm laborers. Given low levels of mechanization until after 1940, the need for laborers was relatively substantial. In the 1940s, however, mechanization and the use of chemical herbicides and pesticides began to reduce greatly the need for labor. No one really knows for certain whether the modernization of agriculture was a response to migration or migration a response to these developments. In any case, they did create the context for massive migrations from the agricultural South of the 1940s and 1950s, as did the expanding economic opportunities of the war economy and the postwar reconstruction of the North. During these two decades, the redefined South, largely corresponding to the South's principal agricultural region, lost nearly 4 million persons through migration. Although migration continued through the 1960s, it dropped to only about one-third the volume it had been during the 1950s.

State of birth data also suggest that not all migrants leaving the redefined South actually left the census region. Major Census South states which grew through migration from other southern states include Florida, Texas, Virginia, Maryland, and most recently Georgia. These states are major centers of service, manufacturing, and heavy construction during the period.

The migration into Virginia and Maryland is easily understandable when viewed within the context of the expansion of the Washington, D.C., metropolitan area. What is equally important in gaining an understanding of recent migration within the region, however, is that the migration into Florida, Texas, and Georgia should be similarly viewed. Metropolitan development there has been very rapid over the last few decades, and there can be little doubt that much of the migration from the redefined South into Florida, Texas, and Georgia represents the centrifugal drift of people which so often accompanies the process of metropolitanization. That is, within the states of Florida, Texas, and Georgia, large metropolitan centers are emerging which pull population from nearby areas. In this sense, it will be particularly interesting in the future to compare the role of migration from outside the region with that occurring within the region to assess the relative contribution of each to both the growth of metropolitan areas and the redistribution of population within the region.

CONCLUSION

In the first section of this paper, we focused upon the contextual consequences of migration in the region. Particular attention was given to the changing distribution of the entire country's population between regions, as well as to the changing rural-urban, racial, and age composition within the Southern Region and between it and other regions. The importance of all four of these factors has been emphasized because each has strongly influenced migration patterns involving the region, and each, in turn, has been substantially influenced by migration. In this way we were able to draw attention to the interrelationship between conditions and consequences of migration.

The South played an important role in the westward movement of population, but, unlike the Northeast and North Central Regions, it did not send a large number of people directly to the West. Rather, many migrants went to the two northern regions, thus helping to offset the latter's losses. To a considerable degree, the interregional migration of people from the South represented a rural to urban migration stream. That is, urban development and industrialization in the South were lagging markedly behind the rest of the country, and many rural Southerners seeking urban life-styles had few alternatives other than leaving the region. Similarly, the demand for unskilled and semiskilled labor in the large urban centers of the North was undoubtedly a strong force pulling many black residents from rural areas of the South. That this pull affected not only blacks was strongly suggested by the data showing that, by and large, white as well as black migrants from the region are heavily concentrated in a few of the most industrialized states in the North.

In more recent years, the dominant pattern of more people migrating from the region has turned around, and in 1980 there was a net flow of people into the region. While it is difficult to quantify all the reasons, a few can be mentioned. First is the post-World War II emergence of large urban centers in the region. As noted, the South was the last urban frontier in the country, and the newness of its metropolitan centers has probably given them an attractiveness and environmental appeal unmatched by comparable metropolitan centers in other parts of the country. Closely related is the Sunbelt phenomenon and its economic and life-style benefits for both individuals and business, as well as the efforts of many states in the region to attract business and families through promotion and tax policy. While the latter has received a considerable amount of attention as a pull attracting the elderly to the region, it is important to bear in mind that this pull has been effective because relatively large numbers of people in the Northeast and North Central Regions have been retiring under systems which make it possible to make such a move at this late stage of the family life cycle. Finally, it is important to note that much of the migration into the region has been concentrated toward a few states (most notably Florida and Texas) where large metropolitan centers are emerging and toward two states (Maryland and Virginia) which are closely tied to the decentralization of the federal bureaucracy and the expansion of the Washington, D.C., metropolitan area.

Indeed, the development of metropolitan centers appears to have been a particularly important force in shaping the pattern of migration within the region. This is suggested by the fact that if we examine intraregional migration patterns, we find the same four states have absorbed the vast majority of migrants from within the region. What role metropolitanization will play in the future devel-

opment of migration patterns both to and within the region is difficult to assess, but it appears that a few other states will soon
attract migrants and that these states are also experiencing metropolitan development. Most notable in this sense is Georgia, where,
in addition to Atlanta, several smaller metropolitan centers with
economic bases extending beyond the traditional service functions
are emerging. Although it appears that many of the states referred
to as the redefined South are likely to be in-migration areas, it
seems highly unlikely that they will be able to maintain that character for long if they do not develop the more diversified economy
usually associated with metropolitanization.

5
An Ecological Explanation of Southern Population Redistribution, 1970–1975

DUDLEY L. POSTON, JR.

During the 1970s the South was the major region of population growth in the United States, primarily because of population redistribution through net migration patterns. The preceding chapter establishes a historical perspective by examining migration both into and within the South during the 100-year period from 1870 to 1970. It is noted that recent migrations to the South have been largely concentrated in those states with large metropolitan areas (most notably Florida and Texas) and in those states closely linked with the expansion of the federal bureaucracy, namely Virginia and Maryland.

However, the migration experiences of southern states since 1970 differ considerably from those of earlier periods. During the 1970s the South (except Louisiana and the District of Columbia) experienced net in-migration. For some states, e.g., Florida and Texas, this represented a continuation of 1950s and 1960s trends. But, for the other states, this was a new development. The other southern states had been steadily experiencing net out-migration. Indeed, the most striking feature of the southern turnaround in net migration during the 1970s has been the extensive population increases through net migration in precisely those southern states which had lost migrants so heavily in the previous decades.

The present chapter considers these post-1970 patterns in greater detail than the preceding chapters and attempts to increase our understanding of them by applying a human ecological approach to the net migration patterns among southern counties during the 1970–1975 interval.

AN ECOLOGICAL EXPLANATION

An explanation of Southern migration patterns could utilize several alternatives. For instance, one could take a psychological (or social psychological) approach to migration and focus on the attitudes and motivational intentions of migrants (cf. Taylor, 1969; Newman, 1965). Or one could develop an explanation of migration by examining political factors and determinants (Petersen, 1958). Along another line, one could follow a purely demographic approach, locating the principal causes of migration in formal demographic variables; e.g., varying levels of fertility and mortality. No one approach need be "better" than the others, and in many instances an investigator's choice of perspectives depends upon personal preferences.

The point of view followed here is that of human ecology. The ecological perspective to migration proposes that human populations redistribute themselves to approach an equilibrium between their overall size and the life chances available to them. From this perspective, migration is the principal measure and mechanism of social change and adaptability for human populations. Therefore, treating the population's size as dependent and its sustenance organization as independent, this approach expects that change in organization—to the extent that it produces change in opportunities for living—will necessitate a change in population size. Because migration is the agent for effecting the change in population size, it is viewed as a demographic response attempting to preserve or attain the best possible living standard by reestablishing the balance between population size and organization.

Harley's views are particularly appropriate in this regard:

> Readjustments to disequilibrium are effected primarily . . . through mobility. Population tends to distribute itself in relation to job opportunities, evacuating areas of diminishing opportunities and gravitating to areas of increasing opportunities (Hawley, 1950:167–168).

> Migration presupposes a condition of disequilibrium in the form of an excess number of people in one locality, and either incompletely used resources or disequilibrium in the form of too few people in an alternative place of settlement. The effect of migration is to permit a restoration of equilibrium at both the point of origin and the point of destination (Hawley, 1950:332).

One of the initial tests of the ecological theory of migration was Sly's study of southern black migration from the "old cotton belt," a group of some 253 counties (with at least 25,000 acres each in cotton as reported in the 1890 census) spread out from South Carolina to Texas. These migration patterns were hypothesized as responses to changes in sustenance organization, as well as in technology and environment. Sly wrote:

> Every population must adapt to its environment; and we assume that adaption is mediated through the population's organization and technology. The environment contains site and situation factors, both of which influence the population's sustenance organization. Site factors limit the sustenance organization because they dictate a population's activities. Furthermore, [the degree of] . . . land cultivation influences the size of the population which can be supported. Now assume some new technological breakthrough makes raw material available from another population; this time, however, the environment factor is a situation factor. . . . A larger sustenance organization . . . [becomes possible, hence allowing] the support of a larger population. . . . An imbalance exists [and] the population can alter itself through a demographic component of change—that is, a demographic response (Sly, 1972:617–618).

This general reasoning was tested with data on southern black migration for the decades 1940–1950 and 1950–1960 and generally received empirical support. In particular, Sly found that migration change during the decade could be viewed as a direct "demographic response to differences in sustenance organization" (1972:615). Ecological organization was also seen as mediating the effects of technology and environment on migration behavior.

Another test of the ecological theory of migration noted that the relationship between sustenance organization and demographic behavior should differ depending upon the particular kind of sustenance activity examined (Frisbie and Poston, 1978b). Specifying ten different components of sustenance organization for the nonmetropolitan counties of the U.S. around 1960, the authors found this general hypothesis to be upheld. Moreover, the sustenance organization components were shown to account for a substantial portion of the overall variation in net migration change (Frisbie and Poston, 1978b: chapter 4).

Thus, there is a developing body of empirical literature providing general support for the ecological statements of Hawley (1950),

Gibbs and Martin (1959), Duncan (1959), and other theorists who have written on the relationship between sustenance organization and migration. Other empirical contributions to this literature include Stinner and DeJong (1969), Sly and Tayman (1977), Poston and White (1978), and Frisbie and Poston (1975, 1978a). In setting forth an ecological accounting of the migration that occurred in the South between 1970 and 1975, we will focus principally on sustenance organization determinants and will address in the next section the basic dimensions of sustenance organization which comprise the explanation. Hypotheses setting forth the ways in which these dimensions should relate with migration will be developed, and, in a final section, the hypotheses will be operationalized and tested with data from circa 1970.

DIMENSIONS OF SUSTENANCE ORGANIZATION

The major proposition of the ecological approach to migration is concerned with a reciprocal relationship between a population's size and its organization for sustenance, which operates through the influence of each on the population's levels of living. To the extent that alterations in the way the population has organized itself for survival produce changes in the opportunities for living, the population will need to change its size. Migration, a principal agent for effecting this change in population size, is thus a demographic response to the population's need for reestablishing the balance between population size and sustenance organization.

Therefore, the concept of sustenance organization is central to the ecological theory of migration. In setting forth the characteristics or dimensions of sustenance organization, we follow the observations of Gibbs and Martin (1959:30), who have noted that a "consideration of what is entailed in sustenance organization can best begin with the conception of a population as an aggregate of individuals engaged in activities that provide them with a livelihood." Or, as Hawley (1950:178) has written, organization particularly refers to the "arrangement of differentiated parts suited to the performance of a given function or set of functions."

The first dimension of sustenance organization we consider is the arrangements of differentiated parts, i.e., *sustenance differentiation*. It is convenient to think of this dimension as consisting of two elements: the number of sustenance activities in the population (i.e., structural differentiation) and the degree of uniformity in the distribution of population members across the sustenance activities (i.e., distributive differentiation). A high degree of sustenance differentiation is present when there is a relatively large number of sustenance activities characterizing the population and when the population members are evenly distributed across these sustenance activities.

A second dimension of sustenance organization is the *volume of sustenance produced* by the population. Given its degree of sustenance differentiation, the concern is now directed to the productivity of its particular configuration. Certainly, some forms or configurations should be more productive of sustenance than others.

The degree of *efficiency of the sustenance organization* is a related dimension. Given the level of sustenance produced by the sustenance organization, how efficiently does this occur? How much effort goes into producing the sustenance, whatever its volume?

There is still another feature of sustenance organization, although not strictly a dimension in the sense of the preceding three. We refer here to the specific functions or strategies whereby populations obtain sustenance. What are the principal sustenance activities, the key functions, which typify the population's quest for survival? A specification of the *components of sustenance organization* should thus be included in any delimitation of its dimensions.

In this section we have attempted to specify some of the dimensions of sustenance organization. Others not entertained here are discussed in detail elsewhere (Poston, 1980). In the next section, these dimensions are operationalized, and hypotheses relating to migration are formulated.

OPERATIONALIZATION OF VARIABLES AND FORMULATION OF HYPOTHESES

The dimension of *sustenance differentiation* deals with the extent to which the acquisition of sustenance is differentiated into discrete sustenance functions; i.e., distributive differentiation and the degree to which the members of the population are evenly distributed in these activities. The greater the number of discrete sustenance functions and the greater the uniformity of the distribution of population members in these functions, the greater the sustenance differentiation.

In the most general sense, one should expect a positive relationship between sustenance differentiation and net migration. Increases (or decreases) in the level of sustenance differentiation in a population suggest that an expansion (or contraction) in the number of niches (or job opportunities) has occurred and that the original balance between population size and life chances needs to be reestablished. Net in- (or out-) migration is the appropriate mechanism through which the population responds to increase (or decrease) its size. Therefore, it is hypothesized that the greater the degree of sustenance differentiation in the southern counties in the circa 1970 period, the greater the net in-migration to these counties between 1970 and 1975.

Many procedures exist for measuring sustenance differentiation (see Gibbs and Poston, 1975), one of which is a measure of diversification, or M_1. It is defined in the following manner:

$$M_1 = 1 - (\Sigma X^2 / (\Sigma X)^2),$$

where X is the number of workers in the population in any one industry. This measure reflects both distributive differentiation and structural differentiation, and it will range from zero to a maximum value depending upon the number of sustenance categories utilized. Six categories are used here. Hence, the maximum value will be .833.

We turn next to hypotheses involving net migration and each of the specific *components of sustenance organization.* Indexes have been developed for four sustenance components: construction; manufacturing; personal services; and educational services. In each case the particular sustenance component index reflects the percentage of the county's employed labor force in the respective industry. Counties with high scores on the construction component should be characterized by net in-migration, and the opposite for those with low scores. The volume of construction in an area and the proportion of the area's labor force in the construction industry are to a considerable degree determined by the current growth and expansion of the area, so much so that some investigators prefer to ignore construction data when developing specialization profiles and location quotients for metropolitan areas (Duncan et al., 1960:204). However, given our interests focusing on the balance between population size and opportunities for living, it would appear reasonable to examine the influence of construction on migration.

Counties where educational services are key functions should be characterized by positive rates of net in-migration. Given the recent shifts toward the service economy (Fuchs, 1968), employment opportunities should be greater in counties where sustenance organization is directed toward the provision of educational and related services than in counties where this is not the case. Conversely, employment and associated opportunities for living should not be particularly prominent in counties where the provision of personal services ranks high. Areas where amusements and recreational services, and hotels and motels, among other services, provide the principal focus of sustenance organization are likely to be resort and tourist-related counties. Thus, permanent migrations are not as likely to occur in these kinds of areas as they would be to areas where the provision of personal services is not the key function.

Predictions involving the relationship between manufacturing and net migration may not be stated definitively because of evidence in research literature of both positive and negative relationships (Tarver, 1972; Frisbie and Poston, 1978b). However, it seems reasonable to predict that the relationship between manufacturing levels circa 1970 and net migration in the 1970–1975 interval should be negative given the capital intensive nature of the manufacturing enterprise.

In summary, we have argued that positive relationships should exist between net migration in the southern counties between 1970 and 1975 and the components of sustenance organization in the circa 1970 period based on (1) construction and (2) educational services. A negative relationship is expected between migration and (3) personal services and (4) manufacturing. Each of the sustenance components is operationalized by taking the number of employees in the particular sustenance (or industrial) activity as a percentage of the total civilian employed labor force in 1970 (see table 5.1).

Another dimension of sustenance organization concerns the volume of sustenance produced by the population at a given time. Given the particular configuration or constellation of sustenance components, the issue here is *sustenance productivity.* Data have been gathered for the circa 1970 period for each of the southern counties for five separate aspects of sustenance productivity: agriculture; retail services; wholesale services; personal services; and mining. Each productivity element is defined as the number of dollars received for the sustenance per sustenance establishment. For example, retail services productivity is the dollar amount of retail sales in an area in 1967 per the number of retail establishments in the area in 1967.

TABLE 5.1 Operationalization of Sustenance Organization Variables

Variable	Operational Definition
Sustenance Differentiation	$1-(\Sigma x^2 / (\Sigma x)^2)$, where X is the number of persons employed in each of six industry categories, 1970[a]
Sustenance productivity variables	
Retail services productivity	Retail sales (thousands of dollars) per retail establishments, 1967
Personal services productivity	Selected services receipts (thousands of dollars) per selected services establishments, 1967
Wholesale services productivity	Wholesale sales (thousands of dollars) per wholesale establishments, 1967
Mining productivity	Mineral industry shipments and receipts (thousands of dollars) per mineral industry establishments, 1967
Agricultural productivity	Value of farm products sold by farms with sales of $2,500 and over (thousands of dollars) per farms with sales of $2,500 and over, 1969
Manufacturing efficiency	Value added by manufacturing (millions of dollars) per manufacturing establishments, 1967

Sustenance components

Manufacturing component — Percentage of employed civilian labor force in manufacturing, 1970

Personal services component — Percentage of employed civilian labor force in selected services, 1970[b]

Educational services component — Percentage of employed civilian labor force in educational services, 1970

Construction component — Percentage of employed civilian labor force in construction, 1970

Source: All data used in the operationalization of sustenance organization variables are taken from U.S. Bureau of the Census, County and City Data Book, 1972 (Washington, D.C.: Government Printing Office, 1973).

Notes: [a]The six industry categories are the following: manufacturing, wholesale/retail, selected services, educational services, construction, and a residual. For information on the development of the sustenance differentiation measure, see J.P. Gibbs and D.L. Poston, Jr., "The Division of Labor: Conceptualization and Related Measures," Social Forces 53:468-476.

[b]Selected services involve the following major groups of services: hotels, motels, camps, and trailer parks; personal services; miscellaneous business services; automobile repair, automobile services, and garages; miscellaneous repair services; motion pictures; amusement and recreational services. These groups closely approximate the groups of services identified as personal services. See H. Browning and J. Singelmann, The Emergence of a Service Society: Demographic and Sociological Aspects of the Sectoral Transformation of the Labor Force in the U.S.A. (Springfield, Va.: National Technical Information Service, 1975).

The more productive the retail services in the southern counties, the greater the net in-migration. As observed earlier, growth in retail services is linked closely with employment growth and associated opportunities for living. Accordingly, areas highly productive of retail sustenance should be characterized by net in-migration. Conversely, areas producing a significant volume of wholesale sustenance should be characterized more by net out-migration than by in-migration, for increases in wholesale volume need not be directly related to increases in wholesale employment. Similarly, counties producing large per capita amounts of sustenance through personal services should be characterized more by net out-migration than by net in-migration. By itself, personal services productivity should not be related closely with general increases in living opportunities.

A positive relationship is expected between agricultural productivity and net migration. Agricultural productivity here refers to the development of agricultural grain and fiber through large-scale enterprises (farms with sales of $2,500 or more in 1969). As such, counties "in which commercial agriculture is pursued successfully [should be expected to] enjoy an expansion of job opportunities [and positive net migration] as a complex of ancillary agribusiness establishments develops. Moreover, farmers with extensive land holdings and high volume production are . . . likely to require, and to be able to afford, labor involved in the actual production of commodities" (Frisbie and Poston, 1978b:48–49). Therefore, unlike the often demonstrated negative relationship between small-scale agricultural activity and net migration, a positive relationship is expected.

The last sustenance productivity variable is mining. A negative relationship is expected with migration owing to a reduced demand for labor in an extractive industry like mining (which comprises metal, bituminous coal, and lignite mining, and oil and gas extraction) as it becomes mechanized, capital intensive, and thus more productive (Frisbie and Poston, 1978b:46; Hawley, 1971; Jones, 1967).

To summarize the hypotheses, positive relationships are expected between migration in the southern counties in 1970–1975 and sustenance productivity circa 1970 based on (1) retail services and (2) agriculture. Negative relationships should exist between net migration and (3) wholesale services productivity, (4) personal services productivity, and (5) mining productivity.

The final dimension of sustenance organization is *manufactur-*

ing efficiency. Following Gordon (1977:57–58), "a production process is quantitatively efficient if it effects the greatest possible useful physical output from a given set of physical inputs, or if it generates a given physical output with the fewest possible inputs." Ideally, a sustenance dimension of this type would be best operationalized by computing a ratio of the amount of sustenance produced to the amount of energy consumed in the production process. Since data of this nature are not available, we have operationalized manufacturing efficiency as the value added by manufacturing per manufacturing establishment. The numerator is derived by subtracting the "total cost of materials (including raw materials, supplies, fuel, electric energy, and cost of resales and contract work done by others) from the final value of shipments" (U.S. Bureau of the Census, 1973b:xliii). In a sense the numerator reflects the dollar value of the shipments after accounting for the manufacturing inputs. The relationship between manufacturing efficiency and net migration could be argued as positive, given the relationship between productivity and efficiency. The more efficient enterprises usually are the more productive. However, manufacturing efficiency as conceptualized and operationalized here is more capital intensive than labor intensive. Almost by definition, the greater the efficiency, the less the requirements for a maximization of personnel labor inputs. For these reasons we are inclined to hypothesize that the relationship between manufacturing efficiency and net migration should be negative. We turn now to the results of the tests of these hypotheses.

RESULTS

The hypotheses delineated in the preceding section were tested by regressing percentage rates of net migration for the 1970–1975 period on eleven sustenance organization variables developed for the circa 1970 period. These variables reflect the four sustenance dimensions of sustenance differentiation, sustenance productivity, manufacturing efficiency, and the components. Five productivity variables and four sustenance components have been identified. Operational definitions for all eleven variables are presented in table 5.1, and their means, standard deviations, and minimum and maximum values are listed in table 5.2

The migration data are taken from components of population change data developed by the U.S. Bureau of the Census for 1970–

TABLE 5.2 Means, Standard Deviations, and Maximum and Minimum Values for Sustenance Organization Variables and Net Migration

Rate: 1,421 counties of the southern United States, circa 1970

Variable	Mean	Standard Deviation	Maximum Value	Minimum Value
Manufacturing component	24.9	13.5	65.8	0
Personal services component	8.0	2.6	40.9	0
Educational services component	7.7	3.8	34.9	0
Construction component	8.1	3.1	57.7	0
Manufacturing efficiency	.446	.700	7.8	0
Retail services productivity	109.0	46.2	444.8	0
Personal services productivity	20.1	13.6	160.7	0
Wholesale services productivity	565.2	489.0	7,198.9	0
Mining productivity	139.5	422.1	6,212.5	0
Agricultural productivity	22.6	22.3	311.4	0
Sustenance differentiation	.741	.051	.850	.488
Net migration	4.35	11.24	97.3	-35.3

TABLE 5.3 Standardized Partial Regression Coefficients Between Net Migration and Eleven Sustenance Organization Variables:
1,421 Counties of the Southern United States, circa 1970

Variable	Standardized Partial Regression Coefficient
Construction component	.249
Sustenance differentiation	.190
Agricultural productivity	.150
Personal services component	-.100
Retail services productivity	.069
Wholesale services productivity	-.062
Educational services component	-.046
Mining productivity	-.035
Manufacturing efficiency	-.028
Manufacturing component	-.022
Personal services productivity	-.001

Multiple Correlation Coefficient (R) .372

Multiple Coefficient of Determination (R^2) (adjusted) .138

1975 (U.S. Bureau of the Census, 1977a). The net migration estimates used are percentage rates of change and were obtained for each southern county by dividing the estimated number of net migrants in the county between 1970 and 1975 by the county's 1970 population. Of course, the net migration percentage rates are based on residual data and thus incorporate any errors resulting from enumeration and estimation procedures, as well as errors in the birth and death components. Nevertheless, these are "fair approximations of the actual level and pattern of migration" (U.S. Bureau of the Census, 1971:4).

Table 5.3 presents the standardized partial regression coefficients from the equation for all 1,421 southern counties of net migration on the eleven sustenance variables. As hypothesized, the construction component is positively related with 1970–1975 net migration. Also as expected, the manufacturing component, the personal services component, and personal services productivity are negatively related with migration. Wholesale services productivity and mining productivity relate negatively with migration, while agricultural productivity and retail services productivity relate positively. Sustenance differentiation is positively associated with migration, and manufacturing efficiency is negatively associated. In each of the above cases, hypotheses have already been generated from the ecological theory of migration predicting precisely these relationships.

One of the sustenance variables—the educational services component—is not positively associated with net migration as hypothesized. Instead its relationship is negative, albeit quite low (-.046). However, as will be noted on the next table, when the effects of this variable on net migration are examined only in metropolitan counties, the relationship is positive and sizable. Apparently, the metropolitan-nonmetropolitan context of the units of analysis mediates in an important way the nature of the relationship. In summary, the relationships with migration of ten of the eleven sustenance organization variables are in the directions predicted.

The sustenance variable with the greatest effect on migration is the construction component, and sustenance differentiation is the next most influential. Agricultural productivity is also associated strongly with net migration. The remaining sustenance variables are related with southern migration rates, but only modestly; each reports a standardized partial regression coefficient of .1 or less. The changes in sustenance organization leading to a demographic response through migration in the southern counties between 1970 and 1975 are best understood through a consideration of the construction component, sustenance differentiation and large-scale agricultural productivity.

Despite the differences among the sustenance variables in the magnitude of their associations with migration, all but one of the hypotheses have found support in the data. Moreover, a not unsubstantial amount of the total variation in net migration has been accounted for by these variables. Nearly 14 percent of the variability in net migration in the southern counties between 1970 and 1975 is explained by dimensions relating to the arrangements and attributes of the sustenance organizations of the counties. These data tend to confirm the suggestion drawn from ecological theory that net migration may be viewed as a demographic response to adjustments in sustenance organization.

TABLE 5.4 Standardized Partial Regression Coefficients
between Net Migration and Eleven Sustenance Organization
Variables:
187 Metropolitan Counties of the Southern United States,
circa 1970

Variable	Standardized Partial Regression Coefficient
Construction component	.404
Personal services component	-.323
Agricultural productivity	.277
Manufacturing efficiency	-.142
Educational services component	.116
Wholesale services productivity	-.076
Sustenance differentiation	.073
Manufacturing component	-.059
Retail services productivity	.058
Personal services productivity	-.045
Mining productivity	-.020

Multiple Correlation Coefficient (R) .605

Multiple Coefficient of Determination (R^2) (adjusted) .326

We turn next to an examination of the effects of the same eleven
sustenance variables on migration within the metropolitan counties of the South. To what extent are the ecological determinants
of population redistribution in metropolitan areas similar to those
in the South as a whole? Table 5.4 presents results from an equation regressing migration on the eleven sustenance variables for
the 187 metropolitan counties of the South. The hypothesized relationships between all of the sustenance variables and migration
find support in the data. The construction component has the major influence, and the personal services and the educational services components follow closely behind. Agricultural productivity
also has a reasonable impact on migration, as do manufacturing
efficiency, wholesale services productivity, the manufacturing
component, retail services productivity, and sustenance differentiation. Whereas only four sustenance variables provide the ma-

jor explanation of migration in the total southern counties, more than that number provide the principal basis in the metropolitan counties.

Of equal importance is the significant increase in the overall ability of the sustenance components and dimensions to account for variation in net migration. These variables collectively explain more than 32 percent of the variation in net migration in the metropolitan counties. The coefficient of determination for the metropolitan counties is more than twice that for the total group of counties.

Finally, we turn to some of the major results of these regression equations in the counties of the South. In both regression equations, the construction component of sustenance organization had the major influence on migration. This finding should not come as a surprise, particularly in light of the close linkages between this component and population growth in general and migration in particular. One would almost anticipate on an a priori basis that the construction component should be a principal explanatory variable in any study of population redistribution. Not only do increases in construction activity mean increases in employment and allied opportunities within the industry, but these increases also reflect the overall growth patterns and potential of the community at large. The fact that the demonstrated relationship between the component and migration was predicted from ecological theory makes the finding all the more engaging.

Another sustenance organization variable having major positive influence on net migration was agricultural productivity; its standardized partial regression coefficient in the metropolitan equation was .277 and in the total county equation, .150. In both it was a major influence. As defined here, agricultural productivity refers primarily to the production of agricultural grain and fiber in large and highly mechanized farming units. The measure is based only on the sales of agricultural products from establishments with at least $2,500 annual sales. These agribusiness activities and their corresponding productivity have been shown to be positively related with net migration, a situation possibly more applicable in the South (and perhaps the West) than anywhere else in the United States, particularly since, in the past thirty years, agriculture has moved more and more in the direction of large-scale activity.

Given this increased participation of corporations in the agricultural industry, it is not surprising that among the chief beneficiaries of these advances is the Southern Region and its numerous agricultural counties, where the climate allows a lengthy growing season, "where crops suitable for large-scale corporate cultivation are grown, and where there are the greatest spaces and therefore the biggest farms" (Sale, 1975:21). The decade of the 1960s was one of substantial growth in large-scale (corporate) agricultural activity, and the southern states have increased their shares of the market significantly, while the Northeast, and even the Corn Belt, have witnessed a decline. These increases in agricultural activity and the associated advances in productivity have opened up numerous opportunities for living and economic advance. Net in-migrations to these southern areas have constituted the demographic response to the ecological imbalance between size and opportunity. Numerous positions have been created in the industry and its ancillary agribusiness establishments, and net in-migration has been the result. The analyses conducted here demonstrate once again the complexity of the agricultural industry in general, as well as the fallacy in presuming that all agricultural activity eventuates in depopulation, principally through out-migration. What has been true of small-scale agriculture (Frisbie and Poston, 1975, 1978b) clearly does not apply in corporate agribusiness, particularly in the South.

SUMMARY

In this chapter a series of hypotheses drawn from the ecological theory of migration were developed and tested in an attempt to provide explanation of the 1970–1975 net migration patterns in the counties of the South. The ecological approach to migration presumes generally that human populations redistribute themselves as they approach an equilibrium between their overall size and the opportunities for living available to them. Given a balance between size and sustenance organization, the theory proposes that disturbances in the latter will require an adjustment in the former, i.e., an increase or decrease in population. Migration is viewed as the agent for effecting these "needed" changes in population size.

Here we have tested the general hypothesis that variation among the southern counties in their rates of 1970–1975 net migration is a function of differentials among them in their sustenance organizations circa 1970. Four dimensions of sustenance organization were developed: sustenance differentiation, sustenance productivity, manufacturing efficiency, and the components of sustenance organization. Empirical indicators were selected for each dimension (one to five indicators for each dimension, for a total of eleven) and the migration rates were regressed on the eleven indicators, first for all the southern counties and then for the metropolitan counties.

The ecological hypotheses advanced found general support in the data. In both examinations the construction component of sustenance organization provided the principal influence on net migration, a finding which is not surprising given the close interrelationships between increases in construction activity and increases in employment and allied opportunities both within the industry and the community at large. Another variable affecting net migration was large-scale agricultural productivity, a reflection of the growth of corporate agribusiness in many southern counties and its close relationship with net in-migration. In concert the ecological variables accounted for more than 32 percent of the variation in the metropolitan counties and nearly 14 of the variation in the total group of counties.

The results presented here provide general support for the ecological statements of Hawley (1950), Gibbs and Martin (1959), Duncan (1959), and other theorists who have written on the relationship between sustenance organization and migration. They also suggest the theoretical and empirical viability of a structural approach to the study of demographic change in general, migration change in particular.

The question why migration occurs is one with many answers and many approaches. We have attempted to provide a response to this question and its application in the South in the 1970s by drawing upon human ecological theory as a point of departure. The evidence presented suggests that the direct attention given by human ecologists to sustenance organization as a predictor of migration has merit. Dimensions of sustenance organization have been shown to be important in explaining population redistribution in the counties of the South in the 1970s.

6
The Metropolitan System in the South: Continuity and Change

OMER R. GALLE AND ROBERT N. STERN

In 1954 Rupert Vance and Sara Smith Sutker wrote one of the definitive works on metropolitan systems, "Metropolitan Dominance and Integration." It remains one of the best-known works in the general area of urban ecology and urban systems of cities. It is unlikely that any student of urban ecology has escaped exposure to this paper or, at the very least, to the figure from the original article which maps the dominance patterns and the lines of integration between southern cities. This classic article is the starting point for the present chapter. First, we briefly review the idea of metropolitan dominance as it has developed over the years in urban ecology and attempt to place the Vance-Sutker article in its proper context. Then, taking that article as the benchmark, we examine changes which have occurred in the urban system of the South since 1950.

THE CONCEPT OF METROPOLITAN DOMINANCE

As human societies increased in size and organizational complexity, the notion of the importance of interrelationships between urban places within a society also began to be developed. As early as 1905, there was an attempt to describe the interrelationships of American cities (Tower, 1905). Since that time, although many discussions and descriptions of the process of increasingly complex urban interdependence have appeared, several stand out as important benchmarks in the development of the notions of metropolitan dominance. N. S. B. Gras (1922), in his discussion of economic evolution, suggested five forms of general economic organization, the last of which was the "metropolitan economy," which was based on "an internal organization of productive forces and an external relationship with other units of either the same order or of more primitive form" (Gras, 1922:184). One of the major ideas expounded by Gras was that of the organization by the metropolis of its surrounding hinterland. "Generally speaking . . . a metropolitan community arises at a favorable conjunction of two circumstances, the economic development of the *hinterland* and the rise of business ability and organization in the center" (Gras, 1922:189). Gras emphasized the interdependence of metropolis and hinterland and also the difficulty of clear delineations of hinterland boundaries. McKenzie (1933) further developed the concept of the "metropolitan community," and, although the major emphasis was again on center-hinterland relationships, he also recognized the difficulties of clear demarcations between metropolitan spheres of influence:

> Each city has its sphere of influence. By laying out these spheres on a map of the United States . . . it is possible to divide the whole nation into metropolitan regions which economically and sociologically have greater reality than the several states. Three dimensions would be required in order to give a clear picture of the metropolitan organization of the country, for some of our metropolises are regional in character, some are interregional, and one or two are international in their influence. Neighboring metropolises compete for trade and prestige, and the boundaries between the territories they control may be as fluctuating and as hotly disputed as though each were an independent principality (McKenzie, 1933: 245).

Bogue (1949), focusing on local spatial relations, executed a landmark study of metropolitan community organizational relationships following these earlier leads. After examining a wealth of data arrayed by metropolitan centers and hinterland zones, Bogue concluded that:

> The metropolitan community thus appears to be an organization of many mutually interdependent and inter-functioning subcommunities oriented about the hinterland cities, which, in turn, are subdominant to and interdependent with the dominant metropolis, and inter-function with it. The entire community organization appears to be held together by a system of community specialization in, and exchange of, locally produced surpluses to fill those needs which cannot be most efficiently satisfied by local institutions (Bogue, 1949:59).

Chronologically, the Vance-Sutker analysis is the next major piece of research to appear in the literature, but we shall postpone discussion of it until the end of this section. As we hope to show at that time, this article was firmly founded on the preceding research and theoretical conceptualizations and, at the same time, was surprisingly prophetic of research to appear much later.

Pappenfort (1959), in a study of the location of branch plants of manufacturing concerns in Illinois, developed the concept of the "ecological field":

A "community" . . . by definition is not a discrete entity. It is an identifiable set of symbiotic relationships which necessarily are involved with and have implications for other such identifiable sets. Several or many such communities constitute an ecological "field," which is the fundamental unit of analysis (Pappenfort, 1959:380).

Building upon this concept as well as others in the literature, Duncan and his colleagues produced in 1960 one of the most complete studies of the complexities of interrelationships between metropolitan areas, their regional and interregional ties, and the multifaceted linkages between urban areas within the United States that has ever been done. This "systematic survey of the industrial composition and regional relationships of the larger cities of the United States" (Duncan et al., 1960:2) is still a model of careful scholarship in the field. The multidimensionality of the urban system of cities is a key element of this work. Ten years later Duncan and Lieberson extended this basic study with *Metropolis and Region in Transition* (1970), an exploration of the historical development of the urban system of cities as outlined in the original work. Here, the importance of historical "inertia" in the development of the urban system was clearly demonstrated.

Other Typological Classifications
Over the years there have been numerous attempts at developing typological classifications of urban areas, and among these are some of the studies already mentioned. But there are others, most of which have been developed with no particular reference to the "system of cities" idea and have, primarily, simply attempted to differentiate types of cities on the basis of a limited number of characteristics, most often labor force characteristics. Harris (1943), for example, developed a "functional classification" of cities based primarily on the labor force employment patterns by indus-

trial category within the metropolitan area. This procedure has been used, with several modifications, over the years as the classification system in the annual series of *Municipal Yearbooks*. Duncan and Reiss (1956) also developed a functional classification of cities based primarily on economic activity and utilized data from the 1950 *Census of Population* and the 1948 *Census of Business and Manufactures*. Hadden and Borgatta (1965) utilized 1960 *Census of Population* data and factor analytic techniques to develop their own schema of American cities. Similarly, Kass (1973), utilizing employment data and "cluster analysis," developed a different typological classification of 1960 metropolitan areas. And, finally, Wanner (1977) extended the Duncan et al. (1960) *Metropolis and Region* schema to 1960, and then South and Poston (1979) to 1970, both employing more refined statistical techniques (Q factor analysis) and showing the viability of that particular classification scheme which was originally constructed in a much more impressionistic and less rigorous way. The progression of the typological attempts is interesting to observe. On the one hand, they utilize more and more sophisticated statistical techniques. At the same time, however, they tend to view (with some exceptions) the creation of the typology of metropolitan areas as an end in itself. Substantially less attention is paid to the *consequences* of a city's position in the typology for other aspects of the city's social structure.

THE METROPOLITAN SYSTEM OF THE SOUTH AT MIDCENTURY

Historical Development

In their attempt to delineate the urban system of cities in the Southern Region of the United States in 1950, Vance and Sutker approached their subject with a historical eye, as well as with an awareness of the existence of an abundance of current statistical data. They began by observing that within the national context southern metropolitan areas tend to be relatively small and less influential than the great industrial concentrations of metropolitan areas in the Northeast and North Central Regions. At the same time, however, they pointed out that these metropolitan areas in the South are important because of their organizational functions in that economy. It is interesting to note that, in the original article written by Vance and Sutker, a substantial portion was devoted to a historical description of the development of the southern urban pattern. They pointed out, for example, that in colonial America the most important urban function was to get raw materials into the channels of world trade, and, as a consequence, the most important cities were ports such as Boston, Philadelphia, and New York. The only southern cities that seemed to be important during this early period were Charleston, South Carolina, and (somewhat later) New Orleans. Charleston, which had a fine harbor, might have been a national contender for metropolitan dominance in those early days except that the plan for a railroad "to reach the rich resources of the Mississippi Valley" (Vance and Sutker, 1954: 119) collapsed and forced Charleston out of the competition for major metropolitan dominance. Somewhat later in the 1800s, New York's most serious rival was New Orleans, the only city in the United States with comparable inland water connections. The outcome of the Civil War, however, settled the question of which city would eventually become dominant.

The major theme in discussion of the development of the urban system in the Vance and Sutker article is (1) the importance of the development of transportation patterns based on railroad technology during the nineteenth century and (2) the long-range impact these transportation patterns had in fixing future growth. They noted, for example, that once the New York/Chicago transportation axis was formed, the supremacy of the northern metropolises over the southern was assured.

The patterning of urban growth in the nineteenth and early twentieth centuries in the South took place under the dominance of the cotton economy and the existing transportation patterns.

> Whereas financial control centered in several future markets and in points of export like New Orleans, the actual buying, collecting, and storing of cotton was spread among many small communities around railroad stations, cotton gins, and crossroad stores. This resulted in very few large cities and many towns of even size, rather than the sharply competitive grading of population in an industrialized area. In the reorganization of the cotton industry, after the Civil War, the same trend can be noted (Vance and Sutker, 1954:120).

The importance both of rail transportation and of the shifting focus of productivity and economic complexity is emphasized in the development of the major metropolitan areas in the South. As Vance and Sutker noted, the focus of metropolitan development began to shift from the gateway cities (which would ship goods away from the region) to those in the interior of the region which were more centrally located. It was in this way that the two great regional metropolises of the South, Atlanta and Dallas, began to develop. Atlanta was originally a depot for supplies and a seat of manufacturing for the Confederacy, but it arose after the Civil War to become the center point in the main currents of traffic and the regional capital for national distributors. In the Southwest, Dallas followed a similar pattern, although its importance and size developed somewhat later.

Throughout the discussion of the historical development of southern urban areas by Vance and Sutker, their major focus was on the organizational aspect of metropolitan areas. These urban centers served to organize the hinterland resources, to provide intermediate processing for products, to serve as transshipment points for goods going to other areas, and to organize the financial flows throughout the region. Another clear underlying theme of this discussion of early development within the South is the long-lasting impact of patterns of interchange once they become established. The rail system, for example, once its initial pattern was established, continued to have a major influence on future growth of specific centers. Similarly, once the Federal Reserve System—with its banks and branch banks—was set up, the flow of money and credit into specific channels was established and maintained. In short, the "inertia" of the system, once it was established, had a very major effect on the future growth and development of the urban and metropolitan pattern. The awareness of this kind of inertia is echoed in later works (Duncan and Lieberson, 1970) and illustrates, we believe, the solid understanding that Vance and Sutker showed of the way in which the metropolitan system developed.

The Southern Metropolitan Pattern of 1950: The Statistical Evidence
Looking at the urban system of the South in 1950, Vance and Sutker attempted to delineate the pattern of metropolitan dominance within the South. To rank southern cities on metropolitan function, they chose six indexes which they felt were related to dominance. The first three were deemed the most important: (1) wholesale sales; (2) business service receipts; (3) number of branch offices (which they saw as an index for the channeling function of metropolitan areas). All these were more important than the next three, which are: (4) retail sales (which they felt was not a metro-

politan specialty but an index of size); (5) bank clearings (used as an index of business activity); and (6) value added by manufacture (the most sensitive index of the volume rather than the type of activity). They saw these last three indexes as reflecting the underpinnings the city has for building its market and amassing wealth.

Utilizing these six indexes, Vance and Sutker ranked the twenty-nine metropolitan areas of the South with central cities of 100,000 population or more in 1950. "So that their relative positions in each factor would be strictly comparable, Z-scores, using the standard deviation were constructed for each index; those of the first three indices were weighted by two; the weighted Z-scores (actually accurate rank scores) were converted to make them all positive numbers, and added, and then divided by six to arrive at an average rank-score for *Metropolitan Function*" (Vance and Sutker, 1954: 127–128). In their classification scheme, they identified four different levels of metropolitan function. At the top were two cities which they labeled second-order metropolises: Atlanta and Dallas. Below these metropolitan areas were five third-order metropolises, twelve subdominant areas with metropolitan characteristics, and ten subdominant areas. "The most certain finding . . . is that Atlanta and Dallas with similar scores on metropolitan function, stand head and shoulder above the other cities. There is no doubt about their being regional capitals. These two cities have been classified as Second Order Metropolises with the idea that First Order Metropolis has a nationwide sphere of influence" (Vance and Sutker, 1954:129). The third-order metropolises and the subdominants with metropolitan characteristics were viewed as cities with descending levels of metropolitan dominance and importance. The fourth class, Vance and Sutker suggested, is a residual as far as metropolitan function is concerned. They noted that the scores within the fourth category, the subdominants, are quite even and speculate that there may be very little difference between these centers and some of the industrial and distribution centers with less population. The original Vance and Sutker classification of metropolitan areas in the South in 1950 is seen in the first column of table 6.1.

METROPOLITAN PATTERNS IN THE SOUTH, 1970

In an attempt to advance the Vance and Sutker typology to 1970, we first of all attempted to replicate their findings for 1950. This

TABLE 6.1   Cities of over 100,000 in the South, Ranked by
Metropolitan Function, 1950

	The Vance and Sutker Ranking System		Galle and Stern Ranking System	
City	Rank	Score	Z-Score	City
	Second-Order Metropolises			
Atlanta	9.91		16.47	Dallas
Dallas	9.71		15.21	Houston
			14.29	Atlanta
	Third-Order Metropolises			
Houston	8.10		7.68	New Orleans
New Orleans	7.36		7.49	Louisville
Memphis	6.62		6.05	Memphis
Louisville	6.43		4.31	Miami
Birmingham	5.94		3.25	Birmingham
	Subdominants with Metropolitan Characteristics			
Richmond	5.34		.44	Ft. Worth
Ft. Worth	5.24		.31	Richmond
Oklahoma City	5.02		-.36	San Antonio
Miami	4.90		-.53	Oklahoma City
Charlotte	4.80		-.88	Tampa-St. Petersburg
Jacksonville	4.79		-1.42	Tulsa
Tulsa	4.60		-1.62	Nashville
Nashville	4.59		-2.24	Charlotte
Little Rock	4.54		-2.26	Jacksonville
San Antonio	4.48		-2.37	Norfolk-Portsmouth
Norfolk-Portsmouth	4.42		-3.45	Chattanooga
El Paso	4.38		-3.56	Knoxville
	Subdominants			
Tampa-St. Petersburg	4.18		-5.75	Little Rock
Chattanooga	4.11		-6.13	Mobile
Knoxville	3.84		-6.37	Shreveport
Shreveport	3.62		-7.06	Savannah
Mobile	3.54		-7.11	El Paso
Savannah	3.46		-7.30	Corpus Christi
Corpus Christi	3.30		-7.44	Montgomery
Montgomery	3.25		-7.55	Baton Rouge
Baton Rouge	3.25		-7.81	Austin
Austin	3.19			

was somewhat difficult, however, because we were unable to obtain two of the indexes used in that original study. We did not have the number of bank clearings and were unable to obtain the number of branch offices (the data for this latter measure came from a study by Dickinson, 1934). As a substitute for the number of branch offices, we substituted the number of manufacturing establishments in the metropolitan area as reported by the *Census of Business and Manufactures* (1948). We could not find a reasonable surrogate for the number of bank clearings and thus ended up using only five measures in our index. We weighted the first three measures (wholesale sales, business service receipts, and the number of manufacturing establishments) by two and the other two indexes (retail sales and value added by manufacture) by one. In addition, we Z-scored our data before the ranking procedure and did not convert all of the Z-scores into positive numbers as Vance and Sutker did. The result of our replication is found on the right-hand side of table 6.1.

Our attempted replication for 1950 is quite similar to the original ordering of metropolitan areas by Vance and Sutker. There are, however, several differences between the two. On the one hand, our ranking system shows a clear break at their theoretical break in levels. That is, the break in Z-scores between second- and third-order metropolises is rather marked, as is the break between third-order metropolises and subdominants in our own ranking system. The breaks in Z-scores in the Vance and Sutker system are not quite as obvious. Several of the metropolitan areas in our ranking system are not in the same category used by Vance and Sutker, but in general these differences appear plausible for several reasons. Houston, for example, is listed higher in our ranking system than it was in Vance and Sutker's. This may result from our lack of information on bank clearings. Houston is listed as a Federal Reserve Branch Bank, whereas both Dallas and Atlanta are Federal Reserve Banks. Similarly, Miami is listed as a third-order metropolis in our system but as a subdominant by Vance and Sutker. All of the other third-order metropolises are Federal Reserve Branches, but Miami is neither a Federal Reserve Branch nor a Federal Reserve Bank. Because of our lack of information on bank clearings, it seems reasonable that these two particular metropolitan areas would be ranked somewhat higher than would otherwise have occurred had we been able to utilize this financial information. Although there are other deviations in the rank ordering of metropolitan areas toward the lower end of the scale, the similarity of our own ranking system to that of Vance and Sutker's justifies the extension of our methodology toward a replication using information for the period around 1970.

Table 6.2 compares our own ordering of the four Vance and Sutker categories of metropolitan areas for 1950 with the ordering of the same metropolitan areas in 1970. The same Z-score ranking methodology utilized for 1950 is used here with data for 1970. (The manufacturing and business service receipt data are from the 1968 *Census of Business and Manufacturers.*) In comparing the 1950 with the 1970 rank orderings, the dominant theme is the stability within the system across the four different categories of metropolitan areas within the South.

The breaks in the Z-scores are still there, especially at the upper end of the distribution. That is, there are clear gaps between the second- and third-order metropolises and between the third-order metropolises and the subdominants with metropolitan characteristics. Several major changes have occurred, however. Houston is now clearly at the top of the rank ordering of all metropolitan areas of the South. Miami's Z-score has increased to the point where it should now belong in the category of the second-order metropolises. Tampa–St. Petersburg has also increased its Z-score ranking and moved up one category, whereas Birmingham has moved down. The downward movement of Birmingham is actually slight, and its movement from the category of third-order metropolises to subdominant with metropolitan characteristics may not be entirely appropriate. In fact, the major breakpoints of the Z-scores for 1970 are more apparent than real throughout the system primarily because by 1970 many more Standard Metropolitan Statistical Areas had populations of 100,000 or more, and these are excluded in table 6.2.

Table 6.3 shows the listing of *all* Standard Metropolitan Statistical Areas within the Southern Region with a population of 100,000 or more in 1970. The Washington, D.C., metropolitan area is also included. Although it was clearly a city of more than 100,000 population in 1950, Vance and Sutker apparently did not consider it southern because of its national importance, even though its location could arguably put it within that region. Again, when comparing the results of table 6.3 with the earlier ranking system of Vance and Sutker, the overall stability of the system remains the major theme. The inclusion of the additional metropolitan areas to the

TABLE 6.2   Changes in the Metropolitan System in the South, 1950-1970

The Vance and Sutker Ranking System		Galle and Stern Ranking System	
City	Z-score in 1950	Z-Score in 1970	City
Second-Order Metropolises			
Dallas	16.47	21.03	Houston
Houston	15.21	17.64	Dallas
Atlanta	14.29	15.45	Atlanta
		11.23	Miami
Third-Order Metropolises			
New Orleans	7.68	3.95	New Orleans
Louisville	7.49	2.89	Louisville
Memphis	6.05	2.89	Memphis
Miami	4.31	2.20	Tampa-
Birmingham	3.25		St. Petersburg
Subdominants with Metropolitan Characteristics			
Ft. Worth	.44	.23	Birmingham
Richmond	.31	.18	Ft. Worth
San Antonio	-.36	-.01	Charlotte
Oklahoma City	-.53	-1.17	Richmond
Tampa-St. Petersburg	-.88	-1.21	Oklahoma City
Tulsa	-1.42	-1.27	Jacksonville
Nashville	-1.62	-1.52	Nashville
Charlotte	-2.24	-1.85	San Antonio
Jacksonville	-2.26	-2.24	Tulsa
Norfolk-Portsmouth	-2.37		
Chattanooga	-3.45		
Knoxville	-3.56		
Subdominants			
Little Rock	-5.75	-4.09	Norfolk-Portsmouth
Mobile	-6.13	-4.28	Chattanooga
Shreveport	-6.37	-4.75	Knoxville
Savannah	-7.06	-5.36	Little Rock
El Paso	-7.11	-5.51	Mobile
Corpus Christi	-7.30	-5.90	Baton Rouge
Montgomery	-7.44	-5.99	El Paso
Baton Rouge	-7.55	-6.06	Shreveport
Austin	-7.81	-6.37	Austin
		-6.44	Corpus Christi
		-6.82	Montgomery
		-6.88	Savannah

TABLE 6.3   Rank Ordering of All SMSAs of 100,000 or More
Population in the South, 1970

City	Z-Score	City	Z-Score
Second-Order Metropolises		**Subdominants (continued)**	
Houston	28.26	Charleston (W.Va.)	-2.70
Dallas	24.54	Raleigh	-2.70
Atlanta	21.96	Huntington-Ashland	-2.72
Washington, D.C.	19.89	Augusta	-3.02
Miami	15.97	Corpus Christi	-3.06
		Austin	-3.11
Third-Order Metropolises		Lexington (Ky.)	-3.22
New Orleans	8.58	Huntsville (Ala.)	-3.23
Memphis	7.89	Lubbock	-3.31
Louisville	7.89	Montgomery	-3.42
Tampa-St. Petersburg	6.45	Savannah	-3.44
Greensboro-Winston-Salem-	5.95		
High Point		**Lower-Order Centers**	
		Charleston (S.C.)	-3.47
Subdominant w/Met. Characteristics		Roanoke	-3.51
Birmingham	4.77	Macon	-3.64
Charlotte	4.66	Amarillo	-3.71
Ft. Worth	4.37	Columbus	-3.74
Richmond	3.19	Steubenville-Wierton	-3.78
Jacksonville	2.87	Newport News	-3.86
Oklahoma City	2.79	Lynchburg	-3.87
Nashville	2.59	Fort Smith	-3.87
San Antonio	1.94	Galveston	-3.87
Tulsa	1.82	Pensacola	-3.90
Ft. Lauderdale-	1.03	Wheeling	-3.96
Hollywood		Asheville	-4.03
Orlando	.20	Durham	-4.05
		Waco	-4.16
Subdominants		Monroe	-4.45
Chattanooga	-.40	Lake Charles	-4.54
Norfolk-Portsmouth	-.58	Wilmington	-4.55
Beaumont-Port Arthur	-.80	Wichita Falls	-4.56
Knoxville	-1.04	Fayetteville	-4.64
Greenville (S.C.)	-1.22	Abilene	-4.68
Little Rock	-1.75	Biloxi	-4.68
Mobile	-1.93	McAllen-Pharr-Edinburg	-4.71
West Palm Beach	-2.09	Brownsville	-4.73
Baton Rouge	-2.41	Tuscaloosa	-4.79
Columbia (S.C.)	-2.42	Gainesville (Fla.)	-5.08
El Paso	-2.56	Tallahassee	-5.12
Shreveport	-2.56	Lawton	-5.34
Jackson (Miss.)	-2.58		

original twenty-nine for 1970 does not significantly alter the relationship of the entire system, particularly at the top. There are, of course, some notable exceptions. Washington, D.C., does appear toward the top of the hierarchy, and its combined Z-score clearly places it alongside Atlanta, Dallas, and Miami. There is a clear break in the Z-score rankings between these metropolitan areas and third-order metropolitan areas. Within the third-order metropolises, there is another new addition, that composed of Greensboro, Winston-Salem, and Highpoint. It should be noted that this particular metropolitan area is a new union of central cities which were not combined as a metropolitan area in 1950. Thus, its inclusion so high in the hierarchy of metropolitan areas within the South may be viewed primarily as an organizational fiat. Had the same cities been combined in 1950, their combined Z-scores would probably have qualified for this higher ranking. Moving down to the subdominants with metropolitan characteristics, two other metropolitan areas have joined this category since 1950. These two areas are the Ft. Lauderdale–Hollywood SMSA and the Orlando SMSA, both located in Florida, an area of extremely rapid population growth during this 20-year period. Within the subdominant category, if we draw an arbitrary breakpoint below the lowest metropolitan area listed by Vance and Sutker—Savannah—there are twelve new and twelve old subdominant metropolitan areas. That is, the twelve metropolitan areas listed as subdominants by Vance and Sutker have been joined by twelve other metropolitan areas which have apparently grown rapidly from relatively smaller sizes from 1950 to 1970. The final category, the lower-order centers, includes all those metropolitan areas not included in the Vance and Sutker analyses, but which by 1970 had achieved a metropolitan area size of more than 100,000 population. Since Vance and Sutker utilized central city size of 100,000 population or greater in 1950 for their lower-level breakpoint, it might be argued that these smaller SMSAs (with a *total* population of more than 100,000) should not be considered metropolitan areas of the same magnitude of importance as those in the original 1950 classification scheme. Accordingly, we will restrict our remaining discussion to the higher-order centers.

In summarizing the information from tables 6.2 and 6.3, several generalizations may be made. First, the significant stability within the system is apparent. The categories delineated by Vance and Sutker still serve to order the types of metropolitan areas within the Southern Region quite well, 20 years after these categories were constructed. At the same time, however, there are exceptions to the system's stability. Miami's growth as a resort, recreation, and retirement area is noted in its increased Z-score and corresponding rise to the highest category of metropolitan areas within the South. Duncan and his colleagues in *Metropolis and Region* classified Miami as a special case because of its resort, retirement, and recreation functions. It seems reasonable to continue to consider this particular metropolitan area as a kind of special case. A similar argument should be made for Washington, D.C., given the rather unique functions it serves for the federal government. Tampa–St. Petersburg has moved from the subdominant category in 1950 to the third-order metropolis category in 1970. Again, this rapidly growing area has considerable importance as a retirement center. However, it also shows strength as a major retail center in the Southern Region. Birmingham is a metropolitan area which has moved down within the metropolitan system. However, it could be argued that Birmingham has not really moved downward but has remained stable during a 20-year period in which there has been generally an upward shift in Z-scores for the entire system. Finally, there is the important case of the emerging dominance of Houston as a metropolitan area at the top of the hierarchy system of the South.

Houston: An Emerging National Metropolis

A case can be made for the fact that Houston has emerged as a type of metropolis not observed in the South in 1950: a truly national metropolitan area. With its specialization in petrochemical industry, Houston's growth over the 20-year period since 1950 is an indicator of its increasing importance in the national economy, as well as in the South itself. As further evidence, data were gathered from the 1967 *Census of Transportation* on the tonnage shipped between twenty-five major production areas within the United States. Only three of those production areas used by the 1967 *Census of Transportation* are located in the South: Atlanta, Dallas, and Houston. Table 6.4 shows the percentage of total tons of commodities shipped from each of the three southern production areas to each of the southern production areas (including their own surrounding area), to the twenty-two other production areas, and to all other areas within the nation.

A substantial percentage of the tonnage from Atlanta and Dallas is shipped within their own production area. Nearly 8 percent of

TABLE 6.4   Selected Figures on the Shipment of Commodities
for Major Production Areas in the United States

Shipping Figures	Major Production Areas in the Southern Region		
	Atlanta	Dallas	Houston
Percentage of Total Tons Shipped to:			
Atlanta	7.6	1.1	--
Dallas	.6	17.0	.6
Houston	.2	7.6	5.1
22 other production areas[a]	9.6	4.7	55.0
All other areas	82.0	69.3	39.3
Percentage of Total Tons Shipped:			
Less than 500 miles	86.4	85.5	16.6
500 to 1,499 miles	13.3	14.1	64.3
More than 1,500 miles	.3	.4	19.1

Source: Census of Transportation, 1967.

[a] Other production areas are Boston, Hartford, New York, North
New Jersey, Philadelphia, Baltimore, Allentown, Harrisburg,
Syracuse, Buffalo, Cleveland, Pittsburgh, Detroit,
Cincinnati, Chicago, Milwaukee, Minneapolis-St. Paul,
St. Louis, Denver, Seattle, San Francisco, Los Angeles.

the tonnage shipped from Atlanta goes to areas within the Atlanta
production area. Seventeen percent of the commodities from Dallas are shipped within the Dallas production area. In contrast, only
5 percent of the commodities from the Houston production area
are shipped to the Houston area. Looking next at the shipments to
the remaining production areas, we find that less than 5 percent of

the total tonnage shipped from Dallas is shipped to these, while less than 10 percent of the tonnage from Atlanta is shipped to the other twenty-two areas. By far the major percentage of tonnage shipped from Atlanta and Dallas is shipped to areas of the United States other than major production areas. The position for Houston is radically different. More than half its total tonnage is shipped to the other twenty-two major production areas in the northern and the western parts of the United States.

Turning next to the bottom panel of table 6.4, note that over 85 percent of the total tons shipped from Atlanta and Dallas are shipped less than five hundred miles from those cities. In contrast, less than 17 percent of the total tons shipped from Houston are shipped within that short radius. In sum, it is apparent that Atlanta and Dallas remain as major metropolitan suppliers for their nearby and surrounding hinterland. In that sense, they deserve to maintain the title of second-order metropolises. Houston, on the other hand, ships its commodities principally to the major production areas in the northern and western parts of the United States and can thus lay claim to the title of national metropolis. Houston's trade is with the nation as a whole (and with other parts of the world), and not with the nearby or surrounding hinterland. Moreover, the importance of Houston as a staging area for the shipment of goods out of the hinterland of Texas and the southwestern area is not a radically new activity. For example, it was noted in one recent history of Houston that:

> the Anderson Clayton Company was brought to Houston in 1916 because, as Will Clayton later explained, "we moved to Houston because Houston was the little end of the funnel that drained all of Texas and the Oklahoma Territory. . . . In other words, we were at the back door and we wanted to be at the front door" (McComb, 1969:112).

Toward a Multidimensional System of Metropolitan Areas in the South

Mention was made earlier of several attempts at building typologies of urban systems that have appeared recently. As an attempt to expand and enrich the unidimensional ordering which the Vance and Sutker methodology necessarily produces on the hierarchy of urban places within the South, we have juxtaposed one of these functional classification typologies upon the Vance and Sutker type of ranking. The typology we have chosen is the one developed

by Kass, whose methodology allows for eight single-function metropolitan areas along with multiple-function metropolitan areas as
well (Kass, 1973). He finds twelve different types of metropolitan
areas within the United States as of 1960. In addition, he has a residual category of metropolitan areas which shows no particular
cluster of industrial concentration. The combination, then, of the
Kass typology with the Vance and Sutker typology is exhibited in
our tentative outline of the urban system of cities in the South as
of 1970 in table 6.5. At the top of our hierarchy, we list two specific
national metropolises—Washington, D.C., which Kass lists as a
center specializing in public administration, and Houston, which
he lists as a retail and finance center. Both, for radically different
reasons, are metropolitan areas of national scope and dominance.
Clearly, Washington, D.C. was not considered by Vance and Sutker because of its importance in the national scheme, and so its
addition in our particular scheme is basically circumstantial. On
the other hand, the emergence of Houston as a national metropolis
is a clear change from the ranking and ordering of metropolitan
areas as shown by Vance and Sutker in 1950. We list Atlanta and
Dallas as the only second-order metropolises in our outline because of the clear difference in their Z-scores from the Vance and
Sutker scheme and because of the evidence from the *Census of
Transportation* on the commodities shipped to and from these
areas. They clearly seem to be the type of areas described, for example, by Duncan et al. in *Metropolis and Region* (1960) as regional metropolises: those areas which have a dominant hold on a
relatively large contiguous hinterland. The Kass typology lists Atlanta as a retail/finance center and puts Dallas in the category of
no cluster of industrial specialization. At the third level of table
6.3—third-order metropolises—there appear to be two different
types within the Southern Region. First, there are those areas
which specialize in retail trade—Miami, New Orleans, Memphis,
and Tampa–St. Petersburg. The second type of center at this level
appears to be those which specialize in nondurable goods manufacturing—Louisville and Greensboro–Winston-Salem–High Point,
North Carolina. As one moves down to subdominants with metropolitan characteristics and the lower subdominants, it is apparent
that more and more specializations within the industrial structure
appear. At the subdominant with metropolitan characteristics
level, there are three clusters of specialization—those of retail/
finance, transportation, and public administration. San Antonio
and Norfolk-Portsmouth are both areas which have major military

installations. Both were noted by Vance and Sutker to be somewhat special because of these characteristics, and they appear to retain that special character. The subdominants show up in five types of specialized function—from retail/wholesale, education, transportation, public administration, and nondurable goods manufacturing. The increasing differentiation of types of specialization as one moves down the urban hierarchy within the South, down both in terms of least scores and size, is reminiscent of a comment made by Duncan et al. when they were describing the metropolitan system as of 1950.

> Perhaps it is not too wild an extrapolation to suggest that, in the United States as of 1950, an SMSA size of roughly 300,000 inhabitants marked a transition point where distinctively metropolitan characteristics first began to appear. Adequately to describe the base of the urban hierarchy consisting of almost all urban centers smaller than this size, one would have to shift the emphasis from metropolism to other principles of functional differentiation (Duncan et al., 1960:275).

That is, as one moves toward the top of the metropolitan hierarchy within the national economy, metropolitan areas appear to serve more general functions within the larger system. As one moves toward the smaller-sized metropolitan areas, there tend to be more *specific* types of functional differentiation.

CONCLUSION

When one looks at the changes within the urban system of cities in the Southern Region from 1950 to 1970, several factors stand out. First of all, there appears to be a great deal of inertia within the larger system. That is, the stability of the ordering of metropolitan areas along the hierarchy suggested by Vance and Sutker seems to be one of the dominating factors of urban life within the South. At the same time, the changes which have occurred are changes which are both significant and logical, given the developing economy of the South in its relationship to the nation. Between 1950 and 1970, the industrial composition of the South has become quite similar to that of the rest of the United States (McKinney and Bourque, 1971). In 1950 this was not the case. Given this close similarity of industrial structure and given the closer integration of the

TABLE 6.5 Tentative Outline of the Urban System of Cities in
the South, 1970

National Metropolises

Houston   (28.26; Million +)
Washington, D.C.   (19.89; Million +)

Second-Order Metropolises

Atlanta (21.96; Million +)
Dallas   (24.54; Million +)

Third-Order Metropolises

Retail	Nondurable Goods Manufacturing
Miami (15.97; Million +)	Louisville (7.89; 500-Mill)
New Orleans (8.58; Million +)	Greensboro-
Memphis (7.89; 500-Million)	Winston-Salem-
Tampa-St.	High Point (5.95; 500-Mill)
Petersburg (6.45; Million +)	

Subdominants with Metropolitan Characteristics

Retail/Finance	Transportation
Birmingham (4.77; 500-Mill)	Tulsa (1.82; 250-500)
Charlotte (4.66; 250-500)	
Ft. Worth (4.37; 500-Mill)	Public Administration
Richmond (3.19; 500-Mill)	Oklahoma City (2.79; 500-Mill)
Jacksonville (2.87; 500-Mill)	San Antonio (1.94; 500-Mill)
Nashville (2.59; 500-Mill)	Norfolk-
Orlando (.20; 250-500)	Portsmouth (-.58; 500-Mill)

Subdominants[b]

Retail/Wholesale	Education	Transportation
Little Rock	Baton Rouge[a]	Huntington-
Shreveport	Jackson	Ashland
Corpus Christi	Raleigh	Savannah
Lubbock	Austin	
	Lexington	

Public Admin.	Nondurable Goods Man.
Mobile, Ala.	Chattanooga
Columbia, S.C.	Beaumont-Pt. Arthur
El Paso, Tex.	Knoxville
Huntsville, Ala.	Greenville, S.C.[a]
Montgomery, Ala.	Baton Rouge[a]
	Charleston, W.Va.
	Augusta, Ga.

Note: Numbers in parentheses are Z-Scores and city size
categories.
[a]Baton Rouge is a dual function SMSA, in both education and in
nondurable goods manufacturing.
[b]All subdominants have negative Z-scores and population of less
than 400,000.

southern economy with the rest of the nation, it is not surprising that we would have the emergence of at least one major national metropolis within the South. And it is not unreasonable to expect further changes will occur. With the increasing movement of population and industry and economic activity from the North to the South, a closer integration of the South into the national economy may occur. Furthermore, the linkages between the metropolitan system of the South (so apparently separated from the rest of the nation in 1950, yet showing signs of closer integration in 1970) may become even more indistinguishable from the larger urban system of the nation in future years. On the other hand, it may be that the apparently growing similarity of the South to the rest of the nation in 1970 is simply the juxtaposition of two crosscutting trends at the same time. That is, the South may continue to become more differentiated from the North through its own unique pattern of growth of industry and services. This southern growth pattern, along with the concomitant decline of the northern metropolitan belt in future years, may lend itself to an *increasing* differentiation of southern and nonsouthern metropolitan systems, but in directions not yet apparent. At this point it is difficult to tell. Data from the census of 1980 and later years will be examined with great interest to test these competing notions.

7
Southern Industrialization

JOACHIM SINGELMANN

The course of a country's economic development is tied to the transformation of its economy from agriculture to services. Generally, a shift from agriculture, with its relatively low productivity, to the higher productivity of manufacturing industries leads to an increase in per capita income that ultimately results in a demand for various services (Fisher, 1935; Clark, 1940; Kuznets, 1966, 1971; Postan, 1971). These changes are reflected in the sectoral transformation of the labor force from primary industries (mostly agriculture) to secondary industries (manufacturing) and, subsequently, to tertiary industries (services). Although this sequence can be observed in many Western European countries, it is absent in countries outside the European continent. In Japan (and in most currently developing countries) the decline of agriculture occurs simultaneously with an increase of employment in service industries (Oshima, 1971). In the United States, secondary and tertiary employment expanded concomitantly when the agricultural sector began to decline. However, since the early part of the twentieth century, the rate of growth of service employment has greatly outpaced the increase of employment in secondary industries.[1] But there is general agreement that during economic development employment will ultimately become concentrated in the various service industries.

The major objective of this chapter is to examine the economic transformation from agriculture to services and its related employment trends in the southern United States during the past 100 years. Three dimensions of this transformation are discussed: (1) changes in the industry structure of employment, (2) occupational shifts and income, and (3) political aspects. Throughout the chapter the development of the South is compared with corresponding trends in other regions of the United States. This comparison per-

mits an examination of the extent to which similarities exist between the South and currently developing countries (see Sharkansky, 1975). In a final section, the likelihood for a continuation of
the differences between the South and the non-South in the near
future is discussed.

THE TRANSFORMATION OF INDUSTRIAL EMPLOYMENT

During the past 100 years, the national labor force has undergone a
sweeping transformation. The share of total employment in agriculture has dropped from 50 percent to less than 4 percent. Manufacturing, which accounted for nearly 18 percent of the total employment in 1870, reached its peak in 1960 (almost 30 percent).
Since then, manufacturing has declined to its current level of
about 25 percent of total employment. Finally, service industries
increased from one-fourth to two-thirds of total employment during this interval, with producer and social services contributing
most to the expansion (Browning and Singelmann, 1975:17–18). By
1970 these two types of services accounted for nearly 30 percent of
the total work force.

This shift of employment toward services has been viewed by
some as a signal for the "coming of postindustrial society" and its
consequent emphasis on the growth of professional and technical
positions, technological knowledge, and the power of the professional and technical class (Bell, 1973). While the postindustrialist
perspective generally does not distinguish between the different
kinds of service activities, it is important to note that much of the
increase in service employment has resulted from the growth of
social service industries. These services either are part of the public sector or are closely linked to it through state policies (e.g.,
medical services, the availability of which in part depends on such
governmental programs as Medicaid and Medicare). The growth of
the social service sector thus is one indication of the extent to
which the role of the state expands in a mature economy such as
that of the United States.[2]

How does the sectoral transformation of the southern labor force
compare with the national pattern? In the South[3] the extractive
sector (agriculture and mining) remained the dominant sector of
employment much longer than in the nation.[4] In 1870 this sector
accounted for more than two-thirds of total employment, and even

by 1920 one-half the southern labor force was employed in these industries.

Unfortunately, the statistical information about labor force trends in the South during the nineteenth century is not complete enough to provide a comparable time series for the past 100 years. Yet, it is clear that the South fell behind the pace of other regions of the United States in its efforts to industrialize, despite its leads in textile manufacturing in the early 1800s. For example, Brooks (1929) notes that southern manufacturing developed slowly during 1880–1925. Similar evidence is presented by Vance (1945) and Thompson (1954). According to Thompson's (1954) data, in 1890 only 9.8 percent of total southern employment was in secondary industries, compared to 29.8 percent for the non-South. This regional difference decreased only slightly to 18.1 percent by 1920. However, since detailed data about the industry structure of employment are only available since 1920 (and even the data for 1920 and 1930 are less than satisfactory), the following discussion of employment changes will concentrate on the past 50 years.

The transformation of employment from 1920 to 1970 is addressed in table 7.1. These data show that the South, throughout the 50-year period, remained more oriented toward agriculture than other regions of the United States. But the more important finding is that the share of employment declined in each decade, with the rate of decline accelerating after 1940. As a result, the difference in the relative proportion between southern and nonsouthern United States has largely disappeared.

The lower level of southern employment in the transformative sector was continued during the twentieth century, but this sector continuously increased its share of employment. These gains were only moderate between 1920 and 1940, but they appear more impressive when compared to the *declines* in other regions. Since 1940 transformative employment has expanded very rapidly and has reached a level comparable to that of the nonsouthern United States. However, the convergence during the 1960s resulted from an *expanding* transformative sector in the South and a *decreasing* sector in other regions.

Many reasons have been given for the belated industrial development of the South, including an inadequate transportation network, charges of railroad rate discrimination, and a large degree of absentee ownership of southern resources. For example, Brooks (1929:6) points to the effects of the industrial revolution in England, which created a higher demand for raw cotton. The condi-

TABLE 7.1   Percentage Distribution of Labor Force by Industry Sectors

Sector and Region	1920	1930	1940	1950	1960	1970
Extractive						
South	49.4	42.1	35.4	23.2	11.8	5.9
Non-South	20.3	16.5	15.0	10.7	6.5	4.0
Difference	29.1	25.6	20.4	12.5	5.3	1.9
Transformative						
South	18.7	20.0	21.6	26.9	31.0	32.0
Non-South	35.9	32.6	33.4	36.8	33.5	33.7
Difference	-17.2	-12.6	-11.8	-9.9	-7.5	-1.7
Distributive Services						
South	13.5	16.1	16.8	20.9	22.0	22.6
Non-South	19.3	22.4	21.9	23.1	21.6	22.5
Difference	-5.8	-6.3	-5.1	-2.2	0.4	0.1
Producer Services						
South	a	a	2.7	3.6	5.5	8.1
Non-South	a	a	5.4	5.6	7.1	9.7
Difference	a	a	-2.7	-2.0	-1.6	-1.6
Social Services						
South	5.7[a]	6.6[a]	8.6	12.0	16.3	20.8
Non-South	7.6[a]	9.2[a]	10.6	12.3	15.7	20.8
Difference	-1.9	-2.6	-2.0	-0.3	0.6	0.0
Personal Services						
South	12.6[b]	15.2[b]	14.6	13.4	13.4	10.7
Non-South	17.0[b]	19.7[b]	13.7	11.5	10.6	9.3
Difference	-4.4	-4.5	0.9	1.9	2.8	1.4

Source: U.S. Censuses of Population, 1920-1970.

[a] For the census years 1920 and 1930, Producer and Social Services are combined.

[b] In the census years 1920 and 1930, the industry classification system included one category called "clerical occupations." Since persons classified in this category could be employed in any industry, I decided to allocate this category to Personal Services. Since the main purpose is to compare the two regions at a given time, this inadequacy of the data is not too serious.

tions for production of this plantation crop were highly favorable in the South and thus made it attractive to southern farmers. More detailed discussion lies beyond the scope of this chapter,[5] but a related aspect may be probed. There is a tendency to compare the development of a lagging region with that of currently developing *countries*. With respect to this latter group, the point has been made that their usually small manufacturing sector should not totally be interpreted as a failure to provide a strong manufacturing base. There is an advantage to being backward, as noted by Veblen, who stated in a different context that England was "paying the penalty for having been thrown into the lead and so having shown the way" (1915:128). Technology that is used by currently developing countries often reflects more the technological sophistication of developed countries than the level of technology of the country in which it is used. An early evaluation of industrialization in the South, in fact, did point to the possibility of such technological advantage (Brooks, 1929:17). Thus, the small share of employment in the manufacturing sector in developing countries may *in part* reflect their higher capital intensity, compared with early industrialized countries at similar levels of economic growth. This argument can be pursued further through a closer examination of the structure of the manufacturing sector.

The data in table 7.2 show that throughout the 1870–1905 period, on the average, southern manufacturing establishments used less capital, had fewer employees, paid lower wages, and produced lower value of products than their nonsouthern counterparts. The data also indicate that these differences between southern and nonsouthern manufacturing establishments were diminishing during that period.

Although the data in table 7.3 are not directly comparable to those in table 7.2, they, too, address differences in productivity between the three southern census divisions and the rest of the United States. Until 1947 the value added per worker was consistently lower in the three southern parts than in the rest of the nation. It can be seen from these data that value added and a large average size of establishment are not always related. In these years the average establishment in the South Atlantic Division had more employees than its counterpart in the West South Central Division or the nonsouthern United States; yet, its value added per worker was lower. By 1947 the West South Central Division overtook the nonsouthern United States in terms of value added and maintained this position through 1972.

TABLE 7.2   Manufacturing: Selected Statistics for the South[a]
as Proportion of U.S. Totals

			Wage Earners		
Year	Establishments %	Capital %	Average Number %	Wages %	Value of products %
1870	15.4	6.6	9.1	5.8	6.6
1880	14.6	6.9	8.2	5.6	6.3
1890	13.1	7.8	9.7	7.1	7.5
1900	15.1	9.0	13.3	9.2	8.9
1905	15.3	11.0	14.0	10.7	10.5

Source: Statistical Abstract of the United States, 1909,
no. 32 (Washington, D.C.: Bureau of Statistics, under the
Direction of the Secretary of Commerce and Labor, 1910).

[a]Southern States: Virginia, West Virginia, North Carolina,
South Carolina, Georgia, Florida, Kentucky, Tennessee,
Alabama, Mississippi, Arkansas, Louisiana, Indian Territory,
Oklahoma, Texas.

A further analysis of the differences in value added between the various regions would require more detailed data about the distribution of employment among individual manufacturing industries. Since industries differ in their capital output ratios, variation in value added can be partially explained by the different industry unit of that sector for the regions. Yet, overall, these data do suggest that the smaller size of the southern transformative sector was *not* due to its higher productivity.

A comparison of employment trends in extractive and transformative sectors reveals that most of the overrepresentation of southern employment in extractive industries is offset by its underrepresentation in transformative industries. In contrast, the differences between the two regions in services are much smaller. By 1970 the South and the non-South differed only in the size of their respective producer and personal services sectors.

The equal representation of social services in the two regions comes as a surprise. Given the lower levels of industrialization, urbanization, and per capita income in the South, we could well have expected the South to have a smaller social service sector than the remaining regions. Apparently, the South was able to compensate for its lower levels in some other ways, and the usual relationship between per capita income and employment in social services that is found among countries does not exist in this case.

In sum, this analysis has shown that the main differences in the industry structure between the South and the rest of the country are accounted for by the extractive and transformative sectors. Also, southern manufacturing employment was traditionally more concentrated in the less productive industries (Dunn, 1962). Except for the West South Central Division, the value added per worker remained lower in the South than in the rest of the nation. The service sectors in the two regions developed quite similarly. Despite its later industrialization, the South was able to expand its transformative sector at a rapid rate after 1940, and, as a result, the industrial structures of the two regions were comparable by 1970. The convergence of the two regions is reflected in the decreasing index of dissimilarity, from .292 in 1920 to .034 in 1970.[6] In other words, by 1970 only 3.4 percent of the southern (or the nonsouthern) workers would have to be redistributed among the industry sectors in order to achieve equal distributions.

OCCUPATIONAL SHIFTS AND INCOME

There is a close link between the industry structure and the occupational distribution of employment. For example, in an agricultural economy, employment is concentrated in farm-related occupations. A shift toward manufacturing industries results in an increase in craftsmen and operatives, and, when service industries expand, the demand for professional, clerical, and service workers increases. Findings for the total United States showed that for 1960–1970 two-thirds of all occupational shifts could be explained by changes in the industry structure (Browning and Singelmann, 1975).

Occupational Shifts
Given the more recent concentration of southern employment in agriculture and the belated development of the transformative sector, the occupational differences between the South and the rest of

TABLE 7.3 Manufacturing: Selected Statistics for Three Southern Districts and the Nonsouthern United States

Year and Region	Number of Establishments	Average Number of Workers per Establishment	Value Added per Worker (Thousands of Dollars)
1914			
South Atlantic	28,925	23.69	0.99
East South Central	14,410	18.34	1.18
West South Central	12,417	17.06	1.30
Non-South U.S.	121,245	47.28	1.47
1921			
South Atlantic	16,427	39.33	1.92
East South Central	7,240	35.78	1.73
West South Central	8,099	28.33	2.50
Non-South U.S.	164,332	35.35	2.76
1927			
South Atlantic	17,029	51.62	2.44
East South Central	7,637	47.07	2.18
West South Central	8,208	32.54	2.82
Non-South U.S.	158,992	43.04	3.49
1935			
South Atlantic	15,408	57.21	1.82
East South Central	6,440	49.48	1.91
West South Central	8,230	27.13	2.59
Non-South U.S.	139,033	42.83	2.80

1947			
South Atlantic	24,001	63.47	4.55
East South Central	10,907	58.10	4.53
West South Central	13,181	41.74	5.50
Non-South U.S.	192,792	60.10	5.31
1958			
South Atlantic	33,425	56.39	7.61
East South Central	13,800	56.74	8.15
West South Central	18,659	42.60	9.80
Non-South U.S.	237,503	52.89	8.99
1963			
South Atlantic	35,546	59.78	9.95
East South Central	14,196	62.48	10.43
West South Central	20,237	42.74	12.68
Non-South U.S.	241,942	54.08	11.53
1967			
South Atlantic	37,961	65.91	11.71
East South Central	15,746	69.35	12.56
West South Central	21,883	49.49	15.34
Non-South U.S.	235,550	62.18	13.81
1972			
South Atlantic	41,535	65.94	16.19
East South Central	16,525	75.58	17.00
West South Central	24,020	51.58	19.85
Non-South U.S.	238,630	57.83	19.11

Source: 1914-1927--Statistical Abstract of the United States, 1930, no. 52 (Washington, D.C.: Department of Commerce, 1930); 1935--no. 59 (1938); 1947--no. 71 (1950); 1958 and 1963--no. 91 (1970); 1967 and 1972--no. 96 (1975).

Note: Number of workers in 1914-1935 are wage earners (average for year). Number of workers in 1947-1972 are all employees (average for year).

TABLE 7.4   Percentage Employment in Major Occupational
Groups: South and Nonsouthern United States, 1940-1970

Occupation	1940	1950	1960	1970
Professionals				
South	5.9	7.6	10.5	13.5
Non-South	8.2	9.4	12.4	16.6
Difference	-2.3	-1.8	1.9	-3.1
Managers				
South	6.9	8.2	8.8	8.3
Non-South	9.0	9.4	8.8	9.0
Difference	-2.1	-1.2	0.0	-0.7
Sales				
South	a	6.5	7.2	7.0
Non-South	a	7.3	7.7	7.8
Difference		-0.8	-0.5	-0.8
Clerical				
South	11.9[a]	9.8	12.9	16.4
Non-South	18.9[a]	13.5	16.1	20.2
Difference	-7.0	-3.5	-3.2	-3.8
Craftsmen				
South	8.3	12.1	13.2	14.2
Non-South	12.6	14.8	14.1	14.8
Difference	-4.3	-2.7	-0.9	-0.6
Operatives				
South	14.9	18.2	19.0	18.3
Non-South	20.0	20.9	19.6	15.8
Difference	-5.1	-2.7	-0.6	2.5
Laborers, except Farm				
South	7.4	7.0	6.0	5.2
Non-South	6.6	5.8	4.7	4.6
Difference	0.8	1.2	1.3	0.6
Farmers				
South	18.9	12.4	5.3	1.9
Non-South	8.2	5.8	3.6	2.0
Difference	10.7	6.6	1.7	-0.1
Farm Laborers				
South	12.5	7.2	3.7	1.8
Non-South	4.4	3.1	1.8	1.2
Difference	8.1	4.1	1.9	0.6
Service Workers[b]				
South	13.3	11.1	13.2	13.3
Non-South	12.1	9.9	11.1	8.2
Difference	1.2	1.2	2.1	5.1
Index of Dissimilarity	20.8	12.9	7.1	9.0

Source: U.S. Census of Population, 1940-1970.

[a] In the 1940 census, sales and clerical occupations were
combined.

[b] Includes private household workers.

the United States are not surprising (see table 7.4). For example, in 1940 southern employment, compared to that of the nonsouthern United States, was mostly overrepresented in the two occupations of farmers and farm laborers and underrepresented in the operative and craftsmen categories and in all white-collar occupations. But, with the convergence of the industry structures of the two regions, the differences in the occupational distribution of employment have diminished. (The differences, as measured by the index of dissimilarity, decreased from .208 to .090. The two regions had the most similar distributions in 1960 with an index value of .070.) Indeed, by 1970 there were proportionately fewer farmers in the South than in the nonsouthern United States. Substantial differences remained in the categories of professionals, clerical workers, and service workers: the South has relatively fewer professionals and clerical workers and more service workers (particularly private household workers).

Income
The greater concentrations of southern employment in low productivity industries and lower-status occupations is also reflected in per capita income of the southern districts (see table 7.5). Historically, the South has had lower incomes than the rest of the nation (with the exception of the West South Central Division in 1840). Between 1880 and 1940, the income pattern of the Southern Region relative to the nation was one of improvement alternating with deterioration. But since 1940 these districts have experienced a continuous improvement in their per capita income vis-à-vis the nation, again suggesting that the development gap between the South and the non-South is closing rapidly. However, unlike the remarkable convergence of the industry structure and the occupational distribution, per capita income in the South remains below the national average by 15 to 25 percent.

This difference results in part from the fact that, aside from the remaining occupational differences between the South and the non-South, wages and salaries for comparable occupations are lower in the South (see table 7.6). But this difference is not constant among occupations: workers in the two occupational groups that are underrepresented in the South (professionals and clerical workers) do much better when compared to their nonsouthern counterparts than do workers in other occupations. The explanation for this finding may be that, due to the more recent industrial development in the South, professionals and clerical workers are

TABLE 7.5   Ratio of Per Capita Income to U.S. Per Capita By
Southern Division: 1840 to 1970

Year	United States	South Atlantic	East South Central	West South Central
1970	100	86	74	85
1965	100	81	71	83
1960	100	77	67	83
1950	100	74	63	81
1940	100	69	55	70
1930	100	56	48	61
1920	100	59	52	72
1900	100	45	49	61
1880	100	45	51	60
1840	100	70	73	144

Source: Historical Statistics of the United States, Colonial
Times to 1970, pt. 1 (Washington, D.C.:   U.S. Department of
Commerce, Bureau of Census), p. 242.

in relatively short supply. This argument seems to be corroborated by the situation of private household workers: these workers are the most overrepresented in the South and, compared to the non-South, their incomes are the lowest.

POLITICAL ASPECTS OF DEVELOPMENT

There is a temptation to compare less developed *regions* within industrialized nations—such as the southern United States, Sicily, or Brittany—with the currently developing *countries*. Both have examples of development to follow or adapt to their own specific conditions; both can make use of technology that was developed by the more advanced regions or countries; and both face the prob-

TABLE 7.6   Median Wage or Salary Income for Males, 1969

Occupation	United States	South	South as % of U.S.
Total	$8,517	$7,365	.865
Professionals, technical, and kindred workers	11,752	11,053	.940
Managers and administrators, except farm	11,747	10,427	.888
Sales workers	9,454	8,533	.902
Clerical and kindred workers	7,973	7,406	.929
Craftsmen and kindred workers	8,730	7,536	.863
Operatives, except transport	7,439	6,148	.826
Transport equipment operatives	7,583	6,074	.800
Laborers, except farm	6,135	4,721	.770
Farmers and farm managers	5,122	4,049	.790
Farm laborers and foremen	3,628	3,096	.853
Service workers, except private household	6,381	5,224	.819
Private household workers	3,118	2,247	.721

Source: U.S. Department of Commerce, 1970 Census of Population, Detailed Characteristics, United States Summary (Washington, D.C.: Government Printing Office, 1973), tables 227 and 296.

lems of having to compete with already established markets. However, Sharkansky (1975) notes that two fundamental differences exist between developing regions and developing countries: (1) even the least developed states in the U.S. have a per capita income well exceeding that of developing countries, and (2) federal assistance to these states, on a per capita basis, is many times the aid received by developing countries. "In 1971–72, federal assistance to state and

TABLE 7.7 Population, Federal Tax Burden, and Federal Outlays in the South

Region and State	1970 % of U.S. Population	Rank	1972 Share of Federal Tax Burden	Rank	1972 Share of Federal Outlays	Rank
South Atlantic	14.66		12.99		14.98	
Delaware	0.15	46	0.34	42	0.22	49
Maryland	1.94	18	2.22	12	2.53	13
Virginia	2.30	14	2.05	15	2.86	9
West Virginia	0.86	34	0.64	33	0.71	36
North Carolina	2.51	12	1.87	17	1.91	16
South Carolina	1.28	26	0.85	30	1.05	31
Georgia	2.27	15	1.82	18	2.21	15
Florida	3.35	9	3.20	10	3.49	8
East South Central	6.33		4.33		5.96	
Kentucky	1.59	23	1.15	24	1.35	26
Tennessee	1.94	17	1.46	21	1.82	18
Alabama	1.70	21	1.13	25	1.61	20
Mississippi	1.10	29	0.59	35	1.18	28
West South Central	9.54		7.85		9.40	
Arkansas	0.95	32	0.60	34	0.84	33
Louisiana	1.80	20	1.31	22	1.38	23
Oklahoma	1.26	27	1.02	27	1.36	24
Texas	5.53	4	4.92	6	5.82	3

Source: Adapted from Barone et al.(1973).

local governments averaged $160.51 per capita in the ten least developed states; an estimate of foreign aid to the developing countries puts the figure at $1.00–$2.00 per capita for recent years" (Sharkansky, 1975:66). And, unlike a large part of today's foreign aid, federal assistance does not need to be paid back. Thus, a comparison of the southern United States with countries of the Third World would not appear to be fruitful. However, the flow of federal outlays can diminish regional differences in income.

Tax Burden and Federal Outlays
A closer examination of the relationship between the federal tax burden and federal outlays reveals some interesting results (see table 7.7). In all southern states but one, the share of the federal tax burden is less than the share of federal outlays. Particularly favorable differences (for the states involved) are found in Virginia, Georgia, Alabama, Mississippi, and Texas.

The reasons for these differences are not entirely clear. Much of it is undoubtedly due to the tax advantage of the South. The Southern Regional Education Board reported recently that the South underutilizes its tax potential more so than any other region (*New York Times*, 1977). Alabama and Texas showed the most tax underutilization in 1975 (24.6 and 21.9 percent) compared to New York's overutilization of 34.8 percent. This tax situation in the South is very favorable for the business community and provides the region with a large competitive advantage in attracting new industries. Another factor might be the political influence and voting behavior of members of Congress from these states. For example, it could be speculated that, due to the prevalence of the one-party system in most southern states (at least until very recently), southern legislators had a greater possibility of remaining in Congress and thus gaining seniority than their nonsouthern colleagues. Since seniority has been the basis for the selection of chairpersonships, southern members of Congress thus may have been able to gain disproportionately high influence. Clarke examines this issue in a later chapter.

Although the data in table 7.7 would need to be further differentiated between outlays for social welfare and other expenditures, they do suggest that transfer of income from higher-income states to the South explains in part the ability of the latter to maintain social services at about the same level as the rest of the country.

ECONOMIC DEVELOPMENT AND REGIONAL
DIVISION OF LABOR

Let us briefly summarize the main findings to this point. During the past 100 years, the economy of the South has been much more oriented toward agriculture than the rest of the nation. In fact, it was the less rapid decline of the agricultural sector combined with a slower growth of manufacturing employment that accounted for the main differences in the industry base of the two regions. If increases in per capita income are viewed as one of the two main goals of economic development (the other being an equitable income distribution), the data show that the South remained behind the rest of the nation throughout the period. A large part of southern employment is still concentrated in low productivity industries and southern per capita income remains below the national average (Hammond, 1972). However, the gap between the South and the non-South has greatly diminished, and, as far as the industry structure is concerned, the similarities in 1970 are more impressive than the remaining differences.[7]

In the past the difference between the two regions in the structure of employment reflected the "backwardness" of the South (as witnessed by lower per capita income), but the remaining differences between the various states should increasingly be viewed in the context of a regional division of labor. To continue to juxtapose the South and the non-South ignores the differentiation among the nonsouthern regions themselves. In a country with the size and geographical diversity of the United States, the economy is likely to be differentiated regionally. Large discrepancies in the standard of living remain among the various regions, but they cannot any longer be analyzed in terms of the internal colonialism model. (The only exception here would be Puerto Rico, which today performs a function that is very similar to that of the South during the last century, including discrimination with respect to transportation tariffs and the maintenance of a reserve labor force. But this chapter concerns only the relationship of the South with the remaining states in the U.S.) Instead, transportation and communication facilities, regional size of markets, tax utilization rates, labor supply, and climatic conditions are among the many factors that influence the industry structure. This regional division of labor is addressed in tables 7.8 and 7.9.

The data in these tables confirm that the South has traditionally been the most agriculturally oriented region. But by 1970 there was

TABLE 7.8   Percentage Employment by Industry Sector and Region

Industry Sector and Region	1920	1930	1940	1950	1960	1970
Extractive						
U.S.	28.9	23.9	21.3	14.4	8.1	4.5
Northeast	10.1	8.0	6.9	5.0	2.7	1.7
North Central	27.6	22.3	21.0	15.0	9.1	5.3
South	49.4	42.1	35.4	23.2	11.8	5.9
West	28.7	23.2	19.4	12.6	7.8	5.1
Transformative						
U.S.	30.8	28.9	29.8	33.9	35.9	33.1
Northeast	43.6	37.9	39.7	41.8	42.4	35.9
North Central	31.5	32.6	31.0	36.2	38.8	36.1
South	18.7	20.0	21.6	26.9	31.0	32.0
West	25.2	23.9	23.3	27.4	31.2	26.4
Distributive Services						
U.S.	17.6	20.3	20.4	22.4	21.9	22.3
Northeast	24.2	22.5	21.8	23.0	21.2	22.2
North Central	18.8	21.3	21.3	22.5	21.6	22.2
South	13.5	16.1	16.8	20.9	22.0	22.6
West	20.6	23.4	24.2	25.0	22.6	23.5
Producer Services						
U.S.	a	a	4.6	4.8	6.6	8.2
Northeast	a	a	6.5	6.6	8.2	11.0
North Central	a	a	4.3	4.5	5.8	8.0
South	a	a	2.7	3.6	5.5	8.1
West	a	a	5.5	5.9	7.8	10.5
Social Services						
U.S.	7.0[a]	8.4[a]	10.0	12.4	16.3	21.9
Northeast	7.6[a]	9.5[a]	11.0	12.3	15.4	20.7
North Central	7.0[a]	8.4[a]	9.9	11.2	14.8	19.6
South	5.7[a]	6.6[a]	10.0	12.0	16.3	20.8
West	9.4[a]	10.7[a]	11.7	15.0	17.9	23.2
Personal Services						
U.S.	15.7[b]	18.4[b]	14.0	12.0	11.3	10.0
Northeast	19.2[b]	22.2[b]	14.1	11.3	10.0	8.4
North Central	15.2[b]	17.6[b]	12.5	10.6	10.0	8.8
South	12.6[b]	15.2[b]	14.0	13.4	11.3	10.7
West	16.0[b]	18.9[b]	15.9	14.1	12.7	11.3

Source: U.S. Censuses of Population, 1920-1970.

[a]For the census years 1920 and 1930, Producer and Social Services are combined.

[b]In the census years 1920 and 1930, the industry classification system included one category called "clerical occupations." Since persons classified in this category could be employed in any industry, I decided to allocate this category to Personal Services. Since the main purpose is to compare the two regions at a given point in time, this inadequacy of the data is not too serious.

TABLE 7.9 Index of Dissimilarity for the U.S. Industry Structure and Four Regional Industry Structures

	1920		1930		1940		1950		1960		1970	
	ID	Rank	ID	Rank	ID	Rank	ID	Rank	ID	Rank	ID	Rank
Northeast	18.75	3	16.00	3	14.35	3	10.25	4	8.20	4	5.65	3
North Central	1.85	1	2.45	1	2.15	1	2.95	1	3.90	1	3.80	2
South	20.55	4	18.15	4	14.90	4	10.15	3	5.95	3	2.35	1
West	5.75	2	5.80	2	8.35	2	8.35	2	4.95	2	6.70	4

Source: Table 7.8

virtually no difference between the Southern, North Central, and Western Regions in terms of agricultural employment. The main difference is now accounted for by the Northeast, from which extractive employment has almost disappeared.

The second major finding is the sharp decline of transformative employment in the West, making it the least manufacturing oriented region. The size of transformative employment in the other three regions has become very similar, largely due to the decline of the sector in the Northeast and its growth in the South.

Third, the Northeast has maintained its lead in producer services, reflecting its historical position as the financial, insurance, and advertising center of the nation. However, the West has been able to attract many producer services as well, and the size of its employment in these service industries comes close to that of the Northeast.

Fourth, the case of the West illustrates that the size of the transformative sector is *not* an absolute indicator of a region's ability to support social services. Throughout the 50-year period studied, the West has had the largest share of employment in social services, even though its transformative sector was one of the smallest.

Finally, when the industry structures of the four regions are contrasted with that of the total United States, the South emerges as resembling the U.S. distribution most closely by 1970. Currently the West has the most divergent distribution of employment among industries. But this trend also confirms the observation made earlier that there is virtually no difference among the regions in terms of service employment. As these industries employed increasing proportions of workers, the difference between the regions diminished.

Whenever two lines approach each other, there also exists the possibility that the lines may diverge again. Thus, it is possible that the South, after having become more similar to the rest of the nation, could reverse the positions and become the leading industrial region of the United States. Although employment data do not exist for the mid-1970s that are comparable to the figures presented earlier in this chapter, industry statistics available for 1975 do not suggest that this has happened yet. By 1975 the manufacturing sector in the South still remained smaller than its size in the northern regions of the country. Even if such reversal in positions should occur, it is not likely to happen before the end of the present century.

As important as present *levels* of employment in the various industry sectors may be, examination of their *rates of growth* suggests additional consequences for industrial redistribution in the United States. We have already commented upon the decline in industrial activity in the Northeast. This trend, in conjunction with population redistribution, has immediate implications for the growth of social services in the various regions. Although the social service sector in the South is now at about the same level as that in the Northeast and North Central Regions, its rate of growth during the 1960s has been much smaller in the South than in the others.

Several factors contributed to this slower expansion of social services. One factor is the favorable business environment which provides many incentives for the formation of new enterprises in the South, the addition of new establishments, or sometimes even the relocation of production facilities from the northern regions. Consequently, the private sector (in manufacturing and construction as well as in distributive and producer services) absorbed most of the increase in the labor force in the South. The differentials in the rate of growth of social services among states *cannot* be explained by family income. In other words, social services in the South did not grow more slowly because family income in this region expanded less rapidly (Singelmann, 1977). Instead, the single most important factor for the expansion of social services is population growth: the higher the rate of population growth, the lower the increase of employment in social services. This finding can be taken to mean that the shift of employment opportunities from the Northeast Region to the South required the state to intervene in the economy by providing public jobs and social services to a growing part of the population whose subsistence cannot be provided for by the private sector.

A second factor is the well-known reluctance of southern states to provide social services to those in need. Although it may be argued that this reluctance affects the level of welfare *payments* more than social service *employment* itself (and that the opposition to welfare might even lead to an elaborate and labor-intensive bureaucracy to control the welfare population), many social service programs that are found in northeastern states do not exist in the South or are provided on a much smaller scale. This ranges from special educational programs to services for migrant workers. For example, without the medical facilities in Wisconsin and Michigan, the health status of Texas migrant workers would be much inferior, for the state of Texas provides very little health care to this employment group. Thus, the rapid industrialization in the South does not necessarily indicate that this region has solved the problems of unemployment and underemployment. There are still large sections of southern workers whose income barely lifts their families out of poverty (and sometimes is not even enough for that). Other persons outside the labor force (particularly from such groups as the elderly, the disabled, and families with small children in which the father either is unemployed or absent) are often cared for less than in other parts of the country.

Thus, given the tendencies for increasing unionization, greater demands for social programs, and emerging signs that southern cities (e.g., Atlanta) apparently will not be spared all the urban woes of northern cities, it seems likely that the pace of southern industrialization relative to other parts of the United States will slow down and that southern governments will come under increasing pressure to provide social services similar to those found in the North and West.

Since these trends are still *in statu nascendi*, their magnitude through the year 2000 remains unclear. Although the current situation in the various regions of the United States does contain the potential for the South to exhibit yet again a distinct pattern of development, the past trends and their rate of change point to more similarities than discrepancies between the South and the non-South in the future. Moreover, whatever dissimilarities may prevail, they will no longer be fruitfully explained by the situation of a region vis-à-vis the *entire* rest of the country but rather by a differentiation among *all* regions and, perhaps increasingly, by states. It is already evident that the differentiation among states *within* one region is as large as the differences *between* the regions.

SUMMARY

This chapter has shown that the industrial development of the South was tied to the agricultural sector for a greater time than was the case in the nonsouthern United States. The counterpart to this situation was a less developed transformative sector. The surprising finding is that, despite these differences, the employment pattern in service industries in the South is very comparable to the national trend. This finding is partly explained by the fact that de-

veloping regions, in contrast to developing countries, receive substantial transfers of income from the more well-to-do regions that
enable them to support a similar level of social services. The
slower expansion of social services in the southern states is largely
due to their more rapid population growth, which reflects a more
favorable employment situation in the South than in other parts of
the United States (for this population growth to a large extent is
made up by migration). Finally, it has been demonstrated that the
contemporary differences between the South and the non-South in
the industry structure of employment are more fruitfully interpreted in the context of a regional differentiation of labor including
all regions than as a continuation of the past when the South was
clearly distinct from the remainder of the country.

NOTES

1. See Singelmann (1978) for a discussion and critique of the three-stage sequence of development.
2. Singelmann (1978) and Browning and Singelmann (1975, 1978) contain a more
   detailed discussion of the employment transformation in the United States
   and its sociological and political significance.
3. A list of southern states is given in table 7.7.
4. For sake of clarity, the changes in the industry structure are discussed on the
   sector level. In order to permit more differentiation than would be possible
   with the traditional distinction of primary-secondary-tertiary industries, this
   study uses the Browning-Singelmann industry classification scheme. This
   scheme is made up of the following sectors: *Extractive* (agriculture, mining);
   Transformative (construction, manufacturing, utilities); *Distributive Services*
   (transportation, communication, trade except eating and drinking places); *Producer Services* (financial services, insurance, real estate, legal services, accounting and bookkeeping, engineering and architectural services, miscellaneous business services except repair); *Social Services* (medical services,
   education, nonprofit institutions, religious and welfare services, public administration, miscellaneous social and professional services); and *Personal Services* (domestic services, eating and drinking places, lodging, recreational and
   entertainment services, repair services, other personal services). See Browning
   and Singelmann (1975) for a full description of this scheme.
5. The growth of the Sunbelt has led to a renewed interest in the economic development of the South during the nineteenth and early twentieth centuries.
   Many different explanations have been offered—the distinctiveness of southern culture, internal colonialism, and monopoly capitalism, to name just a
   few models. Since these models provide competing claims, a thorough evaluation of their relative merits cannot be given in this space. (Gregory Sampson
   and I are discussing these various models in an essay in progress, "The Politi-

cal Economy of Southern Development.") Besides the classic work by Vance (1935, 1945) and Nicholls (1960), interesting recent approaches can be found in Dowd (1977), Greenhut and Whitman (1964), and Perry and Watkins (1977).

6. See Poston and Passel (1972) inter alios for a discussion of the index of dissimilarity and its computation.

7. Obviously, not all states have been able to share in this new economic boom, and many parts of Appalachia and the Deep South remain behind in their development.

8
An Economic Approach to Population Change in the South

WILLIAM J. SEROW

This chapter examines changes in the demographic behavior of Southerners from the point of view of concomitant changes in economic behavior. Because the chapter is essentially an overview, the "South" is implicitly treated as a homogeneous collection of political entities called states. In fact, the South is an extremely heterogeneous collection of economic entities which may bear little correspondence to artificial political boundaries. A great deal of insight could be gained by expanding this general analysis to focus on the much smaller economic units. Unfortunately, the amount of disaggregation required to accomplish this is beyond the scope of this chapter.

Four basic issues are addressed: (1) to what extent has economic change in the South occurred at a rate different from that experienced by other portions of the nation? (2) to what extent are differences in the demographic behavior of Southerners the result of the relatively late transformation of the South from an agrarian to an industrial society? (3) to what extent is the model of demographic transition applicable to southern demographic history? and (4) what economic-demographic differences between the South and the rest of the nation are likely to exist by the end of the century?

ECONOMIC VARIABLES

This section presents a basic overview of economic change in the South since 1870. A discussion of levels of labor force participation and the degree of agricultural employment is followed by a consideration of trends in the industrial composition of the labor force and of trends in the level of income. In all cases, the discussion focuses upon a comparison between the southern and nonsouthern portions of the nation.

Labor Force Participation and Agricultural Employment

While the United States was still a predominantly agricultural nation in 1870, the South was a great deal more agrarian than the rest of the country. More than 85 percent of employed males and more than 50 percent of employed females followed agricultural pursuits. By contrast, for the remainder of the nation, the corresponding figures were 45 and 1 percent. The South contained less than 30 percent of the nation's work force but nearly half of the nation's agricultural employment.

During the interval from 1870 to 1950, the share of total agricultural employment declined in the South as well as the rest of the nation, but the South remained more agricultural than the non-South. In 1950 about one-fourth of all southern males were engaged in agriculture vis-à-vis only 10 percent in the balance of the nation. The 1950 share of southern males in the agricultural industry was about the same as that of the non-South in 1910.

Since 1950 the situation has changed dramatically. By 1970 the proportion of southern males in agriculture exceeded that of nonsouthern males by less than 2 percent. Indeed, the North Central Region had a higher proportion of males in agriculture than did the South. The longtime characterization of the South as an intensively agricultural region had vanished rather sharply.

Despite the earlier concentration of employed persons in agriculture, trends in labor force participation rates (the percentage of population aged 10 and over who are in the labor force)[1] in the South have corresponded quite closely to those in the non-South, especially during the present century. Since 1950 rates for southern as well as nonsouthern males have declined by about 8 percent, while rates for southern as well as nonsouthern females have increased by about 10 percent.

Employment by Industry

The industrial composition of southern workers is shown in table 8.1. These data show the percentage distribution of employment by industry for the South and the rest of the nation for the years 1880, 1900, and 1940–1970. Location quotients for the South are also shown. A location quotient is ". . . a device for comparing a

TABLE 8.1   Industrial Composition of the Labor Force, South and

		Agri-culture	Forestry & Fisheries	Mining	Con-struction	Manu-facturing
1880	South[a] (%)	71.8	0.3	0.4	2.8	4.7
	Non-South (%)	38.5	0.3	2.6	6.9	17.8
	Location Quotient,South	1.45	1.19	0.19	0.50	0.35
1900	South (%)	62.8	0.7	1.2	3.3	7.0
	Non-South (%)	28.4	0.2	3.2	7.5	18.5
	Location Quotient,South	1.59	1.96	0.47	0.54	0.47
1940	South (%)	30.7	0.4	2.9	5.4	16.1
	Non-South (%)	12.3	0.2	1.9	6.0	27.1
	Location Quotient,South	1.72	1.77	1.33	0.93	0.68
1950	South (%)	18.8	0.4	2.7	7.0	18.2
	Non-South (%)	8.7	0.2	1.2	6.2	29.2
	Location Quotient,South	1.61	1.70	1.66	1.09	0.70
1960	South (%)	9.7	0.3	2.0	7.7	22.3
	Non-South	5.6	0.1	0.7	6.2	31.0
	Location Quotient,South	1.42	1.67	1.79	1.16	0.78
1970[b]	South (%)	4.3	0.2	1.4	7.5	23.3
	Non-South (%)	3.2	0.2	0.6	5.7	27.3
	Location Quotient,South	1.22	1.13	1.76	0.89	0.89

Sources: Lee et al. 1957: table L-5; U.S. Bureau of the Census, 1963

[a]Excludes Oklahoma.

[b]Persons not reporting are allocated.

Non-South

Trans- portation	Trade & Finance	Private Household	Other Series Pub.Admin.	Total Employment (thousands)	χ^2
2.7	5.1	7.1	5.2	5,698	
5.8	11.5	6.8	9.9	11,681	28.01(p<.001)
0.56	0.54	1.03	0.62	---	
4.3	7.2	7.1	6.4	9,173	
7.8	15.7	6.8	12.0	19,525	26.96(p<.001)
0.65	0.55	1.03	0.63	---	
5.6	15.8	6.9	16.1	14,421	
7.5	21.9	3.9	19.3	33,703	13.37(p<.10)
0.81	0.79	1.44	0.88	---	
6.8	19.8	4.1	22.2	17,193	
8.1	23.0	1.9	21.5	41,249	8.12(N.S.)
0.88	0.90	1.60	1.02	---	
6.8	22.8	5.1	23.3	18,798	
7.2	23.4	2.3	23.6	46,309	4.59(N.S.)
0.97	0.98	1.64	0.99	---	
6.7	24.3	2.5	29.8	23,627	
6.7	25.3	1.1	29.9	56,099	1.59(N.S.)
1.0	0.97	1.66	1.0	---	

able 259; and U.S. Bureau of the Census, 1973: table 298.

region's percentage share of a particular activity with its percentage share of some basic aggregate" (Isard, 1960:124). Computationally, it is:

$$\frac{S_i/N_i}{S/N} \quad \text{or} \quad \frac{S_i/S}{N_i/N}$$

Where: S_i is the number of workers in a region employed in industry i

S is the total number of workers in the region $(S = \sum\limits_i S_i)$

N_i is the number of workers in the nation employed in industry i

N is the total number of workers in the nation $(N = \sum\limits_i N_i)$.

Thus, location quotients are descriptive indicators of the degree to which industries are concentrated in particular regions. An example of this might be found in the share of the labor force employed in agriculture. From 1880 to 1960, the share of the South's labor force in agriculture declined from 72 to 10 percent, while that for the rest of the nation fell from 40 to 5 percent. Both of these declines are probably attributable to technological changes, such as the mechanization of many agricultural functions. That agriculture remained concentrated in the South is suggested by the equivalence of the location quotient for southern agriculture in 1880 and 1960, with the intervening years showing an increasing concentration of agriculture in the South followed by gradual deconcentration after 1940. By 1970 the concentration of agriculture in the South had fallen even more.[2]

The degree of economic integration between the South and the rest of the nation may be seen by comparing the quotients of 1880 or 1900 with those of 1970. In the beginning of the period, agriculture was heavily concentrated in the South, while secondary (manufacturing) and tertiary (service) activities were heavily concentrated in the non-South. By 1970, apart from employment in private households, the only industry with a remarkable degree of concentration in the South was mining, a sector including petroleum and gas production—as well as the extraction of minerals—which reflects the great concentrations of coal and oil in the region. As of 1970 the South showed levels of employment in the manufacturing and service sectors similar to those of the nation as a whole.

In order to test the significance of differences between distribution of employment by industry, a chi-square test was performed for each census year under consideration. As is shown in table 8.1, the differences between the distributions were highly significant for both 1880 and 1900. Statistical significance was maintained in 1940, but only at the p=.10 level. For 1950–1970 there has been no statistically significant difference in the industrial composition of the South and the non-South. Again, it should be noted that the degree of aggregation for the data in table 8.1 is very high. For example, within the manufacturing sector, the South tends to specialize in resource-intensive activities due to its comparative advantage in both labor costs and resources (Moroney, 1975).

Income
The estimation of income levels and differentials has occupied economists for many years. While numerous problems still exist at the national level, difficulties are even greater at the regional or state level. These are partly due to the relatively large share of goods and services produced in one area and consumed elsewhere and, conversely, to the relatively large share of goods and services consumed in one area and produced elsewhere.

Moreover, analysts of income have developed a myriad of income-related measures, none of which are identical. The best-known measure at the national level is probably gross national product, a measure of the gross value of goods and services produced in the nation during a given period. The subnational analogue, gross state product, does not exist in a uniform measure for all states. These and many similar problems are discussed in Hanna (1957).

Those data which are available at the state level for an extended period of time are limited to basic series: (1) census money income, determined from income-related question(s) in the decennial census of population (also available since 1970 from the census in the so-called "revenue sharing estimates"); and (2) personal income, which has been produced on a regular basis since 1929 by the (now) Bureau of Economic Analysis of the U.S. Department of Commerce. Conceptual differences between these series are relatively minimal. The census series excludes various types of imputed and in-kind income, such as net rental value of owner-occupied homes and net value of food and fuel produced and consumed on farms (Miller, 1966:169–212). The census series goes back only to 1940. In addition, in 1940 individuals who had received more than $5,000 in 1939 were asked only to report that they had received more than that amount (U.S. Bureau of the Census, 1943). Because the B.E.A. series goes back farther and because analogous estimates to 1880 have been made by Lee et al. (1957), this series will provide the basis for the discussion below.

Table 8.2 shows estimated per capita personal income for the South and the balance of the nation for selected years from 1880 to the present. The estimates are not adjusted for temporal fluctuations in the cost of living. Consistent with many of the demographic and economic indicators discussed earlier, the income data reflect a long period after the Civil War of stability in the income of the South relative to the non-South. Per capita income in the South was approximately half that of the remainder of the nation over this period (save 1900, when the industrial Northeast was still feeling the effects of a depression during the middle of the 1890s which did not greatly affect the agrarian South). Since World War II, income in the South has risen dramatically, and by 1975 its per capita income was 86 percent of that of the rest of the nation. This reflects the upgrading in the occupational mix of southern workers into higher paying categories and the consequent increase in the number of the region's workers who are relatively well endowed with human capital. Although partly attributable to differential migration, most of the improvement in the educational attainment of workers in the South Atlantic Division resulted from natural attrition—i.e., the replacement of older workers by younger and better-educated workers over time (Bouvier and Cahill, 1975).

However, these data do not tell the entire story because they assume that cost of living differentials between regions are minimal. There is some evidence to suggest that this is not the case. The consumer price index is routinely gathered for a market basket of goods that might, at some time, be purchased by an urban family. In the fall of 1975, the index for an urban family of four living at an intermediate level was $15,638 for metropolitan areas and $13,886 for nonmetropolitan areas. The average budget level of southern metropolitan areas was $14,584—about 6.5 percent lower than the national level. For nonmetropolitan areas, this budget was $13,253, or about 4.5 percent lower than the national level (U.S. Bureau of Labor Statistics, 1976). The average metropolitan budget for the non-South is approximately 10 percent higher than the corresponding level for the South. Computation for nonmetropolitan urban areas yields a similar figure. Finally, although cost of living data are not gathered in rural areas, it seems probable that the cost of living

TABLE 8.2   Per Capita Personal Income

	South	Non-South	South as % of Non-South
1880[a]	$ 94[c]	$ 214	44
1900[b]	173	216	80
1919-1921[b]	421	762	55
1929	412	823	50
1940	384	686	56
1950	1,129	1,653	68
1960	1,768	2,435	73
1970	3,436	4,219	81
1975	5,299	6,185	86

Source: Lee et al., 1957:table Y-1; and U.S. Department of Commerce, August 1956 and August 1976.

[a]Excludes Oklahoma and District of Columbia.

[b]Excludes District of Columbia.

[c]Current dollars.

in such areas is less than that of urban areas. Because the South remains rural to a greater extent than does the balance of the nation, this would tend to lower the cost of living in the South.

Thus, it is reasonable to assume that the cost of living in the South is about 10 percent lower than that of the remainder of the nation. Bearing this in mind, the level of per capita income in the South, as measured by purchasing power, is perhaps about 95 percent of the level prevailing in the balance of the nation. This difference persists due to differences in racial and rural-urban composition in the South and the non-South. This conclusion is supported by Coelho and Ghali (1971) and by Bellante (1979), who report that the North-South real wage differential is not significantly different from zero.

Thus, in the past few decades, the South has undergone a transformation from a primarily agrarian to a primarily industrial economy. Since 1950 there have been no significant differences in the industrial composition of southern and nonsouthern labor forces. The disappearance of regional economic differences is also quite evident in the rapid gains in relative per capita income in the South. When allowances are made for differences in the cost of living between the South and the balance of the nation, differences in the level of income per person are reduced to near insignificance.

THEORETICAL CONSIDERATIONS

We turn now to issues involving the application of demographic transition theory to southern demographic history. As a field of study, demography tends to weigh heavily toward the empirical vis-à-vis the theoretical (Vance, 1952; Nam, 1979). The absence of "grand" theory in the discipline is symbolized by the recognition that the so-called theory of demographic transition is really a descriptive paradigm of the demographic history of Western Europe and areas of European settlement (United Nations, 1973:60). Credit must go to Thompson (1929) for introduction of the transition concept, while Blacker (1947) modified it into the form in which it is usually found at present. Notestein (1945) is apparently responsible for coining the phrase "demographic transition" and for suggesting that the demographic history of Western Europe might be repeated in presently developing nations.

The theory initially postulates: (1) a condition of fluctuating but high mortality and fertility rates, followed by (2) the decline of mortality, with fertility remaining high (creating the beginning of population expansion). Eventually, (3) birth rates begin to fall, but mortality is lower, so population growth continues. Sooner or later, (4) birth rates fall until a level of approximate equilibrium is reached again and population remains stationary. Blacker identifies a fifth state of low mortality and even lower fertility, where population begins to decline.

At the same time, economic changes were occurring that have been variously described as industrialization, modernization, or economic development. There is incomplete agreement on whether increased population growth enhanced economic development or whether the converse was the case. There is not even complete agreement on whether it was increasing fertility or decreasing mortality that sparked the initial upsurge of population during the industrial revolution (Habakkuk, 1953; McKeown and Brown, 1955). However, there is agreement that the demographic transition is a generalized statement of what did in fact happen in Western Europe, North America, and Oceania (Cowgill, 1962; Satin, 1969). The degree to which this experience can be generalized is questionable. As Teitelbaum (1975) notes:

> . . . a high level of development was ultimately *sufficient* to establish these three preconditions for a decline in marital fertility in Europe. However . . . it is apparent that the preconditions for fertility decline existed under situations of little social and economic development, as in parts of rural France and Hungary (Teitelbaum, 1975:421).

He goes on to note that despite the success of the theory in explaining fertility decline in Latin America

> . . . little success is achieved in predicting the timing of onset and the rate of progress of fertility decline on the basis of transition theory (Teitelbaum, 1975:423; also cf. Beaver, 1975).

Similarly, a recent study by Gregory and Campbell (1976) urges caution in applying the fertility experiences of one set of countries to another. Despite this, the notion of a transition continues to be of great interest to demographers (e.g., Coale, 1975; Morgan et al., 1976; Caldwell, 1976) and seems to appear with great regularity at international population conferences (the so-called development is the best contraceptive argument), despite the fact that modern science can ". . . reduce death rates markedly without a major reorganization of a peasant economy" (Coale and Hoover, 1958:14).

However, the theoretical efforts to explain why demographic behavior changes as it does during the course of modernization are more interesting than efforts to generalize transition theory itself. Fertility and mortality behavior have received a great deal of attention. Easterlin (1975a, 1975b) has reformulated demographic transition theory in light of recent advances in the economic theory of fertility behavior. (See Sanderson, 1976, for a brief account of these developments.) Easterlin presents a series of models using several

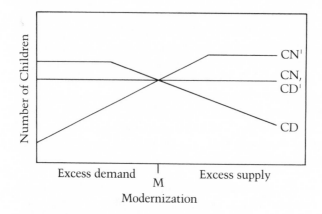

Source: Adapted from Easterlin, 1975a, p. 60
CD,CD¹: Desired number of surviving children in a perfect contraceptive society.
CN,CN¹: Number of surviving children in an unregulated fertility situation.

Figure 8.1. Hypothetical variations in fertility associated with modernization

assumptions which are illustrated in general terms in figure 8.1. Three possible situations are contained in this figure: the first utilizes lines CD¹ and CN¹; the second, lines CN and CD; and the third, lines CN¹ and CD.

In all three situations, the early period (i.e., points close to the Y-Axis) is characterized by an excess demand situation (i.e., CD > CN). As modernization ensues, an equilibrium point, M, is reached (CD = CN); to the right of M, at even higher levels of modernization, an excess supply situation develops (CD < CN). The basic situations differ according to the mechanism which triggers the shift from excess demand to excess supply. In the first case (CD¹, CN¹), demand for children remains constant, while supply increases. This may be attributable to a rise in natural fertility, e.g., through improvements in maternal health. In essence, this represents demographic transition theory in its simplest form. In the second case (CN, CD), the supply, or output, of children remains constant, but demand declines, perhaps due to an increase in the relative cost of children. The final case (CN¹, CD) represents perhaps the most likely case where supply or output increases, while demand decreases.

According to Easterlin, each of these three situations creates an obvious motivation for fertility limitation to the right of M. This is a necessary, but not sufficient condition, however. In an excess supply situation, the actual use of fertility regulation depends upon the costs (market and subjective) of this regulation.

Using the third (CN^1, CD) case as an example, there are three possibilities outlined by Easterlin. At one extreme is the situation when fertility costs are prohibitively high. In this case there is no fertility regulation, and actual fertility behavior is depicted by line CN^1. The perfect contraceptive society where the cost of fertility regulation is zero is at the other extreme. This case is depicted by the line CN^1 from the Y-Axis to its intersection with line CD at M; to the right of M, this case is depicted by the line CD. The final, and most realistic, case is the intermediate one. The most likely course of events has actual fertility following CN^1 for some distance to the right of M (where motivation is still not great enough to offset costs), but then turning sharply downward toward CD as the welfare loss of unwanted children begins to exceed that associated with the costs of fertility control. Thus, this general model covers not only the general transition but also cases where fertility decline preceded mortality decline (Coale, 1969) and others where fertility increased during the early stages of modernization (Sinclair, 1974).

In addition to the traditional definition of the demographic transition in terms of the interaction of fertility and mortality rates with economic change, Zelinsky (1971) has hypothesized the existence of a mobility transition as part of the overall modernization process. Specifically, Zelinsky suggests the following:

> There are definite, patterned regularities in the growth of personal mobility through space-time during recent history, and these regularities comprise an essential component of the modernization process (Zelinsky, 1971:221–222).

Zelinsky goes on to hypothesize that the cause of this mobility transition closely parallels that of the demographic or vital transition. Zelinsky outlines a five-stage theory of the mobility transition which parallels the transition of vital rates. These stages may be summarized as follows: (1) little mobility; (2) massive rural-urban migration, along with movement to "colonization frontiers" and emigration to "available and attractive foreign destinations"; (3) slackening of the above, but increases in circulation and structural complexity; (4) oscillation of residential mobility about a fixed (but high) level, with further reduction in rural-urban flows and emigration, accompanied by considerable interurban migration, and significant immigration from underdeveloped lands. There is also a "vigorous accelerating circulation, particularly the economic and pleasure-oriented." Finally, Zelinsky (5) hypothesizes a decline in residential migration and deceleration in some forms of circulation as communications are improved, with almost all residential mobility becoming intraurban and interurban. There is also the possibility of strict control of internal and international migration on the part of political authorities. Rogers (1978) modifies the final stage somewhat by suggesting that at this point the pattern of residential mobility might become somewhat deconcentrating, with residential moves taking place from larger to smaller places.

Beale (1975) also deals with changing migration patterns as part of the demographic transition. He writes that after fertility and mortality have declined to the low levels Notestein and others have identified as signaling the completion of the demographic transition that

> . . . another aspect of demographic transition may emerge, in which the distribution of population is no longer controlled by an unbridled impetus to urbanization. General affluence, low total population growth, easy transportation and communication, modernization of rural life, and urban population massings so large that they diminish the advantages of urban life—these factors may make a downward shift to smaller communities seem both feasible and desirable (Beale, 1975:14).

In contrast to this social demographic view, most of the economic theory concerning migration deals with the mobility of labor. As Long (1976) points out, many economic models of migration of the total population are flawed by their failure to remove from the migration streams in question such obviously noneconomic migrants as those entering the armed forces and college students. Moreover, as the population ages, a larger portion of total migration will be retirees whose motivation may also be essentially noneconomic (Barsby and Cox, 1975; Heltman, 1975). Although much research focuses upon individual decision making, it is important to remember that some portion of migration results from corporate or governmental decisions regarding the location of some economic activity (Taeuber and Taeuber, 1942; Mickens, 1977; McKay and Whitelaw, 1977; Long and Hansen, 1979).

Much of current migration theory stems from works by Lee (1966) and Sjaastad (1962). Both allow for migration in a personal decision-making context to be influenced by perceived costs and benefits associated with migration. Lee distinguishes between four relevant factors: (1) those associated with the area of origin, (2) those associated with the area of destination, (3) intervening obstacles, and (4) personal factors. Decisions about whether to move and, if so, where result from each individual's own personal calculation of these sets of factors.

Most analyses of the determinants of migration have focused upon the aggregate characteristics of areas or individuals and have not dealt with individual motivations (as an example, see Poston's chapter in this volume). The comparatively few exceptions to this tendency have found that the majority of moves among persons in the labor force occurs at least partially for economic reasons (Butler et al., 1969; Lansing and Mueller, 1967; Long and Hanson, 1979). However, persons not in the labor force are considerably less likely to move for economic reasons. For instance, Lansing and Mueller (1967:60) report that 77 percent of the moves by persons in the labor force are for these reasons, as opposed to only 23 percent of the moves by persons not in the labor force.

Generally speaking, studies in this vein assume an investment or human capital approach (Bodenhofer, 1967; Speare, 1971; Bowles, 1970; David, 1974; and Schwartz, 1976). In general, we would expect migration from low to high income areas and from high to low unemployment areas, but the data do not always support these expectations. Indeed, Greenwood (1974a:411) suggests that "one of the most perplexing problems confronting migration scholars is the lacking of significance of local unemployment rates in explaining migration." This failure may be attributed to specification problems—i.e., simultaneity bias (Greenwood, 1975b)—and to the fact that those who move with new employment already assured are not affected by overall levels of unemployment in the area of destination (Navratil and Doyle, 1977). Fields (1976) reports that a model of labor turnover yields more satisfactory results in explaining migration than does a comparable model using unemployment.

For general purposes, the primary emphasis in this literature is on changes in migration over time as part of a transitional framework and possible changes in the determinants of migration over time. Two of the basic hypotheses advanced by Lee (1966:53–54) are directly relevant to this point: (1) "unless severe checks are imposed, both volume and rate of migration tend to increase with time" and (2) "the volume and rate of migration vary with the state of progress in a country or area."

The first of these hypotheses is based upon a consideration of a variety of factors, such as increasing diversity of areas and people as well as the diminution of the strength of intervening obstacles. Modernization directly enhances this diversity, both on an areal (differential rates of regional growth) and an individual (specialization of labor) basis. Likewise, modernization tends to improve the efficiency and reduce the relative costs of transportation and communication, thus lowering many historical barriers to migration based upon uncertainty or ignorance. Additionally, there is some momentum to migration itself, for a person who has already migrated is more prone than other persons to migrate again (Morrison, 1971).

Lee's second hypothesis follows directly from his first. In some cases the result can be a great deal of gross migration but relatively little net change (Shryock, 1964; Morrison and Relles, 1975). Spengler and Myers (1977) consider migration to be the result of the interplay of centripetal and centrifugal forces. They believe that, over time, the former has exceeded the latter. Hence, population has tended to become more concentrated. They note that

> when there is a range of comparably efficient plant sizes, concern with congestion costs may favor the choice of smaller sizes. Furthermore, miniaturization of optimum plant size . . . could contribute to this result. . . . Increases in output per worker tend to reduce plant size in terms of workers. Increases in the relative importance of services reduces centripetal tendencies. Improvement in means of transportation and communication can have a similar effect. In so far as competition is restrained and larger communities are allowed to exploit smaller communities, removal of constraints upon competition will favor deconcentration of economic activities (Spengler and Myers, 1977:25–26).

In other words, at a relatively late stage in modernization, some movement from larger to smaller areas might be anticipated, a position also assumed by Beale (1975) and Zelinsky (1971). Given the general tendency of average income to be positively associated with size of place, this hypothesis is quite consistent with the statement by Long and Hansen (1977:12) that recent research

". . . seems to suggest that to an increasing degree persons make migration decisions on the basis of factors other than level of income at destination areas." Survey data certainly suggest a residential preference of individuals for smaller places, although close to a larger area (Fuguitt and Zuiches, 1975). However, there is some question of the extent to which persons actually move in response to these desires (DeJong, 1977). That recent population growth in the United States has been concentrated in nonmetropolitan areas is certainly true (Beale, 1976; Fuguitt and Beale, 1976), despite the fact that overall mobility rates have been relatively stable and there is little prospect for appreciable increase in this mobility (Long and Boertlein, 1976:27–30). These factors have also contributed to the changes in patterns of net migration to the South which have been present in the recent decades.

This section has briefly outlined the demographic and economic theory which may explain the very complex interactions of demographic and economic change. Demographic transition is not so much a theory as a descriptive statement of the more or less simultaneous change in economic and demographic variables that have characterized the history of most presently developed nations. The "theory" says nothing about the time of occurrence or duration of change. Perhaps theories of demographic change or response to economic change are fruitful. In a broad sense, as an economy is transformed from an agricultural to an industrial base, fertility generally declines due to increases in the supply of children (i.e., greater probability of survival to adulthood) or decreases in demand (i.e., while children satisfy a variety of needs, their ability to affect economic needs are usually reduced during modernization). Similarly, as economic change transpires in the region at a rate greater than that of another, economic theory postulates that, other things being equal, individuals will move to the faster growing region in order to improve their own well-being.

SYNTHESIS

Our purpose now is to analyze the data on the changed demographic and economic characteristics of the South and of its people in light of the preceding discussion. Specifically, this section will seek to provide answers to the following questions: (1) to what extent have economic change and modernization in the South occurred at a rate different from that experienced by other portions of the country, and (2) to what extent are differences in the demographic behavior of Southerners a result of the relatively late transformation of the South from an agrarian to an industrialized society.

The Tempo of Economic Change

As recently as 1960, Nicholls was able to state:

> The South has been poor for a century. Relative to the rest of the nation, it is still poor today . . . the South has made considerable economic progress, but in doing so it has held with surprising tenacity to traditional values . . . the South has been traditional because it was poor . . . it has also remained poor in part because it was traditional (Nicholls, 1960:87).

Nicholls goes on to cite five major elements of what might be termed "southern tradition" which he feels have seriously hindered the economic development of the region: (1) dominance of agrarian values, (2) rigidity of the social structure, (3) undemocratic political structure, (4) weakness of social responsibility, and (5) conformity of thought and behavior. He posits that these all combined to form an immobile, static, almost caste-ridden society in which upward mobility was possible only through out-migration. Although some elements of southern tradition undoubtedly remain (Reed, 1972), the South is now essentially no different from the remainder of the nation in terms of economic variables such as income and industrial composition of the labor force. See the preceding chapter for further evidence on these points.

From the data presented earlier, there can be no doubt that in the 30–35 years from World War II to the present the South has joined the nation in terms of economic and demographic characteristics. Such a transformation was, in fact, relatively rapid when compared with the remainder of the nation. As noted earlier, the status of the South vis-à-vis other regions of the nation was relatively constant from the end of the Civil War to the onset of World War II. Most changes during this period were due to technological change which did not affect the South to any greater extent than other regions. Since then, regional differences have more or less disappeared.

There exist several theories in economics to "explain" such transformations. One of these is a thesis developed independently by Allen Fisher (1935) and Colin Clark (1940) which has come to be called the Clark-Fisher hypothesis. This theory hypothesizes that increasing per capita income will be accompanied by a decline in the share of resources (labor and nonlabor) employed in primary activities and an increase in the proportion employed in secondary and tertiary activities. The greater the shift in industrial composition, the greater the rate of economic growth. This approach can be questioned on many grounds, including excessive rigidity and its failure in dealing with the causes of economic growth and change (Richardson, 1969). However, it does offer an adequate descriptive tool or transitional model of economic change which reflects the experience of most presently developed countries.

More important for present considerations are the underlying forces which fostered such rapid economic change in the South. The bonds of southern tradition were probably loosened, if not forever shattered, by World War II. For the first time, many rural Southerners had the opportunity to leave their native region. Conversely, many equally parochial non-Southerners experienced their initial exposure to the South.

The rapid change in industrial patterns after the war are the direct consequence of changing patterns of industrial location. A variety of factors exists which influence industrial location: cost of labor, cost of transportation of raw materials and finished products, and tax incentive, to name a few. Fuchs (1962:177) finds that the most important industrial shifts during the twentieth century ". . . occurred in labor-oriented industries such as textiles and apparel, or in industries oriented to natural resources such as chemicals, lumber and paper." In both cases these are areas in which the South may be viewed as holding a comparative advantage over other regions. Thus, Meyer (1963) suggests that a natural conclusion of Fuchs' study is that location decisions are a cause rather than a consequence of population redistribution.

While this conclusion suggests that only low wage industries locate in the South, the rapid closing of regional income differentials makes this a difficult hypothesis to support. Patrick and Ritchey (1974) have demonstrated that deconcentration of economic activity is continuing in the South in about the same pattern as what they term the "Old Manufacturing Belt" (New England, Middle Atlantic, and East North Central census divisions), although differences in the degree of metropolitanization and urbanization cause the South to contain less deconcentrated employment (i.e., central city versus suburb) than the Northeast (see also Kasarda, 1976). Till (1974:309) suggests that, for the nonmetropolitan South at least, the development process is a two-stage one ". . . in which the low-wage, labor intensive firms of the first state prepare a factory-trained labor force which then attracts the relatively higher-wage, more capital intensive firms in the second state." Thus, Wheat (1976:149) finds that within the South places with capital-intensive manufacturing display greater growth than do labor-intensive manufacturing places. Still, nonmanufacturing places grow faster than both, perhaps because ". . . new plants prefer places where they can 'cream' the labor supply, avoid wage competition, and perhaps influence community affairs."

Through the selective exercise of their taxing authority, states are able to reduce or even eliminate the burden of taxation to industry as an incentive for location or relocation. The Advisory Commission on Intergovernmental Relations (1967) identifies six possible tax-related options available to state and local governments to attract industry: (1) property tax exemption for new industry; (2) locally negotiated property tax concessions; (3) "Freeport" laws to minimize personal property tax loads; (4) corporate income tax sales destination apportionment; (5) corporate income tax preferential write-offs; and (6) special sales tax exemptions for new industry. Yet, the commission's findings suggest that despite differences in tax rates among states, and despite the fact that the load of taxation can represent a significant cost of operation, tax incentive schemes play relatively little role in interstate location decisions but a much more important role in intrastate and, especially, intrametropolitan areas. Between distant states, economic (e.g., transport) costs appear to be much more important than tax factors. Between proximate states, the commission was able to find no clear-cut relationship between differential rates of taxation and differential rates of industrial growth. Apparently states have sufficient statutory taxing authority to effectively neutralize any tax differential advantage produced by neighboring states.

Considerations relating to supply of inputs and costs of production (including transportation to markets) underlie industrial location decisions. In addition to labor supply, the relatively abundant natural resource base of the South (fuels, wood, water) provides some incentive for the relocation and creation of certain industrial sectors (e.g., textiles) in the region.

The South has always been a relatively low wage region and interstate tax differentials seem to play only a minor role in decisions affecting the location of industrial activity. Neither of these factors alone can explain the dramatic changes in the industrial composition of the South since World War II. That period has witnessed a variety of closely related phenomena: the use of motor vehicle transportation as the prime mover of American life, population deconcentration, and the rapid relative growth of the South. Trucking has become the primary intercity mover of goods and freight, while automobiles serve the same function for persons (Tobin, 1976). Growth of individual places has been found to be greatly influenced by the proximity of these places to highways, particularly interstate highways (Sturgis, 1973; Wheat, 1976). The South in particular has benefited tremendously from the construction of the interstate highway system. As Barabba notes:

> One of the major reasons for the shift to net in-migration in the South and to net out-migration in the Northeast has been the nation's reliance on truck transportation in recent years instead of rail transportation. This changeover was stimulated by the massive highway construction in the 1950's and 1960's which opened many parts of the South to relatively small manufacturing plants which did not have to rely on rail lines (Barabba, 1975:59).

One might argue that the development of the highway system in its present form greatly affected the timing of industrial shifts toward the South, while the relatively low wages made the South an obvious area of destination. Recent gains in educational attainment of Southerners, particularly the younger workers, add to this attractiveness. Movement toward the South creates its own momentum. Industries related to other industries already relocated in the South have found it advantageous to move, and existing industries have expanded to meet the needs of the new industrial workers.

Demographic Behavior of Southerners in Light of Recent Economic Change

We turn to an examination of the demographic behavior of Southerners and the degree to which it reflects a conscious decision-making process in light of perceived economic and social change. In demographic behavior we include fertility and mobility decisions, but not, in general, mortality (an exception to the latter statement is found in Hamermesh and Soss, 1974). Differences in these variables according to socioeconomic status do exist and, to the extent that the socioeconomic characteristics of Southerners differ from those of non-Southerners, these differences may be important. However, the interest here is with the relationship between changing behavior and changing circumstances.

Fertility. Overall fertility levels in the South are now approximately the same as they are elsewhere in the nation after allowance is made for differing racial composition and degree of urbanization. For black women, fertility is consistently higher among Southerners, although for younger women the margin of excess is only about half as great as the excess in the older age groups. Birth expectation data show that, despite declines over the past decade, the number of lifetime expected births among blacks exceeds that of whites at all ages (U.S. Bureau of the Census, 1976c). Thus, assuming a convergence of actual and expected births, as long as a disproportionately large share of blacks live in the South, the region's overall fertility is likely to remain higher.

With the South now fully integrated into the nation's economy, there is every reason to suppose that the current decline in fertility among Southerners has occurred for precisely the same reason that it has elsewhere. The only real difference between the South and non-South in terms of fertility lies in the higher proportion of nonwhites in the South and, more specifically, the much higher portion of nonwhite Southerners who are rural residents when compared with nonwhite non-Southerners.

Are there differences in the nature of costs and benefits associated with children for rural and urban residences? Theoretically, at least, there are. Phillips et al. (1969:300) suggest that while consumption benefits of children accrue to all, benefits of children as productive assets and as old age security accrue only to rural (specifically, rural-farm) residents. On the other hand, both the actual and opportunity costs of children range from being low for rural-farm residents, intermediate or uncertain for rural nonfarm residents, to high for urban residents. In this context a potentially important finding is that, after accounting for urban-rural residence and income differentials, race ceases to contribute significantly to fertility differences. A lower standard of living thus lowers costs of children, making them more economically viable. However, the more recent findings of Gardner (1972) show statistically significant, but opposite, signs for the nonwhite variable in testing differences in rural-farm and urban fertility levels.

On the other hand, despite the lower cost of living in the South, Espenshade (1977:24) finds that the direct costs of children in the South are higher than those of the entire nation at a moderate standard of living, for rural farm, rural nonfarm, and urban residents, and also higher, at a low standard of living, for farm residents. Hence, the current fertility behavior of Southerners, vis-à-vis non-Southerners, is economically rational from this point of view. Unfortunately, a consistent time series of regional cost differentials is not available, so relationships between relative costs of children and regional fertility differentials over time cannot be evaluated.

Over time, aggregate levels of fertility in the South have reached the levels of the rest of the nation due to (1) reductions in the level of fertility among rural Southerners vis-à-vis those of rural non-Southerners and (2) increasing levels of urbanization in the South. In 1910, the year for which rural-urban fertility data are first available, the rural South had a child-woman ratio of nearly 700 in rural areas, compared with a ratio of slightly more than 500 in rural portions of the predominantly urban non-South. Rural fertility reductions in the South and non-South were very rapid between 1960 and 1970 after little movement (except as a result of low fertility in the 1930s) during the preceding half century. Thus, fertility declines in the South are the result of rapid urbanization in the South since 1950, not the result of any changes in fertility differentials between the South and non-South, when urban-rural distributional differences are held constant.

In 1937 Spengler suggested that as the lag in occupational and rural-urban distribution of the South versus the remainder of the nation was reduced

> . . . and in proportion as urbanization, industrialization, and education spread, there will be a greater frequency of incentive to curtail family size and a greater capacity to effect such curtailment. Southern fertility will approach that observed outside the South in proportion as cultural characteristics associated with low fertility . . . are diffused through the Southern population through improved rural education, improved rural economic conditions, and shifts of the population from rural into non-rural areas and occupations (Spengler, 1937:406–407).

As is reflected in the discussion in the first chapter, this is precisely what has happened, when viewed from the perspective of 40 years of economic change in the South.

Migration. In considering the sudden and dramatic turnaround in migration to the South, it is useful to follow the lead of Long and Hansen (1975), who divide this change into four components. These may be described as follows: (1) increases in in-migration of the nonsouthern born, (2) increases in return migration of persons born in the South, (3) decreases in the out-migration from the South of persons not born there, and (4) decreases in out-migration of the southern born. According to Long and Hansen's calculations, these factors accounted for 27.3, 22.0, 18.4, and 32.1 percent, respectively, of the 650,000-person increase in net in-migration during the interval between 1955–1960 and 1965–1970. Half of the net change, then, is attributable to increased in-migration and half to decreased out-migration.

While a great deal of migration to the South has been of older persons, probably for noneconomic reasons, the patterns of migration among persons of primary labor force age (20–54) have been more important. In 1955–1960 the South experienced a net loss through migration in these age groups of 184,000. In 1965–1970 there was a net gain of 200,000. The only age group in this range with net out-migration between 1965 and 1970 was the 25–29 group. This was caused by departures from the military. Similarly, the disproportionately large net in-migration (100,000 persons) among those aged 20–24 was the result of entry into the military (Long and Hansen, 1975:607).

In a more recent study, Long and Hansen (1977) follow up their earlier work on return migration by studying differing determinants of migration according to whether the individual is leaving place of birth (primary migration), returning to place of birth (return migration), or moving between two other areas (repeat migration). Again, the bulk of their analysis is for 1955–1960 and 1965–1970.

With particular reference to the South, their findings of changes over time and differentials by race are of considerable importance. Although Anne Lee (1974) has found that blacks are less likely than whites to make any of the three types of moves under consideration here, among blacks each type continues to be responsive to differences in income at the areas of origin and destination (i.e., going from low to high income areas) for all types of migration. Among whites this was true only of return migrants. The difference in the importance of income as a determinant of migration by race is summarized by Long and Hansen as follows:

> In the 1965–70 period only 47.1 percent of all whites moving interregionally were going to a region with a higher per capita income than the region they left. But 66.8 percent of blacks moving from

one of the nine regions to another were moving in the direction of higher income (Long and Hansen, 1977:21).

This, of course, reflects the continuing net outflow of blacks from the South during this period. However, since 1970 net out-migration of blacks from the South has fallen close to zero. It would appear that the relative unimportance of income in the migration decision is now becoming a phenomenon of both races.

Using an aggregate income measure as a determinant of migration behavior conceals the fact that an individual's prospects may be totally unrelated to local levels of income and regional differences in costs of living. To determine the degree of success of migration decisions, one needs access to data which trace earnings records of individual migrants over time. One such data source available for this purpose is the Social Security Administration's Continuous Work History Sample (CWHS). In a recent study utilizing these data for the Southeast, Kiker and Traynham (1977) study trends in the level of real earnings for nonmovers, return migrants, and nonreturn migrants during the 1960–1970 period. For males, white and black, increases in income over the period are greater for return migrants than nonmovers but less than that of nonreturn migrants. (For white males only, the level of income of return migrants exceeds that of nonmigrants, and nonreturn migrants have consistently higher income). Looking only at the migrant population, the relative income differences do not develop until after the act of return migration. In other words, their findings do not support the idea that the return migration stream is composed of persons who could not "make it" elsewhere. Increases in income, adjusted for cost of living differentials, would appear to be insufficient to overcome the psychic costs of migration from the region of birth.

Since 1970 two relatively unexpected demographic phenomena have occurred: the movement of population away from large metropolitan areas (Tucker, 1976) and the movement of population to the Sunbelt. These two phenomena are in fact closely related. The South has slightly less than one-third of the entire national population but more than 43 percent of the nonmetropolitan population (and less than 20 percent of the population residing in large—1.5 million or more—metropolitan areas). Thus, the increasing nonmetropolitan redistribution of population at the national level implicitly favors those regions with relatively large nonmetropolitan populations. From 1970 to 1974, the nonmetropolitan population of the South, regardless of size, grew at a greater rate than the metropolitan population, but, within each size category, the southern population grew faster than the corresponding nonsouthern population (U.S. Bureau of the Census, 1976b). Still, the resurgence of nonmetropolitan growth is not exclusively a southern phenomenon.

Between 1970 and 1975, about 4.1 million persons moved to the South from other regions. Total interregional in-migration to all other regions combined was only 1 million persons larger. As shown in table 8.3, three-fourths of migrants to the South came from metropolitan areas, but only 60 percent settled in the metropolitan areas of the South. Relatively fewer (about 70 percent) migrants to other regions were from metropolitan areas (at least partly because this stream includes out-migrants from the South), but substantially more (75 percent) settled in metropolitan areas at their destination.

On balance the South received a net interregional in-migration of 1.8 million persons between 1970 and 1975. In each of the possible origin-destination combinations, net in-migration was the rule. The exception involved a small net out-migration from nonmetropolitan southern areas to central city nonsouthern areas. Of total southern net interregional in-migration, more than half settled in nonmetropolitan portions of the South. Thus, while deconcentration of metropolitan population is a nationwide phenomenon, the South benefits more than other regions from this trend. To a large extent, deconcentration and the emergence of the South as a growth region are two sides of the same coin.

In contrast to our conclusion that changes in the aggregate fertility patterns of Southerners reflected regional urbanization and modernization, the reversal of secular migration trends must be regarded as both a cause and a consequence of this economic change. The basic economic change of the postwar period gradually reduced out-migration and induced in-migration by the provision of more nonagricultural jobs in the South. The presence of these industries ultimately induced the migration of other industries, as well as the creation of some industries in the region. The continued expansion of employment opportunities in the region further reduced out-migration and introduced in-migration so that, at present, a complete reversal for whites and a cessation of net out-migration for nonwhites has evolved. Coupled with this was expanding noneconomic migration for defense or retirement purposes. These also tend to induce further in-migration and reduce

TABLE 8.3   Migration Flows by Metropolitan-Nonmetropolitan
Residence

Origin	Central City	Destination Other Metropolitan	Non- metropolitan	Total
Interregional Migration to South				
Central city	344	564	565	1,473
Other metropolitan	323	746	558	1,627
Nonmetropolitan	221	321	440	982
Total	888	1,631	1,563	4,082
Interregional Migration to Other Regions				
Central city	667	876	373	1,916
Other metropolitan	392	886	367	1,645
Nonmetropolitan	427	590	559	1,576
Total	1,486	2,352	1,299	5,137
Interregional Migration from South				
Central city	267	429	201	897
Other metropolitan	131	280	108	519
Nonmetropolitan	266	275	297	838
Total	664	984	606	2,254
Interregional Migration from Other Regions				
Central city	744	1,011	737	2,492
Other metropolitan	584	1,352	817	2,753
Nonmetropolitan	382	636	702	1,720
Total	1,710	2,999	2,256	6,965
Net Interregional Migration-South				
Central city	77	135	364	576
Other metropolitan	192	466	450	1,108
Nonmetropolitan	-45	46	143	144
Total	224	647	957	1,828

Source: U.S. Bureau of the Census (1975), table 29.

Note: Figures are in thousands of persons.

out-migration by creating employment. A recent study by Pursell (1977) demonstrated that for 1965–1970 the South received a net inflow of human capital in terms of the different age and educational composition of in-migrants vis-à-vis out-migrants. This is likely to be even more pronounced in future periods.

THE FUTURE OF THE SOUTH

Economic trends in the nation during coming years will be shaped by a host of political and social forces. In the long run, two forces are likely to emerge as having the most profound and far-reaching influence. These are the gradual slowing down and possible cessation of national population growth and the increasing cost of energy. Both factors will have profound consequences for the future of the South.

Because of slower growth, the national population will undergo a considerable degree of aging over the coming decades. Although there is the suggestion, based on the Easterlin hypothesis, that fertility in the United States will soon begin to increase, the outlook for the next several decades is for a period of population growth slower than that which has typified recent demographic experience in this country. While these profound demographic changes will influence almost all aspects of the nation's economic structure (Serow and Espenshade, 1978), there are two conditions which should most affect the future of the South. These aspects, which are somewhat interrelated, are shifts in the composition of demand and continuing population redistribution.

One of the consequences of an aging population is a marked decrease in the overall dependency ratio or an increase in the ratio of persons of labor force age to the total population. Unless there is strong impetus to drastic reductions in the age of retirement, a rise in the ratio of the labor force to the population will increase per capita income, under ceteris paribus assumptions, simply because there are proportionately fewer dependents to be supported. This increase in real per capita income will increase discretionary income (that available for expenditures above and beyond necessities) and probably also cause an increased trade-off for leisure relative to work. In turn this suggests a strong increase in demand for travel and other recreational activities. The South, with its generally moderate climate and abundance of recreational resources, should profit considerably from this shift in demand.

Population projections of the distribution of metropolitan area population to the year 2000 show continuing population expansion in the southern region (Pickard, 1972). As Morrison (1972) notes, there is presently great divergence, on a regional basis, in the growth rates of large metropolitan areas. Those regions (the South and the West) with rapidly growing metropolitan centers are favored in terms of future growth in any event, and their relative gain should be even greater in the event of sustained low fertility. As the population ages, it may be anticipated that persons at or near retirement age could constitute a larger portion of the migration stream. In choosing a retirement destination, these persons are apt to respond to stimuli very similar to those mentioned previously regarding the South's comparative advantage in recreational activities. Furthermore, the comparative cost of living values, if present regional differentials are maintained, will add further to the attractiveness of the South as an area of destination for this segment of the population.

Although many persons might find it easy to blame the OPEC cartel for the present high price of energy, simple economic reasoning suggests that if supply is fairly constant (at least in the short run) but demand is increasing at a rapid rate, then the price is very likely to rise. As the search continues for a permanent replacement to the fossil fuel economy of the present, the cost of such fuels will continue to rise. These price increases should greatly benefit the South, for a majority of known reserves of petroleum and natural gas are located in southern states. Most of the coal deposits currently under exploitation are also in the South, although this situation may be expected to change as large-scale extraction from largely underdeveloped reserves in the West come into being (Howard, 1977). For climatic and other reasons, the South, on a per capita basis, consumes less energy than does the remainder of the nation for household purposes (85 million BTUs per year versus 103 million) but consumes more per capita for all purposes—399 million BTUs versus 330 million—due in part to the fact that the production of energy is, in itself, highly consumptive of energy (Hoch, 1977). (Excluding energy production, annual per capita energy use is 252 million BTUs in the South and 238 million in the rest of the nation.) Due to relatively rapid depletion of petroleum and natural gas reserves in the South, Rice (1977) feels that the region's comparative advantage in this sphere is short-lived. Counteracting this, though, is Bohm's (1977) suggestion that recent legislation should enhance the position of the South in reestablishing traditional markets for southern coal and in halting the trend toward western coal. All in all, it seems likely that over the balance of the century the economic position of the South will continue to rise vis-à-vis the remainder of the nation, particularly with respect to the energy-poor Northeast and North Central Regions. It is not implausible, as Miernyk (1976) suggests, that regional economic development policy, which has long favored the South, will shift its emphasis toward these regions. Jusenius and Ledebur (1976) note that such actions would be premature at present.

It is not unreasonable to suppose that by the end of the century the economic position of the South will be at least as good, and probably better, than that of other regions (excluding the West). The availability of relatively inexpensive energy will serve as a further stimulus for the relocation and establishment of economic activity in the region. Ironically, in light of the Clark-Fisher hypothesis, the driving force of this expansion and increase in economic well-being will be in the primary sector.

While the long-term outlook for the South is very good, some economic and social problems do remain. On top of these, new ones (such as the equitable distribution of available energy resources) will come into being. For example, Lockhart (1977) is pessimistic about the probability of significant gains in income redistribution within the region in the near future. The expansion of economic activity there will prove a stimulus for unskilled migrants from the North to come to the South in search of employment. Unless appropriate steps are taken by the end of the century, some parts of the South could find themselves in a position similar to that now faced by large urban areas elsewhere in the nation.

NOTES

1. This definition is employed to insure compatibility of recent with earlier data. Using more conventional denominators yields essentially identical results.
2. It should be noted that labor requirements vary by agricultural commodity and by level of technology. These differences will have some effect upon a region's demand for agricultural labor.

9
A Political Perspective on Population Change in the South

SUSAN E. CLARKE

The common theme of locational advantage unifies macro and micro perspectives on political factors affecting population change and the importance of population changes on political factors in the South. Discussion of the perceived and real effects of federal and state policies on regional structures of locational advantage constitutes a macro approach to questions of allocating locational advantage. A focus on differential perceptions of, and most likely sources of information about, the locational advantage of living and working in the South by those who previously lived there constitutes a micro approach and draws attention to intraregional mobility and return migration in the South. This concept facilitates understanding these interactions without restricting their meaning and incorporates both perspectives on the relationship between demographic and political factors. The following discussion addresses the causes and consequences of changing locational advantage, particularly the political implications of population change.

Locational advantage refers to the costs of access associated with a particular point in space. In its most frequent use as an economic concept, locational advantage is generally determined by the costs of access to markets, resources, labor, and situational factors that influence productivity and profits. These costs are revised as changes occur in technology and communications. For instance, with sophisticated communications technology, the proximity of producers to their markets and subsidiary operations may become less essential and the locational advantages offered by concentrated industrial and commercial areas may diminish.

In addition to market factors, public policies—particularly taxation and zoning policies—are frequently cited as influencing the structure of locational advantages in an area. Indeed, much of the recent Sunbelt/Snowbelt debate centers on the contention that current federal policies enhance the locational advantage of the South to the detriment of the North.

However, the concept of locational advantage has a broader scope than merely expressing the comparative economic worth of real property. Spatial arrangements also structure access to desired societal goals. Because spatial arrangements are differentially advantageous, the process of allocating locational advantage is a critical social and political issue. In the United States, economic market mechanisms—expressed as private investment decisions—are the primary means of allocating locational advantage. Although not intrinsically linked, this process of distribution can distort the allocation of other basic societally valued items, such as education and environmental quality. Therefore, questions of spatial patterns are often also questions of spatial equity and justice.

Recent population changes in the South reflect the enhancement of the locational advantages offered by the region as a whole and revisions by both firms and individuals in estimates of the advantages of living and working in the South. While the economic objective in calculating costs of access is to determine the location that offers greatest access at least cost, social and political objectives may differ. For example, cultural and family links with an area may be a primary determinant of its locational advantage for those who emigrated in an earlier period. The political significance of return migration is considered below in comparisons of political cultures among migrant cohorts.

Whatever the factors involved in calculations of locational advantage, the policy response to the resulting population change in many areas has been expressed through a spatial strategy: state growth management policies. The adoption of state growth management policies signals a different explicit state government role in the allocation of locational advantage. What characteristics of the situation encourage policymakers to seek a spatial strategy? (For discussion, see Williams, 1977.) The following discussion contends that not only is there a political economy of growth but a political economy supporting growth management policies as well. Furthermore, while the politics of locational advantage affect immediate access to socially valued goals, they also structure future political environments. The components of southern population change and the policy responses to population changes in the South, therefore, may presage new spatial and social politics.

PUBLIC POLICY AND POPULATION CHANGE: THE NATIONAL CONTEXT

Recent media and congressional debates over Sunbelt/Snowbelt disparities in federal outlays have renewed interest in the influence of political factors on regional locational advantage. However, determining whether direct relationships exist between political factors and policies and population change (much less whether specific policies do lead to population change) is a complex undertaking. A brief review of some of the arguments and assumptions involved in this relationship precedes a fuller discussion of the political impact of population change.

American political history is replete with areal competition for governmental assistance in providing infrastructure—railroads, waterways, communications—that would improve areas' locational advantage. But, in the absence of comprehensive systematic policy efforts to redirect explicitly the location of economic activity or populations, the notion of politics as a direct causal factor in population change remains untested. At best we have research indicating some association between population change and public policies with "unintended" demographic consequences, such as migration streams and levels of welfare benefits, urban dispersion and federal highway systems, and the like.

In the United States, there have been numerous public policies designed to stimulate development of physical infrastructure for national expansion and regional development. These programs of public works projects are characteristically distributive in nature, with divisible benefits and invisible costs (Lowi, 1970). As such, they provide multiple political resources to politicians but not necessarily the multiplier effects essential for development. Conflicts over distributional policies often concern the definition of appropriate distributive criteria, but the selection of these criteria varies by issue and over time. Distributive criteria frequently serve as the basis for distinguishing among "good" and "poor" policies. The distribution of resources in an efficient economical manner is identified as "good" policy, whereas inefficient distribution in which the costs outweigh the benefits is "poor" policy and is often attributed to what is called pork barrel politics. While these are not the only relevant criteria for evaluating the merits of public policies, they are salient in evaluating development policies and central to the Sunbelt/Snowbelt controversies.

In the Sunbelt/Snowbelt debate it is charged that the South is receiving aid on an asymmetrical basis when the need no longer exists. Furthermore, the existing geographical distribution of federal program benefits is described as inefficient, inequitable, and detrimental to the demand for assistance elsewhere. Consequently, northeastern regional advocates argue that the need for projects to provide the infrastructure essential to the development of primarily agricultural regions no longer exists in the South. Inequities in development programs and in defense expenditures are purportedly sustained because of the historical congressional strength of the South in these policy areas. When the distributional attributes of current federal fiscal policies are examined, there are clear imbalances among regions, although both Sunbelt and Snowbelt regions are receiving per capita payments below the national average. When the South as a region is compared with the Northern Industrial Tier, it appears that there is greater per capita spending in the South than in the North. But this is not so on a program level or on a systematic basis. Moreover, variations within regions are as substantial as differences between the two regions (Jusenius and Ledebur, 1976:29).

With major physical infrastructure now in place, contemporary political debate centers on whether such distributive policies should continue to be defined in terms of regional development or should be reoriented toward infrastructure rehabilitation. Congress is the primary forum for this debate, and the structure of this policymaking body influences the distribution, as well as type, of programs adopted.

Federal Political Factors Influencing Population Change
Before the political reforms of the 1960s, congressional seniority advantages accruing to one-party states allowed dominance of some congressional committees by southern congressmen. The low degree of interparty competition in the South insured the continued reelection of many southern congressmen and control of important congressional committees for significant portions of the postwar decade. Whether this dominance led directly to greater outlays of discretionary funds to the South, particularly public works projects and contracts, is not easily traced, although there is widespread assumption that this is so. Construction of summary accounts of the outlays generated by congressional committees, and determination thereby of the relationship between patterns of influence and benefits, is hindered by the unbounded nature of the

decision-making process and the divisible nature of the benefits themselves. Public works benefits are divisible in that they can be allocated independently of each other and are imprecise in that some, like contracts, lead to further subcontracts and fragmentation on a nonjurisdictional basis.

In a major empirical examination of pork barrel politics, John Ferejohn (1974) urges that features of Congress—geographic representation, majority rule, and committee systems—combine to structure, indeed, almost guarantee, inefficient policies and geographically inequitable distribution of divisible benefits. In his analysis of congressional Public Works Committee decisions on Corps of Engineers projects, Ferejohn found that committee and subcommittee members, particularly the leadership, were able to direct more new projects to their states than were nonleaders and noncommittee members (Ferejohn, 1974:234). Furthermore, Democratic states profited more than Republican states in appropriations subcommittees. On both counts, Democratic party strength and committee leadership, the South has held significant advantages since World War II. But Ferejohn contends that pork barrel politics are engendered not by situations, such as the overrepresentation of the South in these strategic positions, but by the functioning of "relative vetoes" in a decision-making system of committees dominated by representatives of "high-demand" districts. The "relative vetoes" encourage logrolling techniques because committee chairmen hold more resources, including veto power, over legislation in their domains. Even though dominant on committees, representatives of districts with a special need for particular projects must enter into coalitions with members from other districts who put lower priorities on those benefits. In most cases formations of coalitions are unstable and thus the directions of outlays vary. However, historically in the South, there have been relatively constant structural coalitions of incumbent Democratic congressmen and relatively constant veto structures centered on civil rights. Thus, the relationship between patterns of influence and patterns of benefits existed at the state level for southern congressmen and was the basis for working relationships among policy areas. More recently, reforms in congressional procedures have weakened the connection between seniority and committee leadership effectively utilized by southern congressmen. Also, southern coalitions and veto structures have been weakened by increased party competition and increased black voter turnout in many areas of the South. Finally, the passage of civil rights legislation has unraveled the threads of regional coalition; just as the capacity to threaten vetoes has diminished, the coherent need to do so has also diminished.

While continued southern congressional dominance is challenged by these reforms, the structural features engendering distributive locational policies persist and shape the contradictions in contemporary policies. There is a political logic to the attention given to internal improvements projects, but there are nevertheless serious questions about the capacity of federal programs to induce directly or alter geographic patterns of economic growth. Federal government activities have influenced the size, location, and composition of the American population since the first settlements, but primarily as "unintended" growth policies. Most policies and programs have been adopted with little attention to their impacts on the size and location of settlements or distribution of economic activity. If congressional behavior is motivated by an effort to maximize expenditures in one's state, given the institutional features of Congress—relative vetoes and policymaking by committee systems—it is not surprising that regional development policies are fragmented and contradictory. The territorial basis of American politics is institutionalized in a Congress based on geographical representation.

With a political system organized on the basis of geographical representation, most problems are solved, if not defined, in specific spatial contexts. Thus, congressional structure affects the type of programs adopted as well as their distribution. Even when recognizing that the problems involve human resources, such as education and health, whose scope does not coincide with political boundaries, the allocation formulas for assisting people are primarily defined in terms of place. Thus, programs to counter unemployment are territorially static, but labor markets are mobile and economic markets are interdependent. The continuing tension between people-oriented and place-oriented development programs is likely to persist as long as these programs are divisible and distributional, designed by congressmen interested in maximizing outlays for their state or district and needing to create a minimum winning coalition among their colleagues to do so. However, the shape of the pork barrel may change as congressmen become aware of the portents of population changes and demand adjustments in distribution formulas that benefit their area.

An example of the formula changes that southern legislators claim northern congressmen advocate to the detriment of the

South is the effort to circumvent the impact of the inverse per capita formula through inclusion of an "age of housing" indicator in formula allocating Community Development Block Grants. Discriminatory program legislation claims are exemplified by HR 76, the National Employment Priorities Act, which would impose penalties on companies which relocate without an extensive prenotification process beginning two years before the actual move (Southern Growth Policies Board, 1978). But these debates are primarily over changes in the shape of the barrel, not over redefining concepts of development policies. To do the latter would mean a different kind of politics, a national politics centered on the distribution of benefits such as skills training and income to people regardless of location.

Public works projects and manpower programs, two major federal program areas aimed at influencing economic development, illustrate the contradictions in development policy formulation. Both involve discretionary programs and payments amenable to the political process and suitable to justification as "response to need." The Public Works and Economic Development Act of 1965 is an example of ambivalent policy efforts to alleviate people and place symptoms of distress. The act was designed to foster economic development in depressed areas and to reduce unemployment. Connecting these two goals effectively has been stymied by ignoring their interdependence. The continuing debate on whether to use public works and public employment as a countercyclical device or as a means to support permanent new jobs creates ambiguity. Friedlander argues that the link between public works and employment programs is attenuated when no job creation programs are integrated into the design. Politically, a multiplicity of small projects with high numbers of new starts enhance a congressman's resources and prestige. But the likelihood of such projects supplying sufficient multiplier effects or leverages to effect any significant economic development through attracting further investment may be slim.

If public works legislation illustrates the problems associated with federal spatially oriented regional development programs, federal manpower programs such as the CETA Act of 1973 exemplify the difficulty attendant to people-oriented regional development programs. Manpower policies are oriented toward increasing opportunities for disadvantaged workers and facilitating labor market mobility, but the programs are defined and administered in jurisdictional terms that frequently have little to do with labor markets or economic areas. The 1973 CETA program exacerbates this fault by extending the general revenue sharing concept to the manpower policy area and shifting manpower responsibilities and funds to local governments. Apparently this was done in hopes that local government would be more attuned to local employment conditions. But defining the labor market in even more discrete, segmented spatial terms makes it even less likely that programs can be responsive to population changes, much less modify or channel them. Furthermore, by ignoring the demand side of the labor market, there is little chance of confronting structural, hard-core unemployment stemming from sectoral transformations. This epitomizes the weakness of current federal development activities in influencing population changes. Those programs designed to enhance capital investment opportunities in economically distressed areas fail to account for the linkup with human resources development, and those designed to enhance the role of labor in economic development concentrate primarily on the supply of the labor market, thus obviating the chance of using labor development as a means of confronting structural unemployment. In consequence, programs designed to correct market externalities have often become the target for disquiet about regional disparities in benefits.

The degree to which the relative growth and decline in regions is transitory and cyclical or indicative of fundamental change in long-term growth prospects is undetermined. If such change is cyclical, then tampering with allocation formulas and program benefits could be detrimental. However, if it is indicative of basic change, then coping with economic transformations will require more than altering the shape of the pork barrel.

PUBLIC POLICY AND POPULATION CHANGE: THE STATE CONTEXT

Growth management policies are analyzed here as one type of programmatic response at the state level to population change. Enactment of such programs is seen as a response to current growth pressures and as a means of structuring future political environments. This section contends that state growth management policies have dual impacts: (1) certain aspects of locational advantage processes are shifted to the public sector and (2) relocated political constituencies are reintegrated into an increasingly diffuse urban and political system through policies defining changes in existing spatial access arrangements as possible primarily through litigation and administrative decision. This is not necessarily to denigrate such a shift. Indeed, some social scientists (see Lowi, 1969) argue that establishing explicit decision rules and structures serves justice more than leaving critical decisions to the interplay of interest groups. However, this perspective on growth management policies does clarify the political economy dimension of this policy area, particularly the salience of who-where relationships and their political consequences (Williams, 1977).

In guiding and responding to economic growth, politicians are in a bargaining context yet enveloped in an atmosphere of uncertainty (see Moran, 1974). Industry has the resources governmental units need for development. For both local and state government officials hoping to develop their resource base, the initial lack of operating and management skills and the uncertainty regarding the comparative advantage of the area give industries an early bargaining advantage. Dealing from uncertainty and impoverishment, governments frequently establish concessionary policies to attract and compete for industries. State economic development activities, often more appropriately described as industrial development activities, frequently rely on subsidies, such as tax exemptions and accelerated depreciation rates, to influence locational choices by reducing the costs of a firm's capital investment. State and industry then become involved in a continuing tension to determine the most advantageous trade-off of state revenue and expenditure resources and industrial development needs. In a prescient analysis, Vance described these subsidy policies in the South as "neo-mercantilism of the most local dimension" (Vance, 1935:487).

The balance of power, however, can potentially shift over time as the state begins to develop its resource base and to reduce uncertainty surrounding this economic sphere and as industries develop sunk costs in particular locations. Thus, states may begin to develop a more effective bargaining role in spatial allocation processes which determine locational advantage and thereby begin to guide future population and economic growth. If industrial development policies exemplify policy efforts to improve market operations, the adoption of growth management policies can be described as sequential policy adjustment (Heclo, 1974) in which nonmarket conditions are imposed on market transactions in order to influence the quality and distributional characteristics of growth patterns and processes. Again, rather than relegate southern growth processes to "the Southern birth rate and Southern re-

altors" (1935:510), Vance ardently advocated "social mastery of regional resources and processes" (1935:491) and argued for "wise
planning" that would anticipate, rather than merely react to,
growth trends and lead to orderly development of the region. A programmatic response to population change and economic growth is
problematic; this section reports descriptive findings of research
on the incidence of adoption of state growth management policies
in the South.

Since states vary in the components of growth and decline that
they confront, to identify a particular program as "the" innovative
or "best" policy approach in order to measure state growth management policies would not accurately reflect the nature of the policy area nor the policy situation with which states must contend.
Thus, an index of adopted state programs was developed, reflecting
five dimensions that would be present in a comprehensive growth
management policy enhancing a state's capacity to intervene in locational advantage allocation processes. These five dimensions of
state growth management capacity are: environmental management, locational controls, economic development, labor force
development, and community development. Within these five
dimensions, programs are identified as enhancing state growth
management capacity if they have the potential to be locationally
selective in their benefits, to anticipate and protect against market
externalities, to represent extralocal concerns in spatial allocation
processes, to impose nonmarket conditions for targeted population
groups and areas, to strengthen and incorporate the capacity to
guide future desired growth and development, and/or to rationalize
and coordinate state growth processes and patterns. The programs
meeting these criteria and constituting the index of state growth
management are:

Environmental Management
1. Critical environmental areas programs
2. State program for control of power plant siting
3. State program for regulation of indirect sources of pollution
Locational Controls
1. State program for control of large-scale development
2. Statewide comprehensive land-use permit program
3. State program to control development of open spaces
Economic Development
1. State loan guarantee program for building and equipment
2. State program establishing office/division to promote international investment

3. State program to promote research and development
Labor Force Development
1. State program for technical training for hard-core unemployed
2. State program of incentives to industry for locating in areas of high unemployment
3. Manpower development established as policy goal in state budget
Community Development
1. State program of funds for city/county development-related public works
2. State program of funds for city/county master planning
3. State program of mandatory local growth management

Although the lack of reliable sampling methods for selecting a representative set of programs as the basis for analysis deters broad generalizations regarding policy innovations (Walker, 1973), these criteria and programs reflect the policy options and concerns dominant in the literature, as well as programs available and actually adopted in several states.

Each *program* component of the five *dimensions* comprising the additive policy *index* is measured by a dichotomy: the state receives 1 if it has such a program, 0 if it does not; thus, a total score of 15 is possible. To determine which states are adopting and experimenting with less tried programs, a weighted score is used. Programs were arrayed according to their total percentages of adoptions in all fifty states in 1975, and weights were assigned inversely, based on their rank order; i.e., the most adopted program received a weight of 1, the least adopted program received the highest weight of 13. Since adoption of programs which suggest that new definitions of "problems" and "solutions" are being employed is of interest here, the weighted composite score is used throughout (see table 9.1).

Table 9.1 describes the rankings of southern states on growth management innovations compared to all states and compared to rankings on Walker's measure of generalized policy innovation (1969). Florida is both a regional and a national leader in growth management innovation. North Carolina ranks above the national weighted median, but all other southern states are substantially below. According to the Walker scores measuring policy innovation leadership across several policy areas, a quite different ranking might have been expected. In the South, Virginia, Louisiana, and North Carolina have the strongest record of generalized policy innovation, but only North Carolina is a growth management inno-

TABLE 9.1 State Rankings on Growth Management Adoption

State	Rank in the South by Weighted Growth Score	National Rank in Growth Management (Ranks = 1-36)	Rank on Walker's Policy Innovation Score (Ranks = 1-46)
Florida	1	2	30
North Carolina	2	10	23
Tennessee	3	22	32
Virginia	4	24	20
Arkansas	5	25	31
Alabama	6	26	29
Georgia	6	26	35
South Carolina	7	27	43
Mississippi	8	33	46
Texas	8	33	42
Louisiana	9	34	18

vation leader. Use of composite policy innovation scores is sometimes criticized (Gray, 1973) as concealing the range of innovations across issue area and this appears to be the case for growth management. Innovativeness by southern states may be issue specific, and the "social mastery" Vance advocated confined to a few states such as Florida, ranked by Vance (1935) as the most enlightened of southern states.

State growth management policies suggest further attention to politicization of the processes allocating locational advantage within the state and thus have political consequences if not explicit political objectives. Recognizing the political biases reflected in, and often determining, who lives where is not a novel analytical approach but such policies have been adopted in the past primarily to isolate and constrain minorities such as Indians, Orientals, and blacks. In a time of significant population redistribution, they may well be serving an integrative function, explicitly or implicitly, for the tremendous number of relocated citizenry. Piven and Cloward (1971) hypothesized that the War on Poverty programs served as a means to politically integrate the thousands of newly arrived black southern immigrants to northern cities and the Democratic party. Similarly, growth management policies may serve to reintegrate return migrants and primary migrants by insuring the current arrangement of spatial advantage. Growth management policies may incorporate valued goals and objectives, but, as the means by which governments define a new policy arena and a more directive and regulatory policy mode, they also engender a new politics of locational advantage.

POPULATION CHANGE AND POLITICS

In this section it is contended that both policy and theory are hampered by a lag between morphological paradigms—political and academic—and contemporary ecological phenomena. Transformations in social and economic structures have changed the social and political meanings of conventional analytic indicators of settlement patterns and economic activity. The following sections illustrate some disjunctures btween conventional assumptions about the relationship of population changes and political factors and contemporary developments through analysis of new political participants in the South today. Contemporary population trends render the analytic linkages between environmental characteristics and political behavior ever less distinct and challenge the present utility of the concept of culture which serves so often as the analytical link between environment and individual. The materials presented here suggest a paradox: as objective indicators of economic and social conditions in the South converge with those of the rest of the United States, indicating that the South is becoming similar to the rest of the United States and seemingly less distinct as a regional and cultural entity, the character of the population changes accompanying this convergence may be reinforcing, at least initially, the distinctive political culture of the region. Just as the convergence of objective indicators challenges a continued focus on topics such as "demography in the South," a closer look at the characteristics of the inhabitants of the New South suggests reasons for continuing to do so.

Models of Population Change and Political Behavior
The expectation that population changes lead to political change is the basis for many social science models. For example, Wirth (1938) posited that the increasing size, density, and heterogeneity characterizing urban areas would force a more instrumental mode of social and political relationships. In urban areas such status attributes as ethnicity and family rank would become less important determinants of mobility and rewards. Economic factors, including political appeals to economically defined coalitions, would become more salient determinants of political behavior. No doubt many of these processes functioned as described in the Wirthian model, but, even if the relationship between form and behavior that Wirth described was isomorphic with earlier experience, the description is time-bound and culture-bound. Contemporary patterns of urbanization and industrialization differ significantly from historical forms. The political implications of these changes are important not because form and behavior have a deterministic relationship but because reversals of earlier population trends and transformations of economic activities lead to an evaluation of existing models and a redefinition of territorially based politics and policies. For example, urban analysis models focused on the conversion of nonurbanites to urban citizens (Williams, 1978) lose their explanatory power both in urbanized societies characterized by nonmetropolitan growth and in areas experiencing return migration such as the postwar South.

In considering contemporary settlement patterns, deconcentration of both industry and population is contributing to nonmetropolitan growth trends. Technological developments in transportation and communications are key factors in the deconcentration of industry. Extractive and manufacturing activities dependent on certain primary materials are still bound to particular sites, but the administrative and marketing divisions of even those sectors are becoming increasingly flexible in their location. With the expansion of private transport, labor-intensive industries need not locate near concentrations of labor supplies. Capital-intensive industries are relatively free to locate at their discretion, and service industries and activities generally develop where substantial economic activity can sustain them. Furthermore, public opinion polls repeatedly reveal a preference among most Americans for smaller urban areas (Zuiches and Fuguitt, 1976). Given the deconcentration of industry in the last 20 years, the deconcentration of population initially described as suburbanization has increased.

Current trends are partially an elaboration of suburbanization but are best described by a distinctive concept. Suburbanization becomes most visible and amenable to measurement when occurring citywide and most politically salient when crossing jurisdictional boundaries. As suburbanization occurs, people locate farther and farther from central city areas. Some cities, such as Houston, extend their boundaries to incorporate this emerging settlement pattern. In areas where this is less feasible, structural reforms are frequently advocated. However, the full impact of population dispersion is often obscured by continued in-migration to central city areas. The scale of this deconcentration was also masked by jurisdictional boundaries and statistical artifacts until the early 1970s but is now evident in many areas of the United States and within the smallest areal units (Berry and Dahmann, 1977). Berry (1976) describes this trend as "counterurbanization," which refers to a spatial configuration that reverses centralizing trends. The decreased dominance of manufacturing and heavy industry and the decreased reliance, within these sectors, on fixed locations has coincided in some areas with counterurbanization of population. Suburbanization begins to resemble counterurbanization when deconcentration—decreasing density, decreasing size, decreasing heterogeneity in urban areas—accompanies growth in nonmetropolitan areas. As an analytical concept, counterurbanization is most salient when used to clarify the political tensions aroused by concurrent intraregional growth and decline. The political pressures and tensions created by counterurbanization processes are separate from those caused by regional imbalances in economic growth yet are often confused in both politics and policies.

The southern experience offers a provocative example of the political complexities of this demographic shift and the need for a concept that will accommodate its distinctive characteristics. Counterurbanization trends were evolving as southern economic development increased, but, what the Northeast is so painfully achieving through economic and social displacement, the South enjoys as bittersweet historical privilege (see Vance, 1935:407). Earlier modernization of agricultural processes in the South displaced thousands of Southerners to more prosperous northern and midwestern cities. In the midst of these push-pull forces stimulating out-migration by whites and blacks, southern urbanization began to increase. Although southern cities increased in size, they did not always increase as significantly in density and heterogeneity as older American cities did. In part this was due to differences in industrial processes and developments, in part to the historical pattern of dispersed urbanization in the South reflecting the historical economic functions of southern cities as trading centers in an agricultural region. This network of small cities with a few major regional markets such as Atlanta and industrial centers such as Birmingham has been embellished rather than transformed by recent economic growth. In developing later than other regions in the United States, the South is sharing in a different form and stage of national economic growth. If the South inherited this settlement pattern characteristic of counterurbanization— deconcentrated, dispersed population clusters—and is experiencing industrialization and postindustrialization simultaneously (Thompson, 1975), the environment differs substantially from that described in earlier ecological models. The relationship of environment to political behavior becomes even murkier. If one assumes some sort of problematic relationship between form and behavior, the form itself is no longer familiar and the predictability of behavior even less so.

In Wirth's model, urbanization facilitated social change and instrumental politics. The implication was that the more an area approximated Wirth's model (i.e., became industrialized and urbanized), the less salient nonrational factors such as race would become as elements influencing political participation. Anticipation that southern industrialization and urbanization would stimulate attitudinal changes and more rational politics based on economic interests rather than racial distinctions is grounded in these earlier interpretations of American urban experiences. In the traditional "urbanism" perspective described above, scores of diverse migrants became Americanized and urbanized through a process of economic and social accommodation and rationalization of intergroup relations in the city. However, especially in the South, the political significance of urbanization and economic development for black political participation historically has been vitiated by segregationist policies obstructing black mobility and political organization. Now, with dispersed settlement patterns and less labor-intensive industry, it is necessary to reconsider the political meaning of contemporary urban morphology. For example, what are the political consequences of counterurbanization and what are the agents of change and politicization in counterurbanizing postindustrial societies?

Suburbanization Models. Models of suburbanization and of political culture offer some guidance in assessing the political impacts of these population trends, but their limited utility in analyzing the political impacts of population change in the South accentuates the need for further development of both models to accommodate contemporary phenomena. Many parallels exist between early suburbanization stereotypes and stereotypes of the New South. For example, in both cases assumptions about the monolithic nature of newcomers, as well as their host communities, frequently precluded analysis of the variations in interactions. Both suburbanization and southern development were assumed to connote social mobility for participants and concomitant changes in political identification and behavior. As in many urbanization studies, ecological and sociological phenomena were confounded in early suburbanization studies, and they threaten to become so with analyses of recent settlement patterns.

Suburbanization coincided with the Eisenhower years; southern population growth has coincided with the Wallace years and disenchantment with the Democratic party's support of civil rights legislation. In the former case, this frequently led to identification of suburbs as Republican strongholds; in the latter case, it has been equated with entrenchment of the Republican party in the South and greater interparty competition. Several earlier analysts explained these apparent political changes brought about by a change in place in terms of *conversion*: migrants to the suburbs connoted their upward mobility by switching party loyalties and voting Republican. The assumption of transient party identification in this thesis of suburban Republican voting was challenged by arguments that suburban newcomers brought their political affiliations with them. These *transplanted* Republicans or Democrats "colored" the migration stream according to the order of their arrival. Initially, when mainly upper- and upper-middle-class citizens could afford to distance themselves from the trials of urban life, suburbs were perceived as Republican enclaves. As middle- and working-class households gained the opportunity to suburbanize, images of suburbia became more diversified (Wirt, 1965).

Parallel analyses of southern development are complicated by the fact that the southern migrant stream is composed of return migrants, most likely southern Democrats, as well as those most able to relocate, who initially may well be Republican. At this point the utility of the conversion and transplantation models wanes, and a variable must be taken into account that is peculiar perhaps to the South in its intensity but germane to all analyses of return migration—the significance of cultural ties including early political socialization in a distinctive regional political culture. It is proposed here that migration to the South may not have the same political impact as primary migration elsewhere because significant proportions of the migrant stream are return migrants who remain "captive" to their culture. In this sense return migrants are captured by their political culture through early political socialization. These political values, attachments, and associations are not easily dislodged, and return migrants may not be all that dissimilar to residents of the home state in their group identity, although this may well vary by race. Thus, the political significance of return migration is not due to the high proportion of return migrants in the migrant stream. Indeed, return migration of whites actually ranked third as a factor accounting for the reversal of the South's protracted pattern of net out-migration, which occurred during the period to be discussed here, although no other single factor offered significant explanatory power (Long, 1975). Rather, the significance of return migration is in its potential modification of the political impact of these population changes. If return migrants are similar in values and attitudes to natives, this common group consciousness and group identity may make return migrants less likely to be agents of unusual political change. On the other hand, even if dissimilar to natives politically, return migrants may have greater impact than natives or nonsouthern migrants because they understand and can manipulate political culture links even if no longer captured by them.

The politically salient phenomenon described here as being "captured by the culture" parallels the concept of location-specific capital. In their analyses of return migration, DaVanzo and Morrison (1978) describe the diverse "ties" to a particular place—real estate, kinship ties, job seniority—which influence migrants' propensity to return to former residences as location-specific capital. They predict that this propensity to return is affected by the migration interval due to the depreciation of location-specific capital over time. The content and value of location-specific capital varies by individual, and, it is argued here, its depreciation may vary by subculture as well. The term "captured by the culture" implies that location-specific capital in relatively homogeneous areas like the South may be particularly persistent and have significant political connotations. Location-specific capital emphasizes the likelihood of return migration, while a focus on political culture directs attention to the political impact of that return migration on the host community.

Political Culture Models. The concept of political culture is appropriate for analysis of the effects of population change but has limited utility due to its imprecise definition and methodological complexity. As defined by political scientists, the concept refers to "patterns of orientation to political actions" (Almond, 1956; Elazar 1970). Whether these patterns are attributes of the political system or of individual citizens is often unspecified or inconsistent. Clearly the concept offers a link between micro and macro units of analysis, but such linkages are often susceptible to fallacies of extrapolation and personification. Since the political orientations of natives and migrants to the South are compared below as indicators of differing political cultures, critiques of the concept are addressed in some detail.

To resolve some of the conceptual difficulties, Pye (1972) suggests a focus on those orientations that are likely to be operant given distinctive performance characteristics of a political system. To a certain extent, this is the approach adopted by some political scientists attempting to account for variation in state political characteristics. Although these analyses are clouded by definitional difficulties mentioned above, there is evidence from a variety of studies that political culture is not a residual variable but a factor whose effect on state political life is independent of socioeconomic characteristics (Elazar, 1970; Sharkansky, 1969; Johnson, 1976; Clynch, 1972). This relationship is especially visible with political behavior characteristics, less so with output measures.

While the notion is increasingly accepted that political culture has a direct and independent effect on politics, attempts to distinguish among political cultures of aggregate units—either spatial or social—on the basis of differences in quantitative measures of attitudes and opinions creates further questions. In addition to the complex relationship between individual attitudes and behavior which continues to be a matter of concern in more aggregate units, there are uncertainties as to the most meaningful indicators of political cultures of groups and areas and the appropriate measures of their differences. The empirical referents adopted differ, but most center on Elazar's identification of moralistic, traditionalistic, and individualistic political cultures (Elazar, 1970). There appears to be some degree of internal validity and reliability to these categorizations, but, as Pye notes, major differences occur in determining questions of degree of differences. In describing single cultures, the capacity to identify necessary but not sufficient conditions limits the possibilities for testing hypotheses on the systemic impacts of political culture factors. The same question of degree pertains to comparisons of political cultures of different areas and groups. If one attempts to account for the intermingling of political cultures empirically, the questions of level of significance for percentage differences within and among groups become complex (Pye, 1972).

Many of these methodological issues stem from conceptual confusion that is especially visible when aggregate units and comparisons are involved. Political culture is a static concept. As Sopher (1972) points out, cultural characteristics are generally attributed to groups or to areas in terms of the characteristics of groups located there. In order to do so, there must be a formal assumption of stability, although it is obvious that groups are not monolithic and that their occupancy is relatively transient and shared. Some assumption of stability is essential heuristically, but, when both an area and a population are classified in cultural terms, the assumptions of stability become an obstacle to analysis of population change. Although we assume that different ideas and attitudes about politics held by migrants and nonmigrants are among the political impacts of population change, the concept of political culture does not suggest any dynamics by which spatial ordering of political culture shifts and changes.

This assumption of stability, however, can be reversed and presented as a question of the conditions in which cultures and culture areas appear to be stable (see Sopher, 1972). Thus, one factor in the potentially continued stability of a regional orientation to politics characteristic of the South is the return migration of people whose early socialization was in that region and the retention of native populations. This suggests further attention to the cultural significance of location—the investment of place with symbols of group identity. This appears to be stronger in the South than in other parts of the United States; in the survey reported below, over 70 percent of southern respondents vis-à-vis 63 percent of the national sample agreed that their own state was "the best state" in which to live.

Extant political culture concepts do not account for return migration, with its implications of potential revision of ideas and attitudes during the migration interval. It is assumed that cultures are transmitted from one area to another but not that the return of "carriers" to their original milieu might be politically significant. The extent to which return migrants differ from those who stayed and those who did not return is an intriguing question. Generally, first-time migrants are positively selected and exemplify the positive images of a venturesome, mobile population. But what of those who return again—are they likely to have "beneficial" or "adverse," conserving or catalytic, effects on the areas to which they return? One clue is offered in DaVanzo and Morrison's research. In assaying these effects, they note that migrants who return after less than one year are likely to be negatively selected; those who return after a longer migration interval are often positively selected. A fuller understanding of the political impacts of return migration would require: (1) information on early political socialization experiences; (2) political experiences of migrants when outside their home state, including the local political culture they move within; (3) exposure to national cultural and educational institutions; (4) the relative weight of potentially different political experiences compared to early political socialization; (5) modes of political participation of return migrants; (6) and a host of other factors. The very notion of "the political consequences of return migration" in the United States is unsettling: our stereotypes are of movement toward new frontiers, or at least toward the suburbs, rather than a return to the point of origin.

As formal education becomes more standardized, as mass transportation and communications cut down on costs of overcoming distance, as the status connotations of location become more diffuse, as socioeconomic conditions converge, is there much justification for a regional focus in analyses? Even though there may now appear to be as much variation within the South as between the South and other regions on certain indicators, consistent and distinct differences between political attitudes and opinions of Southerners and the rest of the U.S. citizens continue to exist. To discern whether that difference is greater than differences within the South, comparison of samples of individual states with a national sample are necessary. The survey data used in the next section allow such comparisons and indicate that these differences exist and persist. Whether this regional distinctiveness will continue in the face of substantial in-migration can best be determined through longitudinal analyses. The data presented below permit distinctions between natives and migrants and present an array of political cultures varying among natives and migrants, by state, and by issue.

MIGRANTS AND NATIVES IN THE SOUTH: THE COMPARATIVE STATE ELECTIONS PROJECT SURVEY

The Comparative State Elections Project (CSEP) provided individual state samples of five southern states with data on approximately five hundred politically relevant variables collected following the 1968 presidential election. (The CSEP 1968 sample is best described as a modified probability sample; the data here were weighted by the State Weight scheme to facilitate comparisons within and between states. CSEP was a project of the Department of Political Science and the Institute for Research in Social Science, University of North Carolina at Chapel Hill.) Although the CSEP data were not based on independent samples of migrants and natives, it is possible to describe and compare the political orientations and activities of natives and migrants, as well as variations in these configurations. The CSEP sample allowed breakdowns by migrancy status for a broad range of political behavior, including but not limited to voting behavior. While the sizes of the individual state samples limited the complexity of the possible data analysis, the contextual richness of the data outweighed such limitations, including the time elapsed since the data collection. The CSEP study involved 7,673 respondents, including relatively large and representative samples in thirteen states. The southern sample states were Alabama, Florida, Louisiana, North Carolina, and Texas. This unique design allowed genuinely comparative analyses of political attitudes among these states and of the political milieus created by population change.

The CSEP data allowed disaggregation by migrant cohort, although they did not fully account for the recency, frequency, or extent of respondents' migration experiences. The following migrant cohorts were identified.

Natives: Born in the state of current residence; this did not preclude migration by the respondent at some earlier period.

Southern Migrants: Those not born in the state of current residence but in a Deep South or Border State; these respondents had migrated to one of the five southern states studied.

Nonsouthern Migrants: Those not born in the state of current residence but in the Northeast, Midwest, Rocky Mountains region, West Coast, or abroad; these respondents had migrated to one of the five southern states studied.

Blacks: Blacks currently residing in the state; the samples of blacks were too small to permit disaggregation by migrancy status.

By using CSEP data, the structures of political beliefs and activities of migrant cohorts in the southern sample are compared over four dimensions of political culture: political orientations, political attitudes, political efficacy and activities, and political behavior. Survey items referring to these four areas are the dependent variables to be explained. The four cohorts described above—natives, southern migrants, nonsouthern migrants, blacks—are the independent variables reflecting differentiation in migrancy status. The objective is to delineate the effects of race and mobility, two significant components of population change in the South, on state political systems.

To guide in interpreting the tables, a ± 3–4 percent sampling error is allowed in determining the likely significance of response category percentages in a single state sample. For ascertaining the significance of percentage differences in comparing response categories across state samples, a 6 percent sampling error is allowed for percentages near 50 percent. The wide estimate interval and the 95 percent confidence level used in its calculation lend credence to an interpretation of percentage differences exceeding these error allowances as statistically significant differences rather than the result of sampling error (see Black et al., 1974:12–16).

Data on the more distinctive findings are presented in tabular form; findings on other items are summarized.

Migrancy Status

The assumption that in distinguishing between natives and migrants we are distinguishing between Southerners and "outsiders" is misleading. Rather than an "invasion" of the South, the sample suggested significant intraregional mobility and return migration: in every state but Florida, more migrant respondents were born elsewhere in the South than were born outside the South.

During the CSEP interview period, the volume of white return migration to the South was reaching its peak; the CSEP southern migrants category included intraregional migrants as well as interregional southern-born migrants returning to a different area in the South. Both relocators and return migrants were probably sensitive to increased economic opportunities in the South, thus promoting an intraregional labor market mobility informed by communal ties. Florida and Texas, both Border South states, were hosts to the largest percentages of nonsouthern-born migrants in the sample.

If migration is to be a source of political change in the South, migrants presumably must differ from natives along politically salient cultural, attitudinal, and behavioral dimensions. When combined with later racial differences in return migration patterns, mixes of political cultures and potential political change are more probable in some states than in others. Since black return migrants are more likely than whites to return to their original state of birth (Long and Hansen, 1975:609), states experiencing the greatest out-migration of blacks and whites may eventually experience the greatest in-migration of blacks but not necessarily of whites. Although all southern states are becoming relatively more attractive economically (thus inviting in-migration), high growth states are most likely to experience changes in racial and political culture composition because of relatively higher influxes of white migrants, even if all black former residents return.

Political Orientations

Three items describe characteristics suggesting cultural influences on political orientations: (1) the configurations of natives, migrants, and blacks in terms of their subjective class identification; (2) their retention of their parents' political party identification; and (3) the focus of their political attention.
Subjective Class Identification. Although majorities of both na-

tive and migrant respondents identified themselves as members of the working class, this subjective working-class identification was much stronger for natives than migrants and also varied by state. In every state larger percentages of migrants than natives claimed middle-class affiliations (see table 9.2). Although a minority perception, middle-class identification is generally stronger among southern migrants than natives, but, overall, southern migrants were more similar to natives in their class orientation than to nonsouthern migrants. The majority of nonsouthern migrants perceived themselves as middle class. Thus, in terms of social class identification, natives, southern migrants, and blacks generally shared a common class orientation and differed markedly from nonsouthern migrants.

Parent's Party Identification. The largest percentage of *all groups* in *all states* (except Alabama) had the same political party identification as their parents. This intergenerational stability in party identification is a significant feature of American politics, but the CSEP sample revealed interstate and intergroup variation. Indeed, the intergenerational pluralities, with few exceptions, were surprisingly low, and a process of partisan dealignment was evident—many voters appeared to be shifting away from their parents' partisan orientation (Beck, 1977). If retention of family partisan orientation is considered an aspect of the continuing impact of cultural networks, it was weakest, although still operant, among nonsouthern migrants. Self-identification as "independents" reflected a loosening of party ties, but the Wallace candidacy may have been responsible for the substantial number of reported independents, almost wholly natives or southern migrants, who grew up in partisan households. Many blacks coming from apolitical or split-party households moved toward the Democratic party and may have counterbalanced these losses in traditional Democratic households.

Intergenerational stability accounted for all the Republican party identification reported: *all Republican respondents came from Republican households.* In this sample the Republican dimension of population change in the South was a question of transplantation rather than conversion. Intergenerational party identification proved to be a political dimension on which natives, southern migrants, nonsouthern migrants, and blacks were similar.

Political Focus. The scope and focus of political attention is another indicator of how closely individuals are linked to their culture and surroundings. Other studies have remarked on the degree to which Southerners manifest a "local" orientation compared to

Table 9.2 Subjective Social Class Identification

	United States			Alabama			Florida			Louisiana			North Carolina			Texas		
	% Middle Class	% Working Class	% Not Sure	% Middle Class	% Working Class	% Not Sure	% Middle Class	% Working Class	% Not Sure	% Middle Class	% Working Class	% Not Sure	% Middle Class	% Working Class	% Not Sure	% Middle Class	% Working Class	% Not Sure
	40%	56%	4%															
Native				31	64	5	44	51	4	34	57	8	33	61	6	31	63	6
Southern Migrant				43	56	1	36	59	5	35	60	5	35	62	3	39	61	0
Nonsouthern Migrant				35	48	17	56	41	3	45	39	16	61	38	1	49	47	4
Black				14	75	11	24	73	4	18	72	10	12	70	18	9	83	9

Note: Figures are in percentages. N=7,662.

non-Southerners (Reed, 1972). The CSEP survey asked respondents whether they followed international, national, state, or public affairs most closely. Those who followed international or national affairs closely are considered "cosmopolitan," and those who follow state and local affairs most closely are identified as "locals" (Merton, 1957), with groups defined in comparison to other groups in their state. Natives were primarily concerned with state and local affairs, as were blacks, compared to migrants in each state. The congruence of the local orientation in both natives and blacks in all states was in sharp contrast to the dominance of the cosmopolitan orientation of nonsouthern migrants in every state. Furthermore, larger proportions of migrants reported having confidence in national government than did natives. Higher percentages of migrants than natives also felt the national government had a "great effect" on their daily lives. Migrants thus appeared to have greater "attachment" to the national government in terms of their attention, confidence, and evaluation of impact.

Political Attitudes
Attitudes regarding the appropriate roles and activities of government are likely to be influenced by prevalent norms and values. The issues described here reflect Pye's (1972) emphasis on critical values and political orientations through analysis of three significant policy issues—government spending, law and order, and civil rights—on which configurations of opinions among natives, southern migrants, nonsouthern migrants, and blacks would be especially telling. They are also policy areas in which state government has a potential role; respondents' answers, therefore, whether in reference to national or state government, were likely to be meaningful for both state and national politics. Significantly, these three issues and the "Vietnam stand" exhibited the broadest range of variation regionally and by state than any others included in the CSEP study.

Government Spending. When asked whether they agreed that "government spending should be cut," a strong majority of all groups—native and migrant, black and white—agreed. No consistent differences between natives and migrants or among migrants was evident; only blacks were consistent, providing the lowest majority within each state to agree.

Police Authority. There were distinct differences among natives, migrants, and blacks regarding law and order issues (see table 9.3). In every state but Florida, southern migrants were the source of the

Table 9.3   "The Police Ought to be Given More Authority"

	United States		Southern Sample		Alabama			Florida			Louisiana			North Carolina			Texas		
	Yes	No	Yes	No	Yes	No	Not Sure	Yes	No	Not Sure	Yes	No	Not Sure	Yes	No	Not Sure	Yes	No	Not Sure
	77	12	78	10															
Natives					92	2	6	87	6	8	74	11	15	85	7	9	87	4	10
Southern Migrants					97	0	3	78	12	10	86	9	5	87	8	5	92	4	4
Nonsouthern Migrants					68	4	28	79	13	8	72	0	28	82	15	3	85	6	9
Blacks					52	29	19	57	21	22	53	18	29	62	16	22	38	34	28

Note: Figures are in percentages.   N=7,641.

strongest sentiment favoring increased police authority; non-southern migrants, except for Louisiana, reported the highest rates of negative response, although the differences between cohorts were large only in North Carolina and Florida. Blacks in every state, however, differed significantly from both national, regional, and state response rates and all white responses. The differences among white approval rates were smaller than the differences between black rates and the lowest white approval of police authority in all states but North Carolina; there seemed little basis for a coalition of blacks and nonsouthern migrants over law and order issues—the racial dimension dominated.

Neighborhood Integration.   When queried whether they "favor letting Negroes move into white neighborhoods," Americans nationwide were more divided than on any other policy issue (see table 9.4). As a region the South expressed outright disapproval, a majority of respondents disagreeing with the statement altogether. But states varied within the region, and, more particularly, migrants, natives, and blacks differed in their responses.

In no case did natives and southern migrants vary in their rate of approval of open housing by more than 5 percent; in every state the strongest support for open housing among whites came from nonsouthern migrants. The nonsouthern migrant rate of agreement was below national levels in Alabama and Florida; nonsouthern migrants in Louisiana, North Carolina, and Texas approximated the national rate of support for open housing and exceeded state and regional rates.

In the configuration in table 9.4, "capture by culture" seems as likely an explanation as racial bias. Clearly natives and southern migrants were more similar to each other in the low degree of approval for open housing than they were to nonsouthern migrants. In this area nonsouthern migrants were clearly outside the dominant regional political culture in every state but Alabama. Even blacks seemed somewhat captured by this norm *if* it is assumed that open housing was viewed by blacks as a goal. If so, it is curious that black support for open housing was not greater, although the majority of blacks in every state but Louisiana approved of residential integration. The high percentage of all respondents saying they were not sure of their position was indicative of the sensitivity and specificity of the issue; in contrast, a more general proposition that "government ought to help Negroes" was approved in each state at nearly double the rate of this less abstract query.

Workplace Integration.   The salience of the degree of issue speci-

Table 9.4   "I Favor Letting Negroes Move into White Neighborhoods"

	United States		Southern Sample		Alabama			Florida			Louisiana			North Carolina			Texas		
	Yes	No	Yes	No	Yes	No	Not Sure	Yes	No	Not Sure	Yes	No	Not Sure	Yes	No	Not Sure	Yes	No	Not Sure
	46	35	29	59															
Natives					10	82	8	17	69	15	15	75	11	15	75	10	24	62	15
Southern Migrants					9	77	14	12	70	18	10	82	8	18	75	7	29	57	14
Nonsouthern Migrants					12	83	6	38	49	13	45	35	21	44	48	8	42	46	12
Blacks					52	32	16	79	14	7	74	19	7	60	11	30	74	9	17

Note: Figures are in percentages.   N=7,614.

ficity and the social distance dimension were apparent when responses to open housing are compared to attitudes regarding integration at the workplace (see table 9.5). In comparison to open housing, positive support for workplace integration outweighed negative attitudes in the southern sample as a whole. Not only did higher percentages of respondents in each group in each state agree that they would "like to work on a job with both Negroes and whites" but there were seven instances where a substantial *majority* of respondents favored such an arrangement. The high percentages of "not sure" responses indicate that perhaps job integration represented less obvious intrusion on the cultural institutions—home, church, school, community—so highly valued in the South (see Reed, 1972).

In every state but Florida, natives and southern migrants supported job integration to similar degrees, but significantly less so than nonsouthern migrants. Generally, southern migrants registered the largest negative response and nonsouthern migrants the largest positive response of whites in each state. The border states of Florida and Texas present deviant configurations. In Texas, natives and southern migrants were evenly split in their degree of support, with a substantial percentage of natives uncertain rather than definitely negative. Coupled with the positive support of nonsouthern migrants and blacks, the rare incidence of a consensual norm, however latent, was evident. In Florida the natives became cultural isolates, with majorities of all other groups favoring job integration. The sense of an insider/outsider alignment in the other states was strengthened when the intensity of black support for job integration is considered. Blacks were generally stronger in their support of job integration than they were open housing, perhaps regarding it to be the more salient issue.

Efficacy and Activity

Several factors influenced an individual's feelings of political efficacy and propensity to participate in politics. Three measures of political efficacy and activity demarcated those areas in which natives and migrants differed most, and most significantly: an index of political efficacy, an index of campaign activity, and the 1968 presidential vote.

Political Efficacy. The political efficacy index compiled responses to four questions on the potential influence of citizens on government, the concern of public officials for public opinion, the complexity of politics and government, and the impact of voting.

Table 9.5 "I'd Like to Work on a Job with Both Negroes and Whites"

	United States	Southern Sample		Alabama			Florida			Louisiana			North Carolina			Texas		
	Yes No	Yes No	Not	Yes	No	Not Sure	Yes	No	Not Sure	Yes	No	Not Sure	Yes	No	Not Sure	Yes	No	Not Sure
	60 20	48	32															
Natives				28	46	26	34	44	22	29	44	27	35	46	19	42	36	22
Southern Migrants				28	49	23	49	36	16	31	55	15	31	57	12	45	43	12
Nonsouthern Migrants				35	16	49	67	20	13	62	14	24	70	21	9	67	8	25
Blacks				84	4	12	88	3	10	79	4	17	78	5	17	83	4	14

Note: Figures are in percentages. N=7,615.

Those respondents seeing citizens as having an effective role in political activities on all four items received a high efficacy score of 4; those seeing no effective role for citizens received a o. Except for Texas, natives and blacks in all states shared feelings of low political efficacy. In every state but Louisiana, southern migrants were more similar to natives and blacks in proportions who thought citizens had no political impact on government. Significantly, in every state nonsouthern migrants felt most efficacious. It seems reasonable to assume that if nonsouthern migrants had greater feelings of political efficacy than other citizens in the state they would be more politically active, but CSEP data did not support this assumption.

Campaign Activity. This greater sense of political efficacy among migrants was reflected in their higher rates of participation in political campaign activities than natives in every state but Florida. Nonsouthern migrants, however, were not significantly more politically active respondents as measured by the CSEP campaign activity index. The CSEP index is a summary score depicting the number of campaign activities respondents engaged in during 1968. Included in the eight types of activities were such acts as displaying campaign buttons, discussing the campaign, working for a candidate or party, and voting. Although the majority of each group in each state reported participating in from one to three different types of campaign activities, there were differences in the order of rankings between natives and migrants. In Louisiana and Florida, for example, nonsouthern migrants were conspicuously absent from the ranks of the very politically active and distinctively visible in the ranks of the nonactive. In addition to the low political activity rate of blacks, the clearest pattern to emerge was the very high level of political activity of southern migrants in each state coupled with their absence from the nonactivist ranks in every state but Florida. Although return migrants or intraregional migrants may remain captured by their culture, this may be their advantage in engaging in political activities.

Presidential Vote. With the exception of Texas, similar proportions of natives and migrants reported voting in the 1968 presidential election. While majorities of both natives and migrants in every state but Alabama think of themselves as Democrats when it comes to national politics, this identification was stronger among natives than migrants. Larger percentages of migrants were likely to see themselves as independents, as in Alabama, or as Republicans. Republican respondents were more likely to be migrants, although the assumption that the migrant stream to the South was a Republican stream was not altogether true. Florida and North Carolina were good examples of the heterogeneity of migrants to the South, as well as the diverse sources of southern republicanism. In the CSEP sample, migrants were the major source of Republican sentiment in Florida; yet, at the same time, the largest percentage of migrants to Florida identified themselves as Democrats. The sources of Republican strength in North Carolina, on the other hand, came from significant proportions of both natives and migrants claiming Republican affiliation.

The loosening of party loyalties suggested by split ticket voting at state and local levels was amplified at the national level in the 1968 presidential election. True nationwide, this was especially salient in the South, where the Wallace candidacy made significant inroads on traditional Democratic party strongholds. Although those who report having voted in elections are always more numerous than those who actually cast votes, we rely on the CSEP data here for political behavior indicators because they allow disaggregation by native/migrant/racial status (see table 9.6). In these sample states, Wallace's strongest support came from natives, shared in some states by southern migrants; the strongest source of Nixon sentiment was among migrants, predominantly nonsouthern migrants in Florida, similar support by both migrant groups in Texas, and predominantly southern migrant support in Alabama, Louisiana, and North Carolina. Among whites, Wallace support was always weakest among nonsouthern migrants; Nixon support always weakest among natives; and Humphrey support weakest among southern migrants. In this region, traditionally a Democratic stronghold, the national Democratic candidate trailed in every state but Texas and with every white group but nonsouthern migrants in Florida and migrants in North Carolina. The black vote for Humphrey was obviously critical in narrowing the gap in the popular vote regionally and nationwide.

An indirect measure of party strength was provided by data reporting the politician respondents would *pick* to be president rather than the candidate they said they had voted for. Natives in Alabama, Florida, and Louisiana continued to prefer Wallace; natives in North Carolina split their support between Nixon and Wallace as did southern migrants in every state. Wallace ran second to the plurality of Texan natives (25 percent) who said they did not know who they would pick to be president. On the other hand, Humphrey was the first pick of all blacks; Kennedy Democrats

Table 9.6 Presidential Vote 1968

	United States			Alabama			Florida			Louisiana			North Carolina			Texas		
	Nixon	Humphrey	Wallace	Nixon	Humphrey	Wallace	Nixon	Humphrey	Wallace	Nixon	Humphrey	Wallace	Nixon	Humphrey	Wallace	Nixon	Humphrey	Wallace
CSEP	45	45	10															
Actual Returns	43.6	42.9	13.6															
Natives				16	6	77	32	24	44	22	14	64	45	24	31	34	40	26
Southern Migrants				27	0	73	42	13	45	43	9	48	62	20	19	53	23	24
Nonsouthern Migrants				22	15	63	62	25	14	37	22	42	55	33	12	51	46	4
Blacks				2	97	1	4	96	0	5	94	1	5	94	1	3	98	0

Note: Figures are in percentages. N=5,897.

were evident among blacks in all states and nonsouthern migrants in Alabama.

The lower percentage for each candidate in every case suggests more diffuse preferences when party cues are not operating. This was especially true for nonsouthern migrants and natives; sizable segments said they did not know who they would pick to be president if they had the choice. Southern migrants appeared to be the most polarized; given the chance to pick the president most southern migrants would have selected either Nixon or Wallace. These data on voting behavior provide further evidence of the effects of population change on partisan dealignment in the South.

The Political Impacts of Population Change
It is apparent that there were significant similarities as well as differences between natives and migrants to the South. Furthermore, there were numerous political differences between southern migrants and nonsouthern migrants, and often between all these white groups and blacks in the state.

Relationship between Migrant Cohort and Political Orientations. Since migrant cohorts are likely to differ in terms of income, occupation, and education, these factors were introduced as controls to determine whether the relationship between migrant cohort and political orientations, strongest in the relationship to presidential vote (Cramer's V = .49), was sustained when cohorts were stratified by income, occupation, and education. To do so, the strength of association between these nominal variables in the original relationships described above is compared to the strength of association when control factors are introduced.

When presidential vote is stratified by level of educational attainment or income, some original distinctions in presidential vote by migrant cohorts diminished; i.e., the apparent overwhelming preference of natives for Wallace and shared support of Nixon and Wallace by southern migrants were not consistent at all educational and income levels. Southern migrants were more similar to natives with similar levels of education and income than to nonsouthern migrants with similar levels of income and education. There was consistently weaker support among southern migrants for the Democratic party candidate, Humphrey. Also, Wallace support declined with education, and more slowly with income, among southern migrants, and Nixon support increased. Among both natives and southern migrants, the Wallace candidacy appeared to have distorted traditional Democratic affiliations, but the erratic Humphrey vote precluded generalizations about the independent effect of education or income. It seemed that poor and poorly educated natives and southern migrants were more likely to be "captured by the culture" than influenced by education or income level in their voting patterns; with high school and post-secondary education, educational attainment began to be influential, less so for natives than for southern migrants.

Nonsouthern migrants, however, reflect a distinctive political culture; the original relationship of majority support for Nixon and low support for Wallace persisted when stratified for education or for income. It was slightly weaker among the lower income and least well educated nonsouthern migrants but apparently was affected by the Humphrey vote among this cohort, rather than the Wallace vote as in the case of deviant patterns of the lower income and least well educated natives and southern migrants. This same phenomenon occurred among better-educated, wealthier nonsouthern migrants: Nixon support was slightly less than expected because of the strength of the Humphrey vote. Finally, the black support for Humphrey was consistent and overwhelming, fragmented only by a negligible percentage of the poorest and least well educated voting for Nixon.

Four Political Groupings. From the interplay of migrancy status and achieved status characteristics, there appeared to be four distinctive groupings in the South whose political orientations consistently differed. While these may not have qualified as four distinct political cultures, they did offer a basis for potential coalitions and conflicts.

I. BLACK SOUTHERNERS. Throughout the South blacks differed from whites in both achieved status characteristics and, frequently, the proportion and direction of their political sentiment.

Black voting patterns were distinctive: the support for Humphrey was maintained across all educational and income levels, was dissimilar to that of every other cohort, and was not diffused among other candidates. The political orientation of southern blacks in the sample was defined by neither cultural contiguity'nor education nor income; the racial component was most apparent. Both blacks and nonsouthern migrants evidenced distinctive political orientations relatively unaffected by levels of educational attainment and income. Low income, poorly educated whites are more similar in political attitudes and behavior to other whites than to blacks in similar circumstances; in 1968 there appeared to be little basis for anticipating a political coalition among whites and blacks based on common economic deprivation. As blacks began to return to the South, the issue of the political impact of population change acquired a new dimension. The political experience of black southern migrants to the North has generally been examined in comparison to the political behavior of their northern neighbors. Now the question is whether political experiences outside the South, as well as possible socioeconomic advancement, will alter political behavior of black return migrants. It is possible that black return migrants may constitute another political grouping, distinguished from whites by race, from other blacks by education, income, and occupation.

2. NONSOUTHERN MIGRANTS. The political orientations of the second group, nonsouthern migrants, were relatively unaffected by income, education, and occupation; they were also generally different from those of natives and southern migrants, although this varied by state. Nonsouthern migrants were dissimilar in voting behavior to other cohorts with equivalent education or income at every level and retained the original proportional distribution of votes across all categories of the control factors. Their political orientation appeared to be delimited more by their migrancy type, and its "nonsouthern" component, than by education or income. "Nonsouthern migrant" was an artifact, of course; some component dimensions of "nonsouthern" were the important factors in delimiting this grouping, although the distinctiveness of the "nonsouthern" group may have been as reflective of the distinctiveness of southern political culture as of any coherent "nonsouthernness." The influx of nonsouthern migrants in 1968 generally was better educated, had higher incomes, and was more likely to be in nonmanual labor occupations than their southern neighbors. In most cases these nonsouthern migrants more closely approximated national socioeconomic averages and political norms than did most southerners.

3. POOR WHITE SOUTHERNERS. The third and fourth groupings reflected historic socioeconomic cleavages among white southerners that overrode cultural affinities or differences between migrants and natives. Lower-paid, poorly educated southern manual laborers were more similar to each other, whether natives or migrants, than to their better-paid, better-educated cohorts in political attitudes and behavior. Poorly educated, lower-income natives and southern migrants thus appeared to be more influenced by similar educational and economic experiences in their political orientations than by dissimilar migration experiences. The neat

distinctions between native, southern migrant, and nonsouthern migrant were, in fact, more salient if one distinguished between socioeconomic groupings among white southerners.

4. AFFLUENT WHITE SOUTHERNERS. The fourth orientation, the better-educated, wealthier natives and southern migrants, is more difficult to describe but a key to understanding the New South. Cultural influences on better-educated, wealthier natives appeared stronger than on southern migrants: education, income, and occupation influenced their political orientations, but natives were sometimes less responsive to these influences than were southern migrants; i.e., it took more education to alter traditional patterns. For example, native high school graduates reflected a pattern of votes among candidates similar to the less well educated in their cohort, whereas southern migrant high school graduates deviated from the less well educated in their cohort in both proportions and pattern of votes. Natives and southern migrants with higher educational attainment and income levels are more similar to each other in their pattern of voting than to others in their migrant cohort, although still distinct in measures of voting behavior from nonsouthern migrants with similar income and education.

Overall, one would expect natives to be less integrated into a national political culture, less "nationalized" than their southern migrant counterparts, but this was not always so. Recall that southern migrants appeared to have the weakest political party attachments, were least likely to support Humphrey, and were persistent in their opposition to integration despite their income, education, and occupation. Considering that this group appeared to be more politically active, their distinct political orientation deserves further attention.

CONCLUSION

In conclusion, these materials, centered on the concept of locational advantage, analyze and compare the interaction of demographic change and political factors at the macro and micro levels of analysis. In some cases intentional policies are designed to increase regional economic health and thus enhance the national economy. Yet, formulation of such locational policies in a geographically based system of congressional representation has resulted to date in continual conflict between principles of efficiency and equity, between economic and political determination of policy goals and instrumentalities. These tensions have hampered intentional policy efforts to guide growth and change; national policy impacts on growth patterns and processes in the United States continue to be primarily the "unintended consequences" of diverse public policies.

State growth management programs represent intentional state policies designed to guide and manage the intrastate distribution of population and economic activity. Conceptualizing this policy arena as one of locational strategies supports comparison and analysis of such policies across state political systems, regardless of the variety of different state growth contexts. It also centers attention on the political dimension of growth management activities, particularly the degree to which the public or private sector determines structures of locational advantage in different states. Also, in states experiencing significant population change, policymakers and politicians may view growth management programs as appropriate solutions to the difficulties of reintegrating relocated political constituencies.

Relocating constituencies is the focus of the last section which emphasizes analysis of the impact of population change on politics in the South. Most studies measure this impact in terms of electoral behavior and do not distinguish among the impacts of intraregional, interregional, and return migration on political systems. In expanding the scope of analysis to include cultural, attitudinal, and behavioral dimensions of southern political culture potentially affected by migration, these data provide important information on the likely political impacts of population change. By defining four cohorts in terms of migrant and racial characteristics, greater specification of the variability in political impacts is possible. Evidence of partisan dealignment in the South, for example, is offered by these data as well as other clues to the fabric of future southern politics.

If political parties become less viable means of structuring political conflict in the South (Beck, 1977), the data on political constructs suggest potential alternative bases for political coalitions and activity. Indeed, Vance visualized the emergence of a "southern party" influenced by cultural emphases although not a formal political grouping (1935:510). Two issue areas, law and order issues and residential and workplace integration issues, touch on aspects of political morality—emotive constructs not based on and often not congruent with partisan attachments. This lack of congruence weakens our ability to predict the tone and direction of political activity in the South on the basis of conventional electoral data analysis. The data here indicate that variable migrancy and racial mixes in the state populations may significantly affect state political systems. The direct effects of these population mixes stem from the distinctions in support for law and order and integration policies among natives, southern migrants, nonsouthern migrants, and blacks. Southern migrants are generally the most enthusiastic supporters of greater police authority and the most reluctant advocates of further racial integration. Given that they also appear to be more politically active than any other cohort and less bound by partisan attachments than natives, their impact on southern politics may well outweigh their number.

The indirect effects of population change are expressed in changes in income and educational levels in the population brought about by migration (Lyons and Durant, 1978). The four political groupings described as components of the changing political culture of the South reflect the interaction of these direct and indirect effects of population change. Rather than presuming an increased "nationalization" of the South through migration of nonsouthern migrants, this research suggests that a key to understanding the politics of the New South lies in a better understanding of the political activities of affluent, educated, intraregional white southern migrants and black southern return migrants.

10
The Demographically Emergent South

GEORGE C. MYERS

> Today's regions are often yesterday's dreams;
> they may be only tomorrow's memories
> (Watson, 1963:239).

Currently the study of the "demography of the South" is an enigma wrapped in a paradox. The enigma stems from the fact that our expectations regarding demographic changes in the light of social and economic advancement within the region have not only been met but have actually been exceeded. The paradox involves the anachronistic manner in which demographers and other social scientists have persisted in depicting this region as a thing apart and in searching for its uniqueness in differentials between the South and the rest of the United States. In this concluding chapter, I want to examine this regionalistic perspective in terms of the empirical findings and observations reported in the preceding chapters. This is followed by a discussion of likely demographic developments in the future and some important avenues of research for demographers who will be dealing with the emergent South.

The term "emergent" has been applied to the South in the title of this chapter to emphasize that the South is no longer "backwards" or underdeveloped—nor, for that matter, developing or emerging—with respect to the rest of the country or even other regions. To be sure, there are still distinguishable characteristics, most notably in geographic terms (e.g., climate, location, topography) and perhaps in certain selected economic and social terms as well. But the overwhelming evidence from the various studies in this volume is that the South as a region no longer lags behind the rest of the nation in the main dimensions of the demographic transition and, in fact, may soon come to pace the country in terms of certain demographic behavior. While monitoring of these trends and further historical studies should continue, the preoccupation of researchers with gross comparisons of the South with the rest of the nation should give way to a broadened perspective on regional studies. This viewpoint would not neglect research among various regions of the country, both geographic and functional, but would emphasize an inward focus on forces operating within the region, mindful of the important linkages with other national regions and neighboring countries. Therefore, the monolithic vision of the South as a region apart should yield to one that views the diversity of the region as an appropriate field for studying demographic variation and trends.

The issue of the proper role of regional studies is one that is invariably addressed in studies of the South and, indeed, in the various selections in this volume. It is noteworthy that studies of this region from a variety of disciplinary perspectives—geography, economics, political science, history, sociology—greatly exceed those of any other region of the country. The strength and vigor of regional professional associations in the South also testify to the regional outlook shared by many of the South's intellectual leaders. Moreover, a plethora of political and special interest groups (e.g., Southern Regional Council, Southern Regional Educational Council, Southern Governor's Conference and its Southern Growth Policies Board, etc.) exist in the region. Thus, it is not surprising that the concept of regionalism and regional studies has been most fully articulated by scholars from the region. To the extent that a traditional regionalism perspective has dominated and fostered social research in the South, it is important to examine how and why the perspective itself emerged and what the implications of this viewpoint have been.

PERSPECTIVE ON REGIONALISM

It is crucial to point out that the concept of regionalism can take various forms, depending on the disciplinary orientation that is adopted. In this discussion primary consideration is given to the school of thought that is associated with Howard Odum, his students, and coworkers at the University of North Carolina at Chapel Hill. Among these persons Rupert Vance should be singled out as one who made notable contributions to the formulation of the perspective and empirical studies of the South. Although the disciplinary affiliations of these professionals were primarily with sociology and, to a lesser extent, demography, the broad perspective on regionalism that characterized the school makes it an appropriate point of departure for assessing the strengths and weaknesses of the approach which gained such strong attention in the 1930s and 1940s.

The concept of regionalism has never been easy to delineate, even for its most vigorous advocates. Odum and Moore (the latter a sociologist with lengthy tenure at the University of Texas at Austin) in their classic *American Regionalism: A Cultural-Historical Approach to National Integration*, published in 1938, list twenty-eight different definitions of the concept and then spend over six-hundred pages providing a detailed exposition of the approach and descriptive application for six major American regions. From this presentation and other writings on the subject, at least three main dimensions can be discerned—theoretical, methodological, and ideological. Let us consider each of these in turn and how they have been applied to the South.

From a *theoretical* point of view, regionalism, according to Odum (1951), is a "multiple approach to the study of total areal-cultural situations." Thus, we begin with the region, an areal or spatial generalization which has flexible boundaries. Nonetheless, the region must have some degree of homogeneity in a number of characteristics and possess some structural or functional aspect through which the region is to be "denominated," to use Odum's term. Finally, there must be some organic unity to the region, and here the term "cultural gestalt" is used (Odum and Moore, 1938: 16). What is also implied is that the region should have some historical foundations that provide a sense of identity. But Odum and Moore were clearly not accepting the "literary concept of regionalism" or, for that matter, "its most common interpretation, namely, localism, sectionalism, or provincialism." Yet, firmly maintained in their perspective is a notion of regions that have had a strong agrarian foundation.

It is this latter criterion that made the South the prototypical case of an American region. The predominantly agricultural basis of the economy, characterized by the quintessential plantation system and its use of slaves, set off the South from the rest of the nation and laid the groundwork for secession. In turn, the economic and political forces were accompanied by the development of common cultural forms and distinctive social institutions, according to the conventional view. (For a balanced view, see Thompson, 1975.) The so-called myth of southern history holds that the southern identity lies in this awareness of the past, reinforced by a strong sense of belonging to a distinctive society and accentuated by conflict or rivalry with the rest of the nation. Although Odum took pains to insist that regionalism was not sectionalism, in dealing with the South, he and his associates clearly shared in the view that the South was not only historically distinct but remained culturally distinct as well. As Vance and Demerath noted in the preface to *The Urban South* (1954:viii), the volume ". . . accepts the American South as something of a cultural and economic entity." What is remarkable about this view is how long it persisted in the light of profound social changes that were occurring within the South and the nation.

The *methodological* dimension of regionalism was closely shaped by the theoretical view, with the region becoming a tool for multidisciplinary research. Vance (1951) indicated four levels of regional analysis: (1) the delimitation of one-factor regions, (2) the delimitation of complex regions, (3) the regional "monograph" that would include the analysis of the forces and processes operating in a complex region, and (4) the analysis of interregional relations. Moreover, it is clear that Vance felt very strongly that studies should include a temporal dimension, especially insofar as the historical factors that operated within regions were of such great importance. Although examples of each type of study can be found, especially for the South, research on differential factors between the region and the rest of the country predominate. Vance and Demerath defended this position specifically in *The Urban South*:

Regionalism (and we can hardly write of the South today without being a regionalist) has been said by its critics to make its point by delineating differences. Our contributors, however, concentrate on ways in which the South is becoming more like the nation and the differentiation is diminishing. . . . If regionalism is dependent on differentiation—and there is no known reason why differentials are not important—such analysis as follows may lead to further refinements. To be explicit, we are finding in many fields, economic and demographic, trends toward the convergence of differentials in fertility, health, and income. Less and less will we be able to think of our regional differences as those of kind—rural vs. urban, for example, rather they will become differences of degree—in this case, degree of urbanization and concentration. To some students this may mean the need is passing for regional analysis; it can hardly mean the attainment of identity. In any case, the possible demise of regionalism does not concern us here (Vance and Demerath, 1954:viii–ix).

Having stated the issue so sharply, it is therefore surprising that Vance and Demerath dismiss it as of little or no concern. Perhaps the answer lies in the ideological premises upon which so much of the regionalism perspective seems to rest.

Vance and Demerath then proceed to praise regionalism as a "social therapy—an attempt to do something as well as to study something . . . the section's conscious effort to use science to escape from its underdeveloped status" (p. ix). From an *ideological* point of view, regionalism can be viewed as a social movement in which research is used as a tool for social action and planning. Odum and Moore (1938) explicitly sought to promote the use of regionalism as an effort to preserve agrarian-based identities for regions of the country in the face of increasing concentration in the hands of the federal government. As Odum (1951:396) notes, regionalism can be an important force by the "degree to which the United States maintains her historical heritage as a federation of states and the extent to which regional planning may be utilized to maintain balance in America of resources and people." In this regard the viewpoint has much in common with the economic regionalism of Lewis Mumford in his *Technics and Civilization*, in which the demise of agrarian culture in the face of manufacturing dominance is viewed with great alarm. In fairness to this position, it should be pointed out that it entailed a strong belief that national unity would be fostered by preservation of the diversity offered by strong, integrated regions—e pluribus unum—in effect.

To summarize, where has this brief discussion of regionalism as a school of thought led us? Lewis Wirth, who had himself written extensively on the subject, had this to say about it.

> Seminal ideas are so rare that when we meet them in the scientific world we tend to embrace them with more than justifiable enthusiasm. Almost invariably, as a consequence, we are disposed to overextend them and to make them the basis of a cult. To a certain extent this has happened in the case of the regionalism concept (Wirth, 1951:381).

Regionalism as dogma can be readily dismissed. Probably it was formulated well past the time in which it had a real possibility of being widely supported, even by those who may have mistakenly viewed it as southern sectionalism dressed up in scientific robes. The notion of regional planning and administration, while it has been revived periodically in the post-World War II period, has seldom been implemented fully, and, when it has, the regional units usually have been functionally determined on a geographic basis (e.g., river basins, Appalachia, etc.). As an active school of thought stimulating research and instruction, regionalism certainly played an important role for several decades, especially in the South. Since the mid-1950s, however, it has steadily declined in importance, even in fields such as sociology and geography. To be sure, there is still considerable interest in studying the South, and no doubt a fair amount of emotional attachment to the regionalism concept still exists. However, the tenor of social research seems to be far less dogmatic in the search for an appropriate model for regional studies.

The primary question that must be resolved centers on the issue that Vance and Demerath raised so cogently in the statement presented earlier—what happens to regional studies when most of the important differentials that distinguish regions no longer seem operant? Vance and Demerath dismissed the matter by stating that the complete identity of the South with the rest of the nation will never be achieved and that the remaining distinctions will serve to mobilize opinions for seeking equality with respect to certain goals. Increasingly, these distinctions seem fewer and fewer. Even in the extensive research included in Reed's *The Enduring South* (1972), there is little in the way of major cultural distinctions that justify his claim for the South as an enduring cultural entity. Indeed, the findings and discussions reported in this volume suggest convincingly that convergence has occurred on most of the major social, demographic, and economic dimensions, although the paths toward this convergence may differ among the dimensions. The forthcoming reports from the 1980 *Census of Population* will no doubt provide even stronger evidence of convergence.

What then remains on the agenda for southern studies and, specifically, for the field we may call the demography of the South? It is my opinion that much remains in terms of explaining the ways in which social changes have come about in the South *and* in the nation; how demographic trends have been affected and, in turn, affect these changes; and, most importantly, how these forces have operated to create so much *diversity* within what was traditionally assumed to be a socially and economically homogeneous region. Although establishing boundaries for regional analysis always remains an issue, for specific purposes of research, especially statistical studies, the delineation of fairly arbitrary boundaries seems justified on heuristic grounds. Moreover, an implicit concern with internal variation helps to put the boundary issue into perspective. Above all, one must guard against what Collingwood (1940) has termed the "fallacy of precarious margins," the drawing of precise boundaries when none exist. In the remainder of this chapter, use will be made of the Census South, the statistical unit defined by the Bureau of the Census, with all of these caveats kept in mind.

THE SOUTH DEMOGRAPHICALLY

Let us begin by considering the aggregate levels of various social, demographic, and economic dimensions for the South compared with the rest of the nation. The contributors to this volume are in agreement that southern fertility and mortality levels currently do not vary to any considerable extent from those of the country as a whole. However, the third major factor determining population change, net migration, has come to play at least as important a role in the South's population growth as natural increase. In the 1960s a remarkable reversal of the traditionally large net out-migration from the South occurred, and the region became a net recipient of migrants. This trend has continued to an even greater extent through the 1970s. The result of these developments has been to increase the South's population, already the largest of the four major statistical regions in the country, by 8.3 percent between 1970 and 1975, compared with the U.S. rate of 4.8 percent. With these trends the age and sex structure of the region's population has come to resemble more closely that of the rest of the nation, especially in the reduced proportion of younger persons and the increased proportion of older persons.

The South has also lost much of its distinctiveness in terms of other aggregate measures. This is true of urbanization, in which the proportion of the population living in urban places has increased greatly in the past few decades and currently is less than ten percentage points below the national level. The overall occupational structure differs very little from the rest of the country in terms of the percentage of males engaged in agriculture (in which it was typically far above the national level), manufacturing, and service. Serow, in his chapter, makes a convincing case that although the estimated per capita income for the South in 1975 was

14 percent lower than for the non-South, in terms of purchasing power it is only 5 percent lower.

To be sure, there are some social and economic factors in particular in which the South stands out in gross comparisons with the rest of the country. The distribution of wealth is still greatly skewed in the South, with higher levels of the population below the poverty line than is true for the remainder of the country. While the similarity of the occupational structure has been noted, the levels of unionization in the region as a whole are extremely low, which no doubt reflects on the lower levels of per capita income. On various measures of education and educational systems—expenditures per pupil, teacher salaries, percentage advancing to higher education—the South lags behind the rest of the nation. Clarke, in her contribution, notes that some of these matters relate to distinctive governmental and political structures that prevail in the region and which are reflected in different political cultures (also see Sharkansky, 1970). Reed (1972) has been cited earlier as one scholar who feels that distinctive attitudes toward violence and fundamentalist religious beliefs held by Southerners suggest that the region be viewed as an ethnic group. No doubt this list could be extended, but an overall assessment of these factors suggests that the primary factors that have been used in the past to distinguish the region no longer do so.

Yet, there are important issues that are not addressed in analyses that concentrate on aggregate-level differentials. Three come readily to mind, the strands of which can be found running through previous chapters. The *first* of these concerns the trends that have brought about this convergence between the South and the rest of the nation. What strikes one immediately is the rapidity with which the convergence has occurred. In fact, for many of the factors that have been examined, in recent decades the rates of change have exceeded those that would have been expected according to conventional wisdom. Moreover, the patterns of change have been complex and often unexpected. As Singelmann observed, the shift has been from primary-dominated (agricultural) to tertiary-dominated (service) occupational structures without the emergence of the secondary or manufacturing sector that was followed by the rest of the country in its economic development. Rindfuss also demonstrates the complex pattern of change in fertility. The convergence came about through the failure of older, less-educated rural white women in the South to increase their fertility during the baby boom period, 1945–1957, in concert with women in other categories of the population in both the South and the non-South. During the period of declining fertility in the 1960s and 1970s, differential changes have been virtually nonexistent between the two areal units, even when controls are introduced. Other contributors have pointed out with respect to the renewed population growth in nonmetropolitan areas that it is the rest of the nation that is coming to share some of the features that have been characteristic of the South in the past. Thus, convergence can come about in a variety of ways. It is also important to recognize that divergence can operate in the same manner.

It is when we come to consider the factors that may be causally related or at least associated with these demographic trends that important theoretical issues arise, especially those pertaining to the tempo of changes. The enigma that was referred to at the beginning of this chapter relates to the fact that many of the demographic changes have proceeded at a pace much faster than changes in many of the social and economic conditions that are usually thought of as crucial structural determinants of these trends. For example, while urbanization, industrialization, and structural transformations in educational and political institutions have certainly occurred in the South in the post-World War II period, modifications in fertility, mortality, and even shifts in migration patterns have not lagged far behind and, in some cases, may be viewed as preceding them. These observations cast doubt on traditional demographic transition theory (in which structural changes are thought to underlie modifications in attitudes, which lead in turn to changes in demographic behavior) for explaining the case of recent demographic changes in the region. Indeed, a modernization of attitudes and life-style affecting demographic behavior appears to have occurred somewhat out of phase with structural transformations in the region, which may reflect the role of communication in the absorption of national culture. This would seem to be the case with fertility behavior, in particular, but it is also reflected in the shift of migration patterns. Comparative advantages certainly do exist to attract migrants (both newcomers and returnees) to the region, as well as to hold potential out-migrants, but noneconomic factors are probably of more importance than economic opportunities in accounting for the movement. The South, therefore, may be undergoing a different form of social and economic transformation, in which the momentum of change affects subjective experience as much as objective reality.

A *second* point regarding further types of analyses concerns the importance of considering compositional differences in examining demographic levels and trends. Although convergence between the South and the non-South on many of these factors has been noted, it is nonetheless true that significant differentials persist in fertility, mortality, and migration patterns *among* segments of the South's population. Fertility differences by race, urban and rural residence, educational attainment, and other measures of socioeconomic status exist. Mortality differences by race, sex, and socioeconomic grouping also may be noted, especially with respect to variations in cause of death. Similar differences are observed for migration levels and patterns. A knowledge of these compositional differences is clearly important in understanding trends, as was brought out in the analysis of the convergence of fertility between the South and the rest of the nation. But it is also true that compositional differences are crucial in the developments that may take place within a region. For example, Clarke has pointed out that very different political cultures appear to exist among native whites, blacks, and migrants of various types in the South. Thus, the region can serve as a medium for examining a range of important issues that may vary among different components of the population. The extent to which these interactions may differ from other patterns found in different regions can, in itself, be a subject of fruitful inquiry.

A *third* and final issue pertains to the great diversity that may exist among areal subunits of a region—states and census subregions. Various contributors point to this diversity with respect to several demographic factors. These include population size, growth, and density on the most general level, as well as variations in fertility, mortality, and migration. These differences, in turn, reflect themselves on population composition with respect to race, age, ethnic background, and the like. Indeed, the overall impression that one gains is that the diversity in the South is of far greater importance today than any comparisons of the region with the rest of the country or other regions. Perhaps this is understandable, considering that the Census South contains such disparate states as Texas, Florida, Mississippi, Maryland, and West Virginia. The main point is that this diversity ought to become a major focus of attention in which, of course, compositional factors should receive ample consideration. This is especially true of migratory exchanges within the region and functional studies, such as the one on metropolitan dominance in this volume.

A PROSPECTIVE VIEW

It is appropriate at this point to suggest some dimensions of changing conditions in the South that are likely to engender particular concern in the future and are, therefore, subjects that may draw the attention of demographers and other social scientists.

1. The South is the most populous major region in the country and is certain to retain this position. Although the rates of reproductive growth have slowed, further reductions in mortality, especially among the older segments of the population and in infant mortality (in which the South lags behind the country) will insure growth from this source. However, the growth that is likely to occur from the continuation of prevailing migration trends will come to play an even greater role. According to recent official projections for the Census South (U.S. Bureau of the Census, 1978), continuation of migration trends for 1970–1975, along with a modest natural increase, will mean a population of 92 million persons by the year 2000. This compares with a population of 68 million estimated for 1975, a gain of nearly a quarter of a million persons. This represents a 36 percent increase over the period for the region in contrast to only a 22 percent increase for the entire country. This growth is by no means evenly distributed throughout the region. The South Atlantic Division would increase by 42 percent, the East South Central by 23 percent, and the West South Central by 33 percent. The states of Texas and Florida are expected to receive a disproportionate share of this growth. The dynamics of this growth and its implications certainly warrant serious attention.

2. A most obvious feature of this change lies in population structure, particularly the growth of the elderly population. The traditionally youthful age structure of the South has given way to one that is becoming increasingly older. The region has caught up with the rest of the country in the proportion of the population that is 65 years of age and above, and all indications are that it will surpass other regions in the next few decades in this respect. An estimated 7.1 million older persons lived in the South in 1975, almost a third of the nation's elderly (U.S. Bureau of the Census, 1976a). Nearly a third of these elderly are 75 years of age and older, which indicates that the aged will be an increasingly dependent group from the standpoint of providing welfare services and medical care facilities. While this trend is clearly manifest on the national level as well, the aged dependency burden is likely to be even greater in the South, especially in states such as Florida, where over 16 percent of

the population is aged. Moreover, although the proportion of blacks who are elderly is substantially lower than among whites for the most part, in certain states such as West Virginia (15 percent) and Arkansas (12 percent), this proportion is very high, thus contributing a further burden of providing services. The aging black phenomenon, as well as the growth caused by extensive postretirement in-migration, deserve extensive research monitoring.

3. Race remains the most distinctive feature of population composition in the South. Although significant changes have occurred in the demographic behavior of southern blacks in terms of fertility and migration and the narrowing of differentials between whites and blacks, important differences exist and are likely to persist in the near future. Moreover, in closing these gaps, other issues may arise that call for public attention. Two examples can be cited concerning migratory shifts. It has been noted that the South in the 1970s has not only been the recipient of net in-migration to the region but that as many as 78,000 of these net migrants per year are low income persons, many of whom are black. This is a reversal of the patterns of earlier decades, in which the South could be thought of as an exporter of poor persons. The implications clearly are that the region must respond with appropriate social and economic opportunities for this influx. A second movement concerns the rapid urbanization of blacks in the South, especially to larger cities. This has produced stressful administrative implications for local and state governments in the areas of educational policy, legal and judicial procedures, public housing, welfare systems, and generally on the extent to which white-oriented political structures have been responsive to the new and emerging demands of a different citizenry. White flight from cities in the South may not be a popular topic for discussion, but studies of this population redistribution should be pursued.

4. Considerable attention has been paid in the past few years to the possible evolution of new ecological patterns revolving around the more rapid growth of nonmetropolitan areas. Clarke captures most tellingly the nature of these changes:

> Counterurbanization trends were evolving as southern development increased, but what the Northeast is so painfully achieving through economic and social displacement, the South enjoys as bittersweet historical privilege. . . . If the South inherited this settlement pattern characteristic of counterurbanization—deconcentrated, dispersed population clusters—and is experiencing indus-

trialization and postindustrialization simultaneously (Thompson, 1975), the environment differs substantially from that described in earlier ecological models.

Whether nonmetropolitan growth in the 1970s reflects out-migration from metropolitan areas, mainly but not exclusively from central cities, or reduced out-migration from nonmetropolitan areas is certainly not established, but there seems to be little doubt that this trend has occurred in the past decade in the nation as a whole and the South as well (Beale, 1977). McCarthy and Morrison (1977) suggest that the main forces operating in this process are: (1) the ease of transport that makes access to the national metropolitan economy available to previously less accessible areas; (2) the decentralization of manufacturing due to reduced transport costs, inexpensive land, and low wage rates in nonmetropolitan areas; and (3) changes in American life-style such as early retirement, new additional sources of income, and stronger leisure orientation. Surely all these factors can be found in the South, especially in the increased use of truck transport, the shift of certain types of manufacturing into areas of high labor supply (particularly female and black), and in many southern states the extensive development of retirement and recreational settlements.

5. One of the potentially serious consequences of this evolving ecological pattern is the increased focus that it puts on competing uses of land. Settlements in nonmetropolitan areas have larger built-up areas per capita, and the amount of land, mainly prime agricultural land, that has been converted per capita has increased markedly through time. Although the gravity of this incursion on prime agricultural land has been the subject of intense debate for some time, especially in California, there can be no questioning the importance that it holds for rational land use management in the face of competing demands for more recreational space, both private and public, the preservation of natural areas, the need for residential expansion for growing populations, and the potential acquisition of extremely large tracts for magna-agriculture. Already the shoreline of the southern states, so desirable for recreational purposes, has been subject to mass commercial development—often without regard to threats posed by tidal erosion and exposure to tropical storms—which influences its very existence. For most of the South, the relatively high density of dispersed settlement and the anticipated population growth bodes ever increasing competition for this most important resource—land itself.

6. Another implication of this emerging form is the increased burden that it puts on energy provision. While the South, as a region, is relatively favored by milder climate, the per capita consumption of energy in the region has been increasing, due in part to the more widespread use of air conditioning and the growth of energy-intensive industry. The South also has been favored by significant sources of energy (e.g., oil and, to a lesser extent, coal) as well as ready access to other fuels such as natural gas. As these sources are depleted, the South may well lose the competitive advantage that it now holds over other regions of the country. The development of solar energy, in which the South is particularly favored, and the availability of Mexican oil and natural gas supplies may well play a critical role in this regard. The development of energy conscious human settlements would hardly seem to be served well by the growth of nonmetropolitan developments, especially if they entail the greater use of private vehicles for commuting to work and journeys to retail facilities.

7. The cities of the South, which have grown so rapidly in the past few decades, will in time be subject to the same diseconomies that have faced older cities in other parts of the country, mainly in the Northeast and Midwest. Even dispersed nodal developments that characterize the suburban sprawl are subject to obsolescence and displacement by newer developments. Similar problems can face smaller southern cities and in fact may have done so already, although the magnitude is never as evident as it is in large metropolitan centers. Therefore, the differences are those of scale and timing rather than generically different conditions. This topic deserves close research attention.

8. The unique geographic position of the South in the country means that it shares borders and seas with countries of Latin America. These countries in South and Central America, as well as the Caribbean, are among the fastest growing in population in the world, and it is wise to keep this in mind in assessing future developments in the South. The region is a contact point with neighboring countries for better and for worse. Better in the sense of trade and commerce; worse perhaps in the strains that it places from the desires of emerging people for a share of the benefits to be enjoyed by life in the United States. In the past the South has mainly adopted an insular view of its position in the Western Hemisphere. The development of close cultural and economic ties between Texas and Mexico and the growth of the Cuban refugee population in south Florida suggest that the trend may be altered in the future

and that the South will assume more importance with stronger relationships with Latin America.

SUMMARY

Does the "South" offer something to study? Yes. Perhaps not so much as a unit of analysis to be compared to the rest of the country but as a geographic region within which great diversity exists and one which has undergone significant demographic change in the past 30 years. The timing and pace of this change differ substantially from the patterns present in other sections of the country and in themselves present unique opportunities for demographic scholars to test and expand their theoretical concepts. The heterogeneity of demographic behavior among the southern population affords similar opportunities. Thus, the "demography of the South" remains a viable concept, even if the South is no longer (if ever) the monolithic entity described in the extensive writings of the regionalists. Yet, we owe an important intellectual debt to such professionals as Rupert Vance, who laid out an agenda for scholarship as well as a challenge for the nation. Indeed, it was fitting that his lifetime encompassed so much of the fulfillment urged in the title of the final chapter of his book *All These People* (1945):
Wanted: The Nation's Future for the South

References

Advisory Commission on Intergovernment Relations. 1967. *State-Local Taxation and Industrial Location.* Washington, D.C.: Government Printing Office.

Almond, Gabriel. 1956. "Comparative Political Systems." *Journal of Politics* 18 : 391–409.

Barabba, Vincent P. 1975. "The National Setting: Regional Shifts, Metropolitan Decline, and Urban Decay." Pp. 39–76 in *Post-Industrial America: Metropolitan Decline and Inter-Regional Job Shifts,* George Sternlieb and James W. Hughes, eds. New Brunswick, N.J.: Center for Urban Policy Research, Rutgers University.

Barone, Michael, Grant Ujifusa, and Douglas Matthews. 1973. *The Almanac of American Politics.* Boston: Gambit.

Barsby, Steve L., and Dennis R. Cox. 1975. *Interstate Migration of the Elderly.* Lexington, Mass.: Lexington Books.

Beale, Calvin L. 1975. *The Revival of Population Growth in Nonmetropolitan America.* ERS-605. Washington, D.C.: Economic Development Division, Economic Research Service, U.S. Department of Agriculture.

———. 1976. "A Further Look at Nonmetropolitan Population Growth since 1970." *American Journal of Agricultural Economics* 58 : 953–958.

———. 1977. "The Recent Shift of United States Population to Nonmetropolitan Areas, 1970–1975." *International Regional Science Review* 2 : 113–122.

Beaver, Steven E. 1975. *Demographic Transition Theory Reinterpreted: An Application to Recent Natality Trends in Latin America.* Lexington, Mass.: D. C. Heath.

Beck, Paul Allen. 1977. "Partisan Dealignment in the Postwar South." *American Political Science Review* 71 : 477–496.

Bellante, Don. 1979. "The North-South Differential and the Migration of Heterogeneous Labor." *American Economic Review* 69 : 166–175.

Berry, Brian J. L. 1976. "Transformations of the Nation's Urban System: Small City Growth as a Zero Sum Game." Paper prepared for the Public Policy Forum of the Joint Center for Political Studies, Washington, D.C.

———— and Donald C. Dahmann. 1977. *Population Redistribution in the United States in the 1970s.* Washington, D.C.: National Academy of Sciences.

Blacker, C. P. 1947. "Stages in Population Growth." *Eugenics Review* 39:88–102.

Bodenhofer, H. J. 1967. "The Mobility of Labor and the Theory of Human Capital." *Journal of Human Resources* 2:431–439.

Bogue, Donald J. 1949. *The Structure of the Metropolitan Community.* Ann Arbor: Horace H. Rackham School of Graduate Studies, University of Michigan.

————. 1959. *The Population of the United States.* Glencoe, Ill.: Free Press.

———— and Calvin L. Beale. 1959. *Economic Areas of the United States.* Glencoe, Ill.: Free Press.

Bohm, Robert A. 1977. "The Competitive Position of Coal in the Southeast to the Year 2000." Paper presented at the annual meeting of the Southern Economic Association.

Bouvier, Leon F., and Edward E. Cahill. 1975. "Demographic Factors Affecting the Educational Level of the South Atlantic States." *Review of Regional Studies* 5:70–83.

Bowles, G., and James D. Tarver. 1965. *Net Migration of the Population, 1950–1960, by Age, Sex, and Color.* Washington, D.C.: Government Printing Office.

Bowles, Samuel. 1970. "Migration as Investment: Empirical Tests of the Human Investment Approach to Geographic Mobility." *Review of Economics and Statistics* 52:356–362.

Brooks, R. P. 1929. *The Industrialization of the South.* Athens, Ga.: Bureau of Business Research, University of Georgia.

Browning, Harley L., and Joachim Singelmann. 1975. *The Emergence of a Service Society: Demographic and Sociological Aspects of the Sectoral Transformation of the Labor Force in the U.S.A.* Springfield, Va.: National Technical Information Service.

————. 1978. "The Transformation of the U.S. Labor Force: The Interaction of Industry and Occupation." *Politics and Society* 8:481–509.

Butler, Edgar W., et al. 1969. *Moving Behavior and Residential Choice: A National Survey.* Washington, D.C.: Highway Research Board, National Academy of Sciences.

Cahill, Edward E. 1976. "Holding Power of the South." *Growth and Change* 7:38–42.

Caldwell, John C. 1976. "Toward a Restatement of Demographic Transition Theory." *Population and Development Review* 2:321–366.

Cho, L. J. 1968. "Income and Differentials in Current Fertility." *Demography* 5:198–211.

————. 1971. "On Estimating Annual Birth Rates from Census Data on

Children." Pp. 86–96 in *Proceedings of the American Statistical Association, Social Statistics Section.*

———, Wilson H. Grabill, and Donald J. Bogue. 1970. *Differential Current Fertility in the United States.* Chicago: Community and Family Study Center, University of Chicago.

Clark, Colin. 1940. *The Conditions of Economic Progress.* London: Macmillan & Co.

Clynch, Edward. 1972. "A Critique of Ira Sharkansky's 'The Utility of Elazar's Political Culture.'" *Polity* 5:139–141.

Coale, Ansley J. 1969. "The Decline of Fertility in Europe from the French Revolution to World War II." Pp. 3–4 in *Fertility and Family Planning: A World View*, S. J. Behrman et al., eds. Ann Arbor: University of Michigan Press.

———. 1975. "The Demographic Transition." Pp. 347–355 in *The Population Debate: Dimensions and Perspectives.* Vol. 1. New York: United Nations.

——— and Edgar M. Hoover. 1958. *Population Growth and Economic Development in Low-Income Countries.* Princeton, N.J.: Princeton University Press.

Coelho, Philip R. P., and Moheb A. Ghali. 1971. "The End of the North-South Wage Differential." *American Economic Review* 61:932–937.

Collingwood, Robin G. 1940. *An Essay on Metaphysics.* London: Clarendon Press.

Collins, Selwyn D., and Josephine Lehmann. 1953. "Excess Deaths from Influenza and Pneumonia and from Important Chronic Diseases during Epidemic Periods, 1918–1951." *Public Health Monograph*, no. 10. Washington, D.C.: Government Printing Office.

Cowgill, Donald O. 1962. "Transition Theory as General Population Theory." *Social Forces* 41:270–279.

DaVanzo, Julie, and Peter A. Morrison. 1978. "Dynamics of Return Migration: Descriptive Findings from a Longitudinal Study." Rand Paper P-5913. Santa Monica: Rand Corporation.

David, Paul A. 1974. "Fortune, Risk, and the Micro-Economics of Migration." Pp. 21–88 in *Nations and Households in Economic Growth*, Paul A. David and M. W. Reder, eds. New York: Academic Press.

Davis, K. 1972. *World Urbanization, 1950–1970.* Vol. 2. *Analysis of Trends, Relationships, and Developments.* Berkeley: Institute of International Studies, University of California.

DeJong, Gordon F. 1968. *Appalachian Fertility Decline: A Demographic and Sociological Analysis.* Lexington: University of Kentucky Press.

———. 1977. "Residential Preferences and Migration." *Demography* 14: 169–178.

Dickinson, Robert E. 1934. "Metropolitan Regions of the United States." *Geographical Review* 24:278–286.

Dowd, Douglas F. 1977. *The Twisted Dream—Capitalist Development in the United States since 1776.* Cambridge, Mass.: Winthrop.

Duncan, Beverly, and Stanley Lieberson. 1970. *Metropolis and Region in Transition*. Beverly Hills, Calif.: Sage Publications.

Duncan, Otis D. 1959. "Human Ecology and Population Studies." Pp. 678–716 in *The Study of Population*, Philip M. Hauser and Otis D. Duncan, eds. Chicago: University of Chicago Press.

——— et al. 1960. *Metropolis and Region*. Baltimore: Johns Hopkins Press.

Duncan, Otis D., and Albert J. Reiss, Jr. 1956. *Social Characteristics of Urban and Rural Communities, 1950*. New York: John Wiley & Sons.

Dunn, Edgar S. 1962. *Recent Southern Economic Development*. Gainesville: University of Florida Press.

Easterlin, Richard A. 1975a. "An Economic Framework for Fertility Analysis." *Studies in Family Planning* 6:54–63.

———. 1975b. "The Effect of Modernization on Family Reproductive Behavior." Pp. 263–277 in *The Population Debate: Dimensions and Perspectives*. Vol. 2. New York: United Nations.

Elazar, Daniel. 1970. *Cities of the Prairie*. New York: Basic Books.

Eldridge, Hope. n.d. *Net Intercensal Migration for States and Geographic Divisions of the United States, 1950–1960*. Philadelphia: Population Studies Center, University of Pennsylvania.

Elkin, Stephen L. 1973. *Politics and Land Use Planning*. Cambridge: Cambridge University Press.

Espenshade, Thomas J. 1977. "The Value and Cost of Children." *Population Bulletin* 32:1–48.

Ferejohn, John A. 1974. *Pork Barrel Politics*. Stanford: Stanford University Press.

Fields, Gary S. 1976. "Labor Force Migration, Unemployment, and Job Turnover." *Review of Economics and Statistics* 58:407–415.

Firey, Walter. 1945. "Sentiment and Symbolism as Ecological Variables." *American Sociological Review* 10:141–148.

Fisher, Allen G. B. 1935. *The Clash of Progress and Security*. London: Macmillan & Co.

Forster, Colin, and G. S. L. Tucker. 1972. *Economic Opportunity and White American Fertility Ratios, 1800–1860*. New Haven, Conn.: Yale University Press.

Friedlander, Stanley L. 1976. *Regional Economic Development and Federal Legislation*. Washington, D.C.: Economic Development Administration, U.S. Department of Commerce.

Frisbie, W. Parker, and Dudley L. Poston, Jr. 1975. "Components of Sustenance Organization and Nonmetropolitan Population Change: A Human Ecological Investigation." *American Sociological Review* 40:773–784.

———. 1976. "The Structure of Sustenance Organization and Population Change in Nonmetropolitan America." *Rural Sociology* 41:354–370.

———. 1978a. "Sustenance Differentiation and Population Redistribution." *Social Forces* 57:42–56.

————. 1978b. *Sustenance Organization and Migration in Nonmetropolitan America.* Iowa City: Iowa Urban Community Research Center, University of Iowa.

Fuchs, Victor R. 1962. "The Determinants of the Redistribution of Manufacturing in the United States since 1929." *Review of Economics and Statistics* 44:167–177.

————. 1968. *The Service Economy.* New York: Columbia University Press.

Fuguitt, Glenn V., and Calvin L. Beale. 1976. *Population Change in Nonmetropolitan Cities and Towns.* Agricultural Economic Report no. 323. Washington, D.C.: Economic Research Service, U.S. Department of Agriculture.

Fuguitt, Glenn V., and James J. Zuiches. 1975. "Residential Preferences and Population Distribution." *Demography* 12:491–504.

Gardner, Bruce. 1972. "Economic Aspects of the Fertility of Rural-Farm and Urban Women." *Southern Economic Journal* 38:518–524.

Gibbs, Jack P., and Walter T. Martin. 1959. "Toward a Theoretical System of Human Ecology." *Pacific Sociological Review* 2:29–36.

Gibbs, Jack P., and Dudley L. Poston, Jr. 1975. "The Division of Labor: Conceptualization and Related Measures." *Social Forces* 53:468–476.

Gibson, Campbell. 1975. "The Contribution of Immigration to the United States' Population Growth, 1790–1970." *International Migration Review* 9:157–177.

Goldstein, Sidney, and David F. Sly. 1975. *The Measurement of Urbanization and Projection of Urban Population.* Liège, Belg.: International Union for the Scientific Study of Population.

————. 1977. *Patterns of Urbanization: Comparative Country Studies.* Liège, Belg.: International Union for the Scientific Study of Population.

Gordon, David M. 1977. "Class Struggle and the Stages of American Urban Development." Pp. 55–82 in *The Rise of the Sunbelt Cities,* David C. Perry and Alfred J. Watkins, eds. Beverly Hills, Calif.: Sage Publications.

Grabill, Wilson H., and L. J. Cho. 1965. "Methodology for the Measurement of Current Fertility from Population Data on Young Children." *Demography* 2:50–73.

Grabill, Wilson H., Clyde V. Kiser, and Pascal K. Whelpton. 1958. *The Fertility of American Women.* New York: John Wiley & Sons.

Gras, N. S. B. 1922. *An Introduction to Economic History.* New York: Harper and Brothers.

Gray, Virginia. 1973. "Innovation in the States: A Diffusion Study." *American Political Science Review* 67:1174–1185.

Greenhut, M., and W. T. Whitman, eds. 1964. *Essays in Southern Economic Development.* Chapel Hill: University of North Carolina Press.

Greenwood, Michael J. 1975a. "Research on Internal Migration in the

United States: A Survey." *Journel of Economic Literature* 13:397–433.
———. 1975b. "Simultaneity Bias in Migration Models: An Empirical Examination." *Demography* 12:519–536.

Gregory, Paul R., and J. M. Campbell. 1976. "Fertility Interactions and Modernization Turning Points." *Journal of Political Economy* 84: 835–847.

Habakkuk, H. J. 1953. "English Population in the Eighteenth Century." *Economic History Review*, 2d ser., 6:117–133.

Hadden, Jeffrey K., and Edgar F. Borgatta. 1965. *American Cities: Their Social Characteristics.* Chicago: Rand McNally and Co.

Hamermesh, Daniel S., and Neal M. Soss. 1974. "An Economic Theory of Suicide." *Journal of Political Economy* 82:83–98.

Hamilton, C. Horace. 1962. "Health and Health Services." Pp. 219–221 in *The Southern Appalachian Region: A Survey*, Thomas R. Ford, ed. Lexington: University of Kentucky Press.

———. 1970. *The Changing Population of the USA South.* Chapel Hill: Carolina Population Center, University of North Carolina.

Hammond, Ross W. 1972. *Economic Development Trends in the 16-State South.* Atlanta: Industrial Development Division, Georgia Institute of Technology.

Hanna, Frank A. 1957. "Analysis of Interstate Income Differentials: Theory and Practice." Pp. 113–161 in *Regional Income.* Princeton, N.J.: Princeton University Press for National Bureau of Economic Research.

Harris, Chauncy D. 1943. "A Functional Classification of Cities in the United States." *Geographical Review* 33:86–99.

———. 1954. "The Market as a Factor in the Localization of Industry in the United States." *Annals of the American Association of Geographers* 44:315–348.

Hathaway, Dale E., J. Allan Beegle, and W. Keith Bryant. 1968. *People of Rural America.* Washington, D.C.: Government Printing Office.

Hawley, Amos. 1950. *Human Ecology: A Theory of Community Structure.* New York: Ronald Press.

———. 1971. *Urban Society.* New York: Ronald Press.

Heclo, Hugh. 1974. *Modern Social Politics in Britain and Sweden.* New Haven, Conn.: Yale University Press.

Heltman, Lynne R. 1975. "Mobility of the Aged in the United States." Paper presented at the annual meeting of the Population Association of America.

Hines, Fred K., David L. Brown, and John M. Zimmer. 1975. *Social and Economic Characteristics of the Population in Metro and Nonmetro Counties, 1970.* Washington, D.C.: Economic Development Division, Economic Research Service, U.S. Department of Agriculture.

Hoch, Irving. 1977. "The Role of Energy in the Regional Distribution of Economic Activity." Paper presented at the Conference on Balanced

National Growth and Regional Change, LBJ School of Public Affairs, University of Texas at Austin.

Howard, Russell L. 1977. *Energy for the Growing South*. Research Triangle Park, N.C.: Southern Growth Policies Board.

Institute for Research in Social Science. 1979. *Survey on Energy and Migration*. Chapel Hill: University of North Carolina.

Isard, Walter. 1960. *Methods of Regional Analysis: An Introduction to Regional Science*. Cambridge, Mass.: MIT Press.

Johnson, Charles A. 1976. "Political Culture in the American States: Elazar's Formulation Examined." *American Journal of Political Science* 20:491–509.

Jones, Lamar B. 1967. "Farm Labor: Shortage or Surplus?" *Southwestern Social Science Quarterly* 47:401–412.

Jusenius, Carol L., and Larry C. Ledebur. 1976. *A Myth in the Making: The Southern Economic Challenge and Northern Economic Decline*. Washington, D.C.: Economic Development Administration, U.S. Department of Commerce.

Kasarda, John D. 1976. "The Changing Occupational Structure of the American Metropolis: Apropos the Urban Problems." Pp. 113–136 in *The Changing Face of the Suburbs*, Barry Schwartz, ed. Chicago: University of Chicago Press.

Kass, Roy. 1973. "A Functional Classification of Metropolitan Communities." *Demography* 10:427–445.

Kiker, B. F., and Earle C. Traynham. 1977. "Earnings Differentials among Nonmigrants, Return Migrants, and Nonreturn Migrants." *Growth and Change* 8:2–7.

Kiser, Clyde V., Wilson H. Grabill, and A. A. Campbell. 1968. *Trends and Variations in Fertility in the United States*. Cambridge, Mass.: Harvard University Press.

Kuznets, Simon. 1966. *Modern Economic Growth*. New Haven, Conn.: Yale University Press.

———. 1971. *Economic Growth of Nations—Total Output and Production Structure*. Cambridge, Mass.: Harvard University Press.

Lansing, John B., and Eva Mueller. 1967. *The Geographic Mobility of Labor*. Ann Arbor: Institute for Survey Research, University of Michigan.

Lee, Anne S. 1974. "Return Migration in the United States." *International Migration Review* 8:283–300.

Lee, Everett S. 1964. "Internal Migration and Population Redistribution in the United States." Pp. 123–136 in *Population: The Vital Revolution*, Ronald Freedman, ed. Garden City, N.Y.: Doubleday Anchor.

———. 1966. "A Theory of Migration." *Demography* 3:47–57.

——— et al. 1957. *Population Redistribution and Economic Growth: United States, 1870–1950*. Vol. 1. *Methodological Considerations and Reference Tables*. Philadelphia: American Philosophical Society.

Linder, Forrest E., and Robert D. Grove. 1947. *Vital Statistics Rates in the United States, 1900–1940.* Washington, D.C.: Government Printing Office.

Lockhart, Madely M. 1977. *Income Distribution in the South.* Research Triangle Park, N.C.: Southern Growth Policies Board.

Long, John F. 1976. "Interstate Migration of the Armed Forces." Paper presented at the annual meeting of the Southern Sociological Society.

Long, Larry H., and Celia C. Boertlein. 1976. "The Geographical Mobility of Americans: An International Comparison." *Current Population Reports,* ser. P-23, no. 64.

Long, Larry H., and Kristin A. Hansen. 1975. "Trends in Return Migration to the South." *Demography* 12:601–614.

———. 1977. "Models of Return, Repeat, and Primary Migration by Age and Race." Paper presented at the annual meeting of the Population Association of America.

———. 1979. "Reasons for Interstate Migration: Jobs, Retirement, Climate, and Other Influences." *Current Population Reports,* ser. P-23, no. 81.

Lowi, Theodore J. 1970. "Decision Making vs. Policy Making: Toward an Antidote for Technocracy." *Public Administration Review* 30:314–325.

———. 1969. *Interest Group Liberalism.* New York: Norton.

Lyons, William, and Robert F. Durant. 1978. "The Impact of In-Migration on a State Political System: The Case of Tennessee." Unpublished paper.

McCarthy, Kevin F., and Peter A. Morrison. 1977. "The Changing Demographic and Economic Structure of Nonmetropolitan Areas in the United States." *International Regional Science Review* 2:123–142.

McComb, David G. 1969. *Houston: The Bayou City.* Austin: University of Texas Press.

McKay, John, and James S. Whitelaw. 1977. "The Role of Large Private and Government Organizations in Generating Flows of Inter-Regional Migrants: The Case of Australia." *Economic Geography* 53:28–44.

McKenzie, R. D. 1933. *The Metropolitan Community.* New York: McGraw-Hill.

McKeown, Thomas, and R. G. Brown. 1955. "Medical Evidence Related to English Population Changes in the Eighteenth Century." *Population Studies* 9:119–141.

McKinney, J., and L. B. Bourque. 1971. "The Changing South: National Incorporation of a Region." *American Sociological Review* 36:3, 399–411.

Masnick, George S., and Joseph A. McFalls, Jr. 1976. "A New Perspective on the Twentieth-Century American Fertility Swing." *Journal of Family History* 1:216–244.

Metropolitan Life Insurance Company. 1973. "Regional Variations in Nonwhite Mortality." *Statistical Bulletin* 54:7–9.

Meyer, John R. 1963. "Regional Economics: A Survey." *American Economic Review* 53:19–54.

Mickens, Alvin. 1977. "Regional Defense Demand and Racial Response Differences in the Net Migration of Workers." *Quarterly Review of Economics and Business* 17:65–82.

Miernyk, William H. 1976. "Regional Economic Consequences of High Energy Prices in the United States." *The Journal of Energy and Development* 1:213–239.

Miller, Herman P. 1966. *Income Distribution in the United States.* Washington, D.C.: Government Printing Office.

Moran, Theodore. 1974. *Multinational Corporations and the Politics of Independence.* Princeton, N.J.: Princeton University Press.

Morgan, Robert W., et al. 1976. *New Perspectives on the Demographic Transition.* Washington, D.C.: Interdisciplinary Communications Program, Smithsonian Institution.

Moriyama, Iwao M. 1964. "The Change in Mortality Trends in the United States." *Vital and Health Statistics.* Washington, D.C.: National Center for Health Statistics.

Moroney, John R. 1975. "Natural Resource Endowments and Comparative Labor Costs: A Hybrid Model of Comparative Advantage." *Journal of Regional Science* 15:139–150.

Morrison, Peter A. 1967. "Duration of Residence and Prospective Migration: The Evaluation of a Stochastic Model." *Demography* 4:2, 553–561.

———. 1971. "Chronic Movers and the Future Redistribution of Population: A Longitudinal Analysis." *Demography* 8:171–184.

———. 1972. "The Impact of Population Stabilization on Migration and Redistribution." Pp. 543–560 in *Population, Distribution, and Policy.* Vol. 5. *Research Reports, Commission on Population Growth and the American Future,* Sara Mills Mazie, ed. Washington, D.C.: Government Printing Office.

——— and Daniel A. Relles. 1975. "Recent Research Insights into Local Migration Flows." Paper presented to the Conference on the Distribution of Population, Center for Population Research, National Institute of Child Health and Human Development.

Nam, Charles B. 1979. "The Progress of Demography as a Scientific Discipline." *Demography* 16:485–492.

Navratil, Frank J., and James J. Doyle. 1977. "The Socioeconomic Determinants of Migration and the Level of Aggregation." *Southern Economic Journal* 43:1547–1559.

Newman, Dorothy K. 1967. "The Negro's Journey to the City." *Monthly Labor Review* May:503–507, June:644–650.

New York Times. 1977. "Economic Gains in South Linked to Under Use of Its Taxing Potential." March 11.

Nicholls, William H. 1960. "Southern Tradition and Regional Economic Progress." *Southern Economic Journal* 26:187–198.

Notestein, Frank W. 1945. "Population—the Long View." Pp. 36–57 in *Food for the World*. Chicago: University of Chicago Press.

Odum, Howard W. 1936. *Southern Regions of the United States*. Chapel Hill: University of North Carolina Press.

———. 1951. "The Promise of Regionalism." Pp. 395–425 in *Regionalism in America*, Merrill Jensen, ed. Madison: University of Wisconsin Press.

——— and Harry E. Moore. 1938. *American Regionalism: A Cultural-Historical Approach to National Integration*. New York: Henry Holt.

Omran, Abdel R. 1975. "The Epidemiologic Transition in North Carolina during the Last 50 to 90 Years: II. Changing Patterns of Disease and Causes of Death." *North Carolina Medical Journal* 36:83–88.

———. 1977. "Epidemiologic Transition in the U.S." *Population Bulletin* 32, no. 2. Washington, D.C.: Population Reference Bureau.

Oshima, Harry T. 1971. "Labor-force 'Explosion' and the Labor-Intensive Sector in Asian Growth." *Economic Development and Cultural Change* 19:161–183.

Pappenfort, Donnell M. 1959. "The Ecological Field and the Metropolitan Community: Manufacturing and Management." *American Journal of Sociology* 64:380–385.

Patrick, Clifford H., and P. Neal Ritchey. 1974. "Changes in Population and Employment as Processes in Regional Development." *Rural Sociology* 39:224–237.

Perry, David C., and Alfred J. Watkins. 1977. "Three Theories of American Urban Development: Introduction." Pp. 13–17 in *The Rise of the Sunbelt Cities*, David C. Perry and Alfred J. Watkins, eds. Beverly Hills, Calif.: Sage Publications.

———, eds. 1977. *The Rise of the Sunbelt Cities*. Beverly Hills, Calif.: Sage Publications.

Petersen, William. 1958. "A General Typology of Migration." *American Sociological Review* 23:256–266.

Phillips, Llad, Harold Votey, and Darold E. Maxwell. 1969. "A Synthesis of the Economic and Demographic Models of Fertility: An Econometric Test." *Review of Economics and Statistics* 51:298–308.

Pickard, Jerome P. 1972. "U.S. Metropolitan Growth and Expansion, 1970–2000, with Population Projections." Pp. 127–182 in *Population, Distribution, and Policy*. Vol. 5. *Research Reports, Commission on Population Growth and the American Future*, Sara Mills Mazie, ed. Washington, D.C.: Government Printing Office.

Piven, Frances Fox, and Richard A. Cloward. 1971. *Regulating the Poor: The Functions of Public Welfare*. New York: Random House.

Postan, Michael M. 1971. *Fact and Relevance—Essays on Historical Method*. Cambridge: At the University Press.

Poston, Dudley L., Jr. 1980. "Regional Ecology: The Macroscopic Analysis of Sustenance Organization." A chapter in *Sociological Human Ecol-*

ogy: Contemporary Issues and Applications, M. Micklin and H. Choldin, eds. New York: Academic Press.

———— and Jeffrey Passel. 1972. "The Texas Population in 1970: Racial Residential Segregation in Cities." *Texas Business Review* 46:1–6.

Poston, Dudley L., Jr., and Ralph White. 1978. "Indigenous Labor Supply, Sustenance Organization, and Population Redistribution in Non-metropolitan America: An Extension to the Ecological Theory of Migration." *Demography* 15:637–641.

Pursell, Donald E. 1977. "Age and Educational Dimensions in Southern Migration Patterns, 1965–1970." *Southern Economic Journal* 44: 148–154.

Pye, Lucian W. 1972. "Culture and Political Science: Problems in the Evaluation of the Concept of Political Culture." *Social Science Quarterly* 53:284–296.

Reed, John Shelton. 1972. *The Enduring South: Subcultural Persistence in Mass Society*. Lexington, Mass.: Lexington Books.

Retherford, Robert D., and Neil Bennett. 1977. "Sampling Variability of Own-Children-Fertility Estimates." *Demography* 14:571–580.

Retherford, Robert D., and L. J. Cho. 1974. "Age-Parity-Specific Fertility Rates from Census or Survey Data on Own Children." Paper presented at the annual meeting of the Population Association of America.

Rice, Patricia L. 1977. "The Petroleum Industry in the South: Progress and Prospects." Paper presented at the annual meeting of the Southern Economic Association.

Richardson, Harry W. 1969. *Regional Economics: Location Theory, Urban Structure, and Regional Change*. New York: Praeger.

Rindfuss, Ronald R. 1976. "Annual Fertility Rates from Census Data on Own Children: Comparisons with Vital Statistics Data for the United States." *Demography* 13:235–249.

————. 1977. "Methodological Difficulties Encountered in Using Own-Children Data: Illustrations from the United States." East-West Population Institute Paper Series, no. 42. Honolulu: East-West Population Institute.

————, John Shelton Reed, and Craig St. John. 1978. "A Fertility Reaction to a Historical Event: Southern White Birthrates and the 1954 Desegregation Ruling." *Science* 201:178–180.

Rindfuss, Ronald R., and James A. Sweet. 1977. *Postwar Fertility Trends and Differentials in the United States*. New York: Academic Press.

Rogers, Andrei. 1978. "Migration, Urbanization, Resources, and Development." Pp. 149–217 in *Alternatives for Growth*, Harvey McMains and Lyle Wilcox, eds. Cambridge, Mass.: Ballinger Publishing Co.

Ryder, Norman B., and Charles F. Westoff. 1971. *Reproduction in the United States, 1965*. Princeton, N.J.: Princeton University Press.

————. 1972. "Wanted and Unwanted Fertility in the United States." Pp. 467–487 in *Demographic and Social Aspects of Population Growth,*

Charles F. Westoff and Robert Parke, Jr., eds. Vol. 1. Commission on Population Growth and the American Future Research Reports. Washington, D.C.: Government Printing Office.

Sale, Kirkpatrick. 1975. *Power Shift: The Rise of the Southern Rim and Its Challenge to the Eastern Establishment*. New York: Random House.

Sanderson, Warren C. 1976. "On Two Schools of the Economics of Fertility." *Population and Development Review* 2:469–477.

Satin, Maurice S. 1969. "An Empirical Test of the Descriptive Validity of the Theory of Demographic Transition in a Fifty-Three Nation Sample." *Sociological Quarterly* 10:190–203.

Schwartz, Aba. 1976. "Migration, Age, and Education." *Journal of Political Economy* 84:701–719.

Serow, William J. 1976. "The Role of the Military in Net Migration for States." *Review of Public Data Use* 4:42–48.

—— and Thomas J. Espenshade. 1978. "The Economics of Declining Population Growth: An Assessment of the Current Literature." Pp. 13–40 in *The Economic Consequences of Slowing Population Growth*, Thomas J. Espenshade and William J. Serow, eds. New York: Academic Press.

Sharkansky, Ira. 1969. "The Utility of Elazar's Political Culture: A Research Note." *Polity* 2:66–83.

——. 1970. *Regionalism in American Politics*. Indianapolis and New York: Bobbs-Merrill.

——. 1975. *The United States—A Study of a Developing Country*. New York: David McKay Company.

Shryock, Henry S., Jr. 1964. *Population Mobility within the United States*. Chicago: Community and Family Study Center, University of Chicago.

—— and Jacob S. Siegel. Rev. ed. 1973. *The Methods and Materials of Demography*. Washington, D.C.: Government Printing Office.

Sinclair, Sonja A. 1974. "Fertility." Pp. 124–168 in *Recent Population Movements in Jamaica*. Paris: Comité International de Coopération dans les Recherches Nationales en Démographie.

Singelmann, Joachim. 1977. "Population, Income, and Employment Growth in Services, 1960–1970." Working paper no. 77-38. Madison: Center for Demography and Ecology, University of Wisconsin.

——. 1978. *From Agriculture to Services: The Transformation of Industrial Employment*. Beverly Hills, Calif.: Sage Publications.

Sjaastad, Larry A. 1962. "The Costs and Returns of Human Migration." *Journal of Political Economy* 70:80–93 (supplement).

Sly, David F. 1972. "Evaluating Estimates of Net Migration and Net Migration Rates Based on Survival Ratios Corrected in Varying Degrees." *Journal of the American Statistical Association* 67:313–318.

——. 1972. "Migration and the Ecological Complex." *American Sociological Review* 37:615–628.

———— and Jeff Tayman. 1977. "Ecological Approach to Migration Reexamined." *American Sociological Review* 42:783–795.

Sly, David F., and R. H. Weller. 1972. "Some Comments on the Changing South: National Incorporation of a Region." *American Sociological Review* 37:227–230.

Sopher, David E. 1972. "Place and Location: Notes on the Spatial Patterning of Culture." *Social Science Quarterly* 53:321–337.

South, Scott J., and Dudley L. Poston, Jr. 1979. "Stability and Change in the U.S. Metropolitan System, 1950–1970." Texas Population Research Center Papers, Series 1.020. Austin: Population Research Center, University of Texas.

Southern Growth Policies Board. 1978. *Problems and Promises.* Research Triangle Park, N.C.

Speare, Alden, Jr. 1971. "A Cost-Benefit Model of Rural-to-Urban Migration in Taiwan." *Population Studies* 25:117–131.

————, S. Goldstein, and W. Frey. 1975. *Residential Mobility, Migration, and Metropolitan Change.* Cambridge, Mass.: Ballinger Publishing Co.

Spengler, Joseph J. 1937. "Population Problems in the South—Part I." *Southern Economic Journal* 3:393–410.

———— and George C. Myers. 1977. "Migration and Socio-Economic Development: Today and Yesterday." Pp. 11–35 in *Internal Migration: A Comparative Perspective,* A. A. Brown and E. Neuberger, eds. New York: Academic Press.

Sternlieb, George, and James W. Hughes. 1975. Prologue in *Post-Industrial America: Metropolitan Decline and Inter-Regional Job Shifts,* George Sternlieb and James W. Hughes, eds. New Brunswick, N.J.: Center for Urban Policy Research, Rutgers University.

Stinner, William F., and Gordon F. DeJong. 1969. "Southern Negro Migration: Social and Economic Components of an Ecological Model." *Demography* 6:455–471.

Sturgis, R. B. 1973. *Selected Factors Influencing City Growth, 1960–1970.* ORNL-UR-109. Oak Ridge, Tenn.: Oak Ridge National Laboratory.

Taeuber, Conrad, and Irene Barnes Taeuber. 1942. *A Research Memorandum on Internal Migration Resulting from the War Effort.* New York: Social Science Research Council.

Tarver, James D. 1972. "Patterns of Population Change among Southern Nonmetropolitan Towns, 1950–1970." *Rural Sociology* 37:53–72.

Taylor, R. C. 1969. "Migration and Motivation: A Study of Determinants and Types." Pp. 99–133 in *Migration,* John A. Jackson, ed. Cambridge: At the University Press.

Teitelbaum, Michael S. 1975. "Relevance of Demographic Transition Theory for Developing Countries." *Science* 188:420–425.

Thompson, Edgar T. 1975. *Plantation Societies, Race Relations, and the South: The Regimentation of Populations.* Durham, N.C.: Duke University Press.

Thompson, Holland. 1919. *The New South*. New Haven, Conn.: Yale University Press.

Thompson, Lorin A. 1954. "Urbanization, Occupational Shifts, and Economic Progress." Pp. 38–53 in *The Urban South*, Rupert B. Vance and Nicholas J. Demerath, eds. Chapel Hill: University of North Carolina Press.

Thompson, Warren S. 1929. "Population." *American Journal of Sociology* 34:959–975.

――― and Pascal K. Whelpton. 1933. *Population Trends in the United States*. New York: McGraw-Hill.

Till, Thomas E. 1974. "Changes in Industries Located in the Nonmetropolitan South, 1959–1960." *American Journal of Agricultural Economics* 56:306–309.

Tobin, Gary A. 1976. "Suburbanization and the Development of Motor Transportation: Transportation Technology and the Suburbanization Process." Pp. 95–111 in *The Changing Face of the Suburbs*, Barry Schwartz, ed. Chicago: University of Chicago Press.

Toney, M. B. 1976. "Length of Residence, Social Ties, and Economic Opportunities." *Demography* 13:297–310.

Tower, W. D. 1905. "The Geography of American Cities." *Bulletin of the American Geographical Society* 37:577–588.

Tucker, C. Jack. 1976. "Changing Patterns of Migration between Metropolitan and Nonmetropolitan Areas in the United States: Recent Evidence." *Demography* 13:435–443.

United Nations. 1973. *The Determinants and Consequences of Population Trends*. New York.

U.S. Bureau of the Census. 1943. *Introduction to the 1940 Census of Population: Vol. III, Part 1, Labor Force: United States Summary*. Washington, D.C.: Government Printing Office.

―――. 1963a. *Statistical Abstract of the United States: 1963*. Washington, D.C.: Government Printing Office.

―――. 1963b. *U.S. Census of Population: 1960, Detailed Characteristics, United States Summary*. Washington, D.C.: Government Printing Office.

―――. 1971. "Components of Population Change by County: 1960 to 1970." *Current Population Reports*, ser. P-25, no. 461.

―――. 1973a. *Census of Population: 1970, Detailed Characteristics, United States Summary*. Washington, D.C.: Government Printing Office.

―――. 1973b. *County and City Data Book*. Washington, D.C.: Government Printing Office.

―――. 1973c. *1970 Census of Population—Subject Reports, State of Birth* (PC[2]-2A). Washington, D.C.: Government Printing Office.

―――. 1975. "Mobility of the Population of the United States: March 1970 to March 1975." *Current Population Reports*, ser. P-20, no. 285.

―――. 1976a. "Demographic Aspects of Aging and the Older Population in the United States." *Current Population Reports*, Special Studies, ser. P-23, no. 59.

———. 1976b. "Estimates of the Population of States with Components of Change: 1970 to 1975." *Current Population Reports*, ser. P-25, no. 640.

———. 1976c. "Fertility of American Women: June 1975." *Current Population Reports*, ser. P-20, no. 301.

———. 1976d. *Statistical Abstract of the United States: 1976.* Washington, D.C.: Government Printing Office.

———. 1977a. "Estimates of the Population of Counties and Metropolitan Areas: July 1, 1974 and 1975." *Current Population Reports*, ser. P-25, no. 709.

———. 1977b. "Estimates of the Population of States, by Age: July 1, 1975 and 1976." *Current Population Reports*, ser. P-25, no. 646.

———. 1978. "Illustrative Projections of State Populations: 1975 to 2000 (Advance Report)." *Current Population Reports*, ser. P-25, no. 725.

U.S. Bureau of Labor Statistics. 1976. "BLS Revises Estimates for Urban Family Budgets and Comparative Indexes for Selected Urban Areas: Autumn, 1975." *News* (May 5).

U.S. Department of Commerce, Bureau of Economic Affairs. *Survey of Current Business*. Various years.

U.S. National Center for Health Statistics. 1971. "Annual Summary for the United States, 1970: Births, Deaths, Marriages, and Divorces." *Monthly Vital Statistics Report* 19:1–19.

Vance, Rupert B. 1929. *Human Factors in Cotton Culture.* Chapel Hill: University of North Carolina Press.

———. 1935. *Human Geography of the South.* 2d ed. Chapel Hill: University of North Carolina Press.

———. 1941. "The Regional Approach to the Study of High Fertility." *Milbank Memorial Fund Quarterly* 19:356–374.

———. 1945. *All These People: The Nation's Human Resources in the South.* Chapel Hill: University of North Carolina Press.

———. 1951. "The Regional Concept as a Tool for Social Research." Pp. 119–140 in *Regionalism in America*, Merrill Jensen, ed. Madison: University of Wisconsin Press.

———. 1952. "Is Theory for Demographers?" *Social Forces* 31:9–13.

——— and Nicholas J. Demerath, eds. 1954. *The Urban South.* Chapel Hill: University of North Carolina Press.

Vance, Rupert B., and Sara Smith Sutker. 1954. "Metropolitan Dominance and Integration." Pp. 114–134 in *The Urban South*, Rupert B. Vance and Nicholas J. Demerath, eds. Chapel Hill: University of North Carolina Press.

Veblen, Thorstein. 1915. *Imperial Germany and the Industrial Revolution.* New York: Macmillan.

Walker, Jack L. 1969. "The Diffusion of Innovations among the American States." *American Political Science Review* 63:880–899.

———. 1973. "Comment: Problems in Research on the Diffusion of Policy Innovations." *American Political Science Review* 67:1186–1191.

Wanner, Richard A. 1977. "The Dimensionality of the Urban Functional System." *Demography* 14:519–537.

Watson, James W. 1963. *North America: Its Countries and Regions*. London: Longmans.

Westoff, Charles F. 1974. "Coital Frequency and Contraception." *Family Planning Perspectives* 6:136–141.

——— and Norman B. Ryder. 1977. *The Contraceptive Revolution*. Princeton, N.J.: Princeton University Press.

Wheat, Leonard F. 1976. *Urban Growth in the Nonmetropolitan South*. Lexington, Mass.: Lexington Books.

Whelpton, Pascal K. 1936. "Geographic and Economic Differentials in Fertility." *Annals of the American Academy of Political and Social Science* 188:37–55.

———, A. A. Campbell, and J. E. Patterson. 1966. *Fertility and Family Planning in the United States*. Princeton, N.J.: Princeton University Press.

Williams, Oliver P. 1978. "Urbanism and Socio-Economic Processes in Space." Pp. 65–75 in *The Social Ecology of Change: From Equilibrium to Development*, Zdravko Mlinar and Henry Teune, eds. Beverly Hills, Calif.: Sage Publications.

Wirt, Frederick M. 1965. "The Political Sociology of American Suburbia: A Reinterpretation." *Journal of Politics* 27:647–666.

Wirth, Louis. 1938. "Urbanism as a Way of Life." *American Journal of Sociology* 44:1–24.

———. 1951. "The Limitations of Regionalism." Pp. 381–393 in *Regionalism in America*, Merrill Jensen, ed. Madison: University of Wisconsin Press.

Woodward, C. V. 1951. *Origins of the New South, 1877–1913*. Baton Rouge: Louisiana State University Press.

Zelinsky, Wilbur. 1971. "The Hypothesis of the Mobility Transition." *Geographical Journal* 61:219–249.

Zuiches, James J., and David L. Brown. 1975. "The Changing Character of the Rural Population." Paper presented at the annual meeting of the Rural Sociological Society.

Zuiches, James J., and Glenn V. Fuguitt. 1976. "Public Attitudes on Population Distribution Policies." *Growth and Change* 7:28–33.

Author Index

Subject Index